LIBERALISM AND THE RISE OF LABOUR 1890-1918

Liberalism and the Rise of Labour 1890-1918

KEITH LAYBOURN & JACK REYNOLDS

CROOM HELM
London & Sydney

ST. MARTIN'S PRESS
New York

©1984 K. Laybourn and J. Reynolds
Croom Helm Ltd, Provident House, Burrell Row,
Beckenham, Kent BR3 1AT

Croom Helm Australia Pty Ltd, First Floor, 139 King Street,
Sydney, NSW 2001, Australia

British Library Cataloguing in Publication Data

Laybourn, Keith
    Liberalism & the rise of Labour 1890-1918.
    1. Labour Party – Great Britain – History
    2. West Yorkshire – Politics and government
    I. Title   II. Reynolds, Jack
    324.24107'09428'1   JN1129.L3

    ISBN 0-7099-1651-5

Library of Congress Card Catalog Number: 83-40700

ISBN 0-312-48342-2

Printed and bound in Great Britain

CONTENTS

TABLES AND FIGURES

Tables and Figures

TO JULIA AND EVELYN

PREFACE

We have two main purposes in writing this book.
The first is to explain why West Yorkshire should
have produced a flourishing Labour movement in the
late nineteenth and early twentieth centuries. The
second is to question the view that the Labour Party
simply emerged as a viable party during the First
World War by stepping into the political vacuum
created by the split within Liberal ranks. We feel
that the evidence of Labour's growth before 1914 -
particularly in securing trade-union support from
the 1890s onwards and in rapidly increasing its
local political successes after 1909 suggests that
the First World War was less significant to Labour's
political rise in West Yorkshire than it might have
been nationally, or in other regions of the
country.
       It is amazing, given the importance of the
West Yorkshire textile area in the embryonic growth
of the Independent Labour Party and the Labour
Party, that there has not, until now, been a detailed published account of the West Yorkshire Labour movement. Most accounts have, hitherto, concentrated upon the famous national events which
occurred in West Yorkshire - the Inaugural Conference of the National ILP at Bradford in 1893 being
the most famous - and not attempted to explain the
complexity of a region in which the ILP caught on
in some areas, such as Bradford and Halifax, but
failed to sustain much of an impact in other areas,
such as Huddersfield and Keighley. Only recently
has detailed research been undertaken to examine
the political record of Labour and Liberalism in the
various industrial constituencies of West Yorkshire
and much of this remains to be published. Therefore, this book is an attempt to fill the gap. Of
course, in a book of a couple of hundred pages it is

impossible to offer a detailed study of all the 22
constituencies and 23 seats which we take as the
West Yorkshire area. Indeed in a good proportion of
these constituencies there is comparatively little
to report, and the evidence of pre-war Labour
growth is sketchy. For this reason, whilst we have
attempted to do justice to the whole West Yorkshire
area we have inevitably had to concentrate upon the
areas of greatest Labour activity, such as Bradford,
Halifax, Leeds, Keighley and Huddersfield, whilst
recognising the significant developments which were
occurring in the surrounding districts.
    As research into the early Labour Party and
the Liberal Party continues so new evidence and
perspectives will appear. In the meantime we offer
our assessment of the main features of Labour history in West Yorkshire. Whilst future research
may qualify our findings, we hope to have provided
a suggestive guide through the quagmire of early
Labour politics in West Yorkshire.

Pudsey and Bradford   Keith Laybourn
                                      Jack Reynolds

ACKNOWLEDGEMENTS

This book could not have been written without the
help of many individuals and institutions. We owe
a particular debt to the staff of many West Yorkshire libraries who have been generous in their
advice and help. Whilst our thanks extend to all
those library staff who have helped us in our research we would particularly like to thank David
James, the Bradford Archivist, Elvira Willmott,
the Local Studies Adviser for Bradford Libraries
Division, Dr. Alan Betteridge, the Archivist for
Calderdale, and their respective staffs for their
unstinting support of our research.
     This research has, of course, been sustained
and illuminated by discussions with many individuals over many years. The enthusiasm and critical
advice of Dr. David Clark MP, Martin Crick, John
Halstead, Bill Lancaster, Cyril Pearce, Robert
Perks and Dr. David Wright has been invaluable to
our work. Tony Jowett deserves particular mention,
having helped to shape some of our ideas for
chapter seven.
     Our thanks must also go to David James and
the Bradford Archives Department for permission to
use the Keir Hardie election card for the 1896
East Bradford By-Election on the front cover.
Elizabeth Dawson patiently typed the camera-ready
copy for this book and David Lawford was responsible
for the artwork.
     The years of research and long hours spent
in writing this book have placed a considerable
burden upon our wives and it is to them - Julia
and Evelyn - that this book is dedicated.

ABBREVIATIONS

ASE	Amalgamated Society of Engineers
BSP	British Socialist Party
BWL	British Workers' League
COS	Charity Organisation Society
CVLL	Colne Valley Labour League
CVLU	Colne Valley Labour Union
CVSL	Colne Valley Socialist League
ILP	Independent Labour Party
ISEL	Industrial Syndicalist Education League
LEA	Labour Electoral Association (Bradford)
LRC	Labour Representation Committee
NAC	National Administrative Council (of the ILP)
NEC	National Executive Committee (of the LRC and Labour Party)
SDF	Social Democratic Federation
SDP	Social Democratic Party
UDC	Union of Democratic Control
WMF	Workers' Municipal Federation (Bradford)

Chapter One

THE RISE OF LABOUR AND THE DECLINE OF LIBERALISM:
THE GENERAL PROBLEM AND WEST YORKSHIRE

The rise of the Labour Party between 1890 and 1924
and the decline of the Liberal Party in the same
period are political events of more than usual
significance for our own times. From a peak of 400
members of parliament in the 1906 General Election
the Liberal Party crashed down to 40 in the general
election of 1924. The Labour Party had made compar-
able gains, rising from a mere handful of members at
the beginning of the century to 191 in 1923 - enough
to form a minority government. Even in the general
election of 1924, the defeated Labour Party had 151
parliamentary representatives and was clearly the
alternative party of government to the Conservative-
s. It was little more than 30 years since the Independent Labour Party, the progenitor of the Labour
Party, had held its first annual conference in
Bradford in 1893.
        The primary cause of the Liberal decline was
obvious. Voters had abandoned the Liberal Party in
favour of Labour or Conservatism. The problem of
the historian was to analyse the timing of this
change. Was the shift in political support before
1914 - the expression in politics of class division
in society - decisive? Or did the Liberal Party
lose a hold on public opinion, which it had recap-
tured after an apparant decline at the beginning of
the century, as a result of the internal battles
between Asquith and Lloyd George during the war and
in the immediate post-war years? In other words,
had the Liberal Party faced the challenge offered by
the 'emergence of the masses' into politics, and
become the natural party of the working classes
before 1914 only to be destroyed in the 1920s by the
conflicting political ambitions of their principal
men. In our view, the evidence of the West Yorkshire textile area overwhelmingly suggests that

1

decline of the Liberal Party was a continuous process from the late nineteenth century onwards and
that this reflected the fundamental change in the
structure and organisation of society. The Liberal
Party was losing its supporters from the 1880s onwards. Despite the radicalism of the great governments dominated by Asquith and Lloyd George before
1914, the intransigence of hardcore Liberalism, as
expressed for instance in the Liberal clubs of the
West Yorkshire textile district, guaranteed that it
did not offer itself as an effective party of social
reform at the local level. Far less would its programme take on that element of crusading passion
needed to arouse the working class into something
like concerted political action. There was a long
history of working-class support for Liberalism but
few middle-class Liberals were unaware of class
distinctions within the party or could bring themselves to ignore the assumptions of working-class
deference this implied. In West Yorkshire, the
Liberal Party never became, for working-class men
and women, 'our party' in the comprehensive sense
the Labour Party achieved.

The strength of nineteenth century Liberalism
lay in its economic philosophy – its faith in the
impersonality of economic forces; its view of the
needs and obligation of the religious life - equal-
ity between the sects and hostility therefore to
the special position of the Anglican church; the
central principle of individualism which gave Liberals their deep-rooted suspicion of the executive
power of the bureaucratic state. By the last twenty
years of the nineteenth century, the value of these
ideas was being challenged. A good many West Yorkshire woolmen were abandoning the economic liberalism which had been the corner stone of Victorian
political consensus. In 1882, Samuel Cunliffe
Lister, one of Bradford's most influential manufacturers, began a nationwide campaign for what he
called 'Fair Trade', the introduction of British
tariffs against those who hampered the movement of
British goods.[1] By 1904, in the Bradford and District Chamber of Commerce there was a majority in
favour of the controlled introduction of tariffs.
In religion also the position was weakening. The
strength of the Liberal Party lay in its connection
with Nonconformity but well-to-do Liberals were
drifting into the Anglican church. As for the
working class, while there was perhaps a significant
increase in their numbers amongst Primitive Metho-
dists, they as a whole remained indifferent to the

claims of religion. And, of course, the importance
of the connection generally diminished as society
became increasingly secular. There were adjustments
also required in the unifying principle of individualism and personal independence. Liberals themselves had contributed to the growth of the power
of the state when they fought to transfer local
power from the hands of self-elected oligarchies to
the democracy of borough and county councils, working under the supervision of central authority. By
the end of the century demarcation lines between
individual and state responsibility were being re-
defined in ways which many Liberals found difficult
to accommodate.

Some Liberals did however respond to the new
circumstances. Recognising the importance of the
spirit of collectivism developing in English society, men like J.A. Hobson, L.T. Hobhouse,
C.F.C. Masterman and Herbert Samuel tried to remould
Liberalism in such a way as to reconcile individualism with the need for social reform which allowed
greater state intervention.[2] Some writers have in
fact argued that their efforts were rewarded and
that the fortunes of the Liberal Party picked up as
the programme developed.[3] There can be little
doubt that in terms purely and simply of parliamentary elections the Liberal Party benefited enormous-
ly from the gratitude felt by working people for the
great advances of the period 1906 to 1910. Indeed
one writer goes so far as to maintain that the
Liberal Party was benefiting from the development
of class politics and was well on the way to count-
ering the ILP/Labour Party claims to be the party
of the working class.[4]

But this view, in our opinion, is based on a
narrow view of the evidence for it concentrates too
exclusively on the evidence of parliamentary elections. It ignores the physical difficulties of
organising a completely new working-class party and
the obstacles in the operation of the franchise
which still hampered the expression of working-class
political opinion. It has been estimated that about
six million adult males could not vote under the
provision of the two franchise acts of 1867 and
1884. Some were disenfranchised under the house-
holder and lodger provisions, some through the
difficulty of operating the seven different franchises and some simply because they could not fulfill
the twelve-month residential qualification - a not
unusual problem given the high level of residential
mobility of working men. It is not enough to say

that this was a question of randam inequality which
affected the Liberal Party as much as Labour.[5]
An election agent was essential if any local party
was to poll its full strength and clearly the
Liberals were far better placed in this regard than
Labour before the First World War. The working
class did not begin to register its true vote until
after the introduction of a new franchise act in
1918.[6]

Much of the discussion in favour of the post-
1914 decline of the Liberal Party centres upon the
work of P.F. Clarke in his book <u>Lancashire and the
New Liberalism</u>. As the title implies the evidence
is drawn almost exclusively from Lancashire and its
politics are not necessarily typical of the country
as a whole. In fact we think that the textile
district of the West Riding of Yorkshire, West
Yorkshire, probably offers a better insight into
the process by which the Labour Party emerged.
Apparently the Liberal Party in Lancashire was in
great difficulty by the end of the century and com-
pelled to look for new policies in the hope of surviving. In the West Riding the Liberal Party was
much more powerful, returning either 19 or 20 of the
23 MPs who represented West Yorkshire between 1906
and 1914.[7] Perhaps inevitably the challenge to
Liberalism in West Yorkshire was keener. Bradford
was the birthplace of the Independent Labour Party,
and the textile district of the West Riding the
main initial centre of the movement which produced
the Labour Party.[8]

A number of the central themes of Liberal and Labour
history are well illustrated in a study of West
Yorkshire. The importance of examining the results
of local municipal and other elections is established for these show a steady, though not entirely
continuous, rise in Labour fortunes before 1914.[9]
Thus in Bradford, working-class candidates standing independently of the two major parties took
22.4 per cent of the municipal vote in 1893, 18.8
per cent in 1900 and 43.1 per cent in 1913.[10]
Labour was in fact the most rapidly rising political
party on Bradford City Council, though the organisation of the municipal political system meant that
it was not yet in a position to take over the administration of the city.
A study of West Yorkshire also provides a
useful insight into the real strength of the new
Liberalism at the grass roots of politics. The new
Liberalism was not well represented in West

Figure 1.1: Map of West Yorkshire Parliamentary
Constituencies 1885 – 1918

Yorkshire. Its most notable and politically active exponent was William Pollard Byles, sometime editor and owner of the <u>Bradford Observer</u>. His advocacy of social reform and his support of the working classes was sustained from the 1880s onwards. Yet working-class opinion never found him entirely convincing and local Liberals as a whole were at least upset by his activities. After a tempestuous career in Bradford, Shipley and Leeds he was obliged to leave Bradford to pursue his political career in Salford. One critical observer commented: 'It is a hard fate, but it is necessary if Mr Byles should fulfill the political role to which he is irresistably drawn'.[11] There were others: E.J. Smith for instance, a friend of Fred Jowett, a passionate advocate of housing reform whose work produced a blue print on which the development of Bradford's post-war municipal housing plan was based; Jacob Moser and his wife Rebecca, who directed the transformation of Bradford's charitable organisations in the years immediately before the First World War.[12] But their political following was slight. A more typical representative of the new Liberalism in the eyes of Bradford's working class was H.H. Bentham, Chairman of the Board of Guardians, a member of the Royal Commission on the Poor Law and a signatory of the Majority report of that inquiry, but best recalled in Bradford for his stern opposition to the introduction of school meals.[13] On the whole it was the 'Alfred Illingworth' figure which still represented Liberalism in the textile area. Free trade, voluntaryism and personal independence remained, for such men, at the heart of their political creed. Illingworth had died in 1907, but his opposition to the Eight-Hour Movement, his reluctance to accept schemes for old-age pensions or health insurance, his refusal to look for the possibility of abolishing half-time working for young children, his bad-tempered intervention against Fred Jowett, the ILP candidate in the West Bradford parliamentary election of 1906 were not forgotten and there were men like George Garnett, the Greengates mill owner, to step into his shoes.[14] Old Liberalism based upon the leadership of a few Non-conformist business families sustained places like Keighley and Huddersfield as Liberal strongholds up to and even beyond the First World War.[15] In the circumstances it is not surprising that time and time again we come across examples of Liberal intransigence - expressed usually by Liberal

executive committees refusing to consider working
men as candidates for local election.

The West Yorkshire region also demonstrated
clearly one of the central features of the situation. Perhaps for the first time in British
history the structure of working-class society
showed real possibilities of unity in political action. The Labour-Capital relationship was clari-
fed and effectively polarised, and the class-based
division of opinion which accompanied the
Manningham Mills strike of 1891 - the catalyst
of events which led to the founding of the ILP -
confirmed it. [16] The paternalism which as a mana-
gerial device had masked the division between
Labour and Capital, persisted in some parts of the
West Riding. In the smaller towns and villages
there was a good deal still, for one or two firms
could generally control most of the facilities of
such areas. J.C. Horsfall exercised in Glusburn
near Keighley the sort of authority that Sir Titus
Salt had exercised in Saltaire. Bairstow and Harley
held between them much the same position in nearby
Sutton. The Fosters of Black Dyke Mills dominated
the village of Queensbury and the proprietors of
the Low Moor Iron Works the district of Wibsey
Low Moor. [17] But in the larger towns there is plenty of evidence of the dimunition of such influences. Some of the oldest and largest established
firms - the founders of West Yorkshire's industrial
greatness - had disappeared. In Bradford, the
Rands went out of business in 1873 for lack of
heirs. [18] The Bowling Iron Company went into liqui-
dation in 1897. [19] In 1892 the Salt family sold
the whole of the Saltaire complex to a local
consortium. [20] One or two large firms emerged to
take their places, but generally they were replaced
by smaller units whose resources could not provide
the sort of quid pro quo on which such relation-
ships depended. Generally the relationship of
Labour to Capital was reaching a more modern polar-
isation. In printing, the Federation of Master
Printers confronted the local branch of the
National Typographical Association, and in the
Dyeing trade, the Bradford Dyers' Association
battled with the Amalgamated Society of Dyers,
and almost everywhere the trade union - though
met with great hostility - was (however
reluctantly) accepted as the bargaining agent of
workingmen. [21]

There were also more general social indica-
tors of the position. The social geography of the

large towns had responded to the development of the
class-divided society and the building speculators
were isolating one class from another. The new
working-class district in Bradford which stretched
across the eastern slopes of the bowl of hills was
a good example of these developments. It was built
between 1870 and 1890 and owned by small owners of
property who held blocks of four or eight houses
each. As an area, it offered few facilities except
those available on the long-existing thoroughfares
it overran. Yet it was not as homogeneous as it
appeared on the surface. The regimental files of
dark-grey-slate roofed houses masked a number of
minor social diversities. These separated those
who lived in the terrace houses on the periphery,
those who lived in the back-to-back houses and
those who lived in the larger side-scullery houses.
All nevertheless shared the same facilities, the
chapels, the churches, the schools, shops and public
houses along Otley Road, Barkerend Road and Leeds
Road. The area never developed into a community in
the way that a place like Saltaire or other earlier
building developments based upon old townships
could. But it drew together a sizeable portion of
Bradford's working class. About a half of the en-
rolled trade unionists of Bradford lived there.
A number of leading members of the Bradford ILP had
their homes within a few minutes walk of each other
in the area.[22]
     By the 1890s much of the antagonism which the
Irish immigration brought into West Yorkshire was
disappearing. The Irish were never to be entirely
assimilated or their culture submerged but within
the framework of their own institutions they were
being effectively integrated into the fabric of
society. They had their own schools, subject, like
other schools, to the control of the school boards.
In school board elections they voted Conservative,
on other matters with the Liberals until the turn
of the century when increasingly the Irish vote
came to the Labour Party.
     By 1890 also a whole generation of working-
class children had shared the common experience of
school board elementary education. The tendency,
noted in J.S. Winder's report on education in
Bradford in 1861, for craftsmen and others of the
better paid to send their children to small and in-
adequate private schools diminished rapidly.[23]
Almost all working-class children savoured the
facilities which the board schools provided; young
working-class adults formed an element in society

linked by the newly-shared experience of education.

We are not of course arguing that the inexorable pressures of sociological change made the rise of the ILP inevitable. We are saying that the material conditions for such a development existed. Why it actually occurred and the manner in which it emerged depended on the way men acted in the complex juxtaposition of old and new in social life. The work of recent historians has demonstrated that the condition of the Liberal Party and its response to the Labour challenge varied from region to region, and in an earlier article we provided what we consider to be a useful framework for the analysis of the problem. A number of questions have to be asked. How strong was the Socialist tradition in the area? How powerful and well-organised was the trade union movement and how firmly was it linked with the local Liberal Party? To what extent did the local Liberal Party respond to the demands of the working class? To what extent could the new Independent movement absorb a wide range of differing opinions, providing a platform for the far-reaching aspirations of Socialism and social reformism of many working-class radicals?

We found that in Bradford, the birthplace of the ILP,there was a small Socialist movement active in the 1880s, largely composed of trade unionists, who gradually won the support of the Bradford Trades Council at a time when the Liberal Party appeared to be blatantly disregarding the interests of the organised working classes. Bradford trade unionists, hitherto prepared to accept the leadership of the well-to-do, became increasingly disillusioned with the effectiveness of the political representation they enjoyed at the municipal and national level and supported the ILP as the vehicle for their political aspirations. Trade unionism was thus the vital factor in the growth of the Bradford Labour movement.[24] Jeff Hill, writing about Manchester, had come to a similar conclusion.[25] Yet research into Rochdale and Bolton has suggested that where the local Liberal Party was able to hang on to trades-council support it was able to blight the growth of the Labour Party.[26] Still further research, into Keighley and Huddersfield, has suggested that if the local trades council was weak then its capture by the Labour Party would not necessarily produce a significant political breakthrough for Labour.[27]

David Howell's recent book on British

Workers and the Independent Labour Party summarises
much of the research and tends to support our contention that the key factor in the growth of Labour
was trade-union, or trades council, support.[28]
Yet there appears to be at least one exception to
this rule. David Clark's book Colne Valley:
Radicalism to Socialism reflects that the success
of Victor Grayson in the 1907 Colne Valley parliamentary by-election was inspired by an individual-
istic, ethical branch of Socialism which was alien
to trade unionism and its emphasis upon collective
action.[29] But even in Colne Valley the importance
of trade unionism cannot be fully ignored, for many
of the early leaders of the Colne Valley Labour
Union/League were in fact trade unionists.

   Like most major debates the one which was
focused on the rise of Labour and the decline of
Liberalism has led to a good deal of academic petti-
ness and belligerence which is anathama to compromise. Yet sober opinion would, even at this
interim stage, reflect that several main conclusions have emerged. In the first place, no one can
be categorical about the timing of the Liberal decline or Labour growth because of the immense regional and local variations which have been observed. Secondly, advocacy of new Liberalism as the
redeemer of Liberalism is no longer tenable; too
much research has indicated the absence of its
influence in many regions of the country.[30]
Thirdly, although the impact of unequal franchise
remains unclear, municipal and parliamentary by-
election results suggest that Labour's electoral
strength was rising rapidly between 1910 and 1914.[31]
But if there is one lesson to learn from this debate it must be that an attempt to apply a general
theory to the whole country will not work.[32] It is
imperative that more research should be undertaken
into constituency politics if a satisfactory conclusion to this debate is to be reached.

   This study of the West Yorkshire textile region is an attempt to deal with one major regional
gap in our knowledge. Apart from a few brief
articles comparatively little has been published on
constituency politics in West Yorkshire.[33] David
Clark's study of Colne Valley is in fact the only
fully detailed study to have been published for a
West Yorkshire constituency.[34] The first purpose
of this book will be to present the political
picture that was emerging in the Yorkshire textile
constituencies between the 1890s and the First
World War. The main thrust of this book will be

directed at answering the questions raised by the recent and current debate. It will be suggested that the Labour movement had broken the traditional two-party political system in some constituencies but that the Liberal Party still held on well in many constituencies. It will also be argued that Liberal resilience was very largely based upon the old, rather than the new, Liberalism and that wealthy Nonconformist families, often rooted in the woollen textile industry, still held sway within the Liberal Party. Trade-union support was also vital in sustaining a growing Labour Party and where it was not a preponderant force the growth of Labour was likely to be fitful. Yet gains were made even in the most unlikely areas. The Labour movement made significant inroads into the position of both the Liberal and Conservative parties in the Yorkshire textile industry, particularly in the early 1890s, between 1901 and 1906 and from 1910 to the First World War. With its political successes it brought hope of an improvement in the conditions of life endured by the working classes, though its real effect upon the lives of most was minimal. Yet at least the Liberal heartland was under threat and the way had been paved for a political takeover by the Labour Party. Labour gains from an obdurate and trenchant old, rather than new, Liberalism was the picture of politics in West Yorkshire before August 1914.

NOTES

1.   Bradford Observer, 3, 7 Feb. 1880; B.H. Brown, The Tariff Movement in Great Britain 1881-1893 (Columbia University Press, Columbia and London, 1943); K. Laybourn, 'The Attitude of Yorkshire Trade Unions to the Economic and Social Problems of the Great Depression, 1873-1896', unpublished PhD thesis, University of Lancaster, 1973, pp. 94-6.
2.   P. Clarke, Liberals and Social Democrats (Cambridge University Press, Cambridge, 1978 and 1981).
3.   P.F. Clarke, Lancashire and the New Liberalism (Cambridge University Press, Cambridge, 1971; H.V. Emy, Liberals, Radicals and Social Politics 1892-1914 (Cambridge University Press, London, 1973); M. Freeden, The New Liberalism: An Ideology of Social Reform (Clarendon, Oxford, 1978).
4.   Clarke, Lancashire and the New Liberalism.
5.   P.F. Clarke, 'Liberals, Labour and the

Franchise', English Historical Review, 1977, pp. 582-9.

6. R. McKibbin, The Evolution of the Labour Party 1910-1924 (Oxford University Press, London, 1974), pp. xv.

7. The West Yorkshire area is taken to include the following constituencies: Bradford Central, Bradford East, Bradford West, Dewsbury, Halifax (two seats), Huddersfield, Leeds Central, Leeds East, Leeds North, Leeds South, Leeds West, Wakefield, Colne Valley, Elland, Holmfirth, Keighley, Morley, Pudsey, Otley, Shipley, Sowerby and Spen Valley.

8. J. Reynolds and K. Laybourn, 'The Emergence of the Independent Labour Party in Bradford', International Review of Social History, Vol. XX (1975), Part 3, pp. 313-46.

9. M.G. Sheppard and J.L. Halstead, 'Labour's Municipal Election Performances in Provincial England and Wales 1901-1913', Bulletin of the Society for the Study of Labour History, 39, Autumn 1979, pp. 39-62.

10. Bradford Trades and Labour Council, Year Books for 1912, 1913 and 1914 (Bradford Trades Council, Bradford, 1912, 1913 and 1914).

11. Bradford Daily Telegraph, 31 Mar. 1903.

12. F. Brockway, Socialism over Sixty Years: The Life of Jowett of Bradford (Allen and Unwin, London, 1946), pp. 58.

13. K. Laybourn, 'The Issue of School Feeding in Bradford, 1904-1907', Journal of Educational Administration and History, Vol. XIV, No. 2, Jul. 1982, p. 31.

14. Yorkshire Daily Observer, 2 Jan. 1907.

15. The Brigg Family, for instance, exercised some paternal powers in Keighley and John Brigg, later Sir John Brigg, was MP for Keighley from 1895 until his death in 1911.

16. E.P. Thompson, 'Homage to Tom Maguire' in A. Briggs and J. Saville, Essays in Labour History (Macmillan, London, 1960), pp. 306-8; C. Pearce, The Manningham Mills Strike, Bradford, December 1890-April 1891 (University of Hull Occasional Papers in Economic and Social History, Hull, 1975); K. Laybourn, 'The Manningham Mills Strike: its importance in Bradford history', Bradford Antiquary, 1976, pp. 7-35.

17. E. Sigsworth, Black Dyke Mills (Liverpool University Press, Liverpool, 1958).

18. Bradford Observer, 10 Jun. 1873.

19. H. Long, 'The Bowling Ironworks',

Industrial Archaeology Vol. 5, no. 2, May 1968, pp. 171-7.

20. _Saltaire and Shipley Times_, 5 Aug. 1893.

21. Bradford Typographical Society, Minutes, Deposited in the J.B. Priestley Library, University of Bradford.

22. Reynolds and Laybourn, 'The Emergence of the Independent Labour Party in Bradford', p. 320.

23. _Parliamentary Papers_, 1861, Vol. XXL, Part II, pp. 175-242: Report of the Assistant Commissioner J.S. Winder Esqu., on the State of Popular Education in Rochdale and Bradford.

24. Reynolds and Laybourn, 'Emergence of the Independent Labour Party in Bradford', p. 313.

25. J. Hill, 'Manchester and Salford Politics and the Early Development of the Independent Labour Party', _International Review of Social History_, Vol. XXVI (1981), Part 2, pp. 171-201.

26. M. Coneys, 'The Labour Movement and the Liberal Party in Rochdale 1890-1906', unpublished MA dissertation, Huddersfield Polytechnic, 1982; P. Howarth, 'The Development of the Bolton Independent Labour Party, 1885-1895', unpublished MA dissertation, Huddersfield Polytechnic, 1982.

27. D. James, 'The Keighley ILP 1892-1900 "Realising the Kingdom of Heaven"' in J.A. Jowitt and R.K.S. Taylor (eds.) _Bradford 1890-1914: The Cradle of the Independent Labour Party_ (Bradford Occasional Papers No 2, Extra-Mural Department, Leeds University, Bradford, 1980); R. Perks is concluding his research on Huddersfield for a PhD at Huddersfield Polytechnic. A.W. Purdue, 'The Liberal and Labour Parties in North-East Politics, 1900-1914: The Struggle for Supremacy', _International Review of Social History_, XXVI (1981), Part 1, pp. 1-24 has made a similar point about the Liberal Party's control of trade unionism in the North East.

28. D. Howell, _British Workers and the Independent Labour Party 1888-1906_ (Manchester University Press, Manchester, 1983).

29. D. Clark, _Colne Valley: Radicalism to Socialism. The Portrait of a Northern constituency in the formative years of the Labour Party 1890-1910_ (Longman, London, 1981).

30. K.O. Morgan, 'The New Liberalism and the Challenge of Labour: The Welsh Experience', in K.D. Brown (ed.) _Essays in Anti-Labour History_ (Macmillan, London, 1974), pp. 159-82; A. Howkins, 'Edwardian Liberalism and Industrial Unrest: a class view of the decline of Liberalism', _History Workshop Journal_, 4 (Autumn, 1977).

31. Sheppard and Halstead, 'Labour's Municipal Election Performance'; K.D. Wald, 'Class and
the Vote before the First World War', British
Journal of Political Science, Vol. 8 (1978), pp.
441-57.
32. Clarke, Lancashire and the New Liberalism,
particularly the introductory remarks.
33. Apart from the articles already cited
there have also been the following publications:
M. Pugh, 'Yorkshire and the New Liberalism', Journal of Modern History, vol. 50, part 3 (1978),
D1139-D1155; A. Roberts, 'Leeds Liberalism and
late Victorian Politics', Northern History, V,
(1970), pp. 131-56.
34. Clark, Colne Valley: Radicalism to Socialism.

Chapter Two

THE ORIGINS OF SOCIALISM AND INDEPENDENT LABOUR

Most students of modern history acknowledge the significance of the revolutionary changes which took
place in the structure of European industrial society towards the end of the nineteenth century.
These were bound up with the growing impersonality
of the business unit, increases in the size and
scope of international markets and the deeper invol-
vements of political authorities in many aspects of
economic life. In the evolution of social activity,
the element with which this study is concerned, the
emergence of the masses into politics, is fundamental.
Universal manhood suffrage came before 1870 in
France and in Germany but in both countries the most
significant developments in working-class politics
came after that date, in France under the Third
Republic and in Germany after the repeal of anti-
Socialist legislation in 1890. Spain, Belgium, the
Netherlands, and Norway all passed manhood suffrage
legislation between 1890 and 1898 and in the last
quarter of the century Socialist parties sprang up
in all Western European countries. The Second
International of the European Socialist parties was
established in 1889.
     In the United Kingdom - as elsewhere - the
struggle for a democratic society was long and pain-
ful, though, generally, after 1850, less violent
than elsewhere. Its success was embodied in a
series of enactments which broke down some of the
authority held previously by a property-owning
oligarchy of middle and upper classes. The act of
1867 conceded the franchise to male householers living in the parliamentary boroughs and another in
1884 extended the privilege to male householders in
the county constituencies. The Secret Ballot Act
of 1872 and the Corrupt Practices Act of 1883 cleared the way for the introduction of proper democrat-

ic procedures. In 1918, all males over 21 and
women over 30 were allowed to vote and all women
were finally included in the franchise in 1928.
Meanwhile the act of 1882 had opened up municipal
government to working men by its abolition of the
property qualification for local councillors and
aldermen.[1]

Between the Reform Act of 1832 and that of
1867, however, the structure of politics was little
changed. By and large membership of the political
nation was confined to males of the upper and middle classes. A small number of working men throughout the country had the vote. In the parliamentary
borough of Bradford, for instance, only about seven
per cent of the electors were working men. There
were about 1,500, however, who had a vote in the
county elections as freeholders. Occasionally,
Chartist candidates appeared at the hustings -
Ernest Jones had stood for Halifax in 1848 - but
generally, like Julian Harney in Bradford in 1852,
they withdrew from the contest after a vote had
been taken by a show of hands and before the ballot
proper.[2] The prevailing mood of the political
nation after 1848 was one of consensus based on a
belief in free trade and an ill-defined concept of
progress. The core of its support in West Yorkshire was found in the votes of non-dogmatic Tories
and Moderate Liberals. Radicalism was powerful and
vocal there for there was a wealthy dissenting
community led by some of the richest industrialists
in the district but it had no automatic majority
over the combined forces of Tory and Moderate Liberal until after 1867. Perhaps the best evidence
of the prevailing harmony was to be found in Bradford. Between 1850 and 1867 there were six parliamentary elections but only two of them were contested in this borough.[3] Of the two seats, one was
held by H.W. Wickham, a director of the great Low
Moor Iron Works, and a convert from Toryism to moderate Liberalism in 1852.[4] The other was held at
different times by Robert Milligan, the first mayor
of Bradford and head of the great mercantile enter-
prise of Milligan and Forbes, Titus Salt, second
mayor of Bradford and the founder of Saltaire, and
W.E. Forster, a prosperous manufacturer in the
neighbouring village of Burley and one of the country's leading politicians.[5] All were classed as
Radicals, though the degree of their commitment was
questioned from time to time. By the 1860s, both
Milligan and Forster had abandoned any belief in
manhood suffrage they may have had, and there were

those who suspected that Salt might even be moving
into the Tory camp. The only permanent political
organisations were the Electoral Registration associations; elections were run by the ad hoc committees of what were known as 'friends of the candidates'.6

The working-class vote, such as it was, and the
support of organised non-electors tended to go to
Radical candidates. There was already in existence
an understanding between working men and middle-
class Radicals that one of the main objectives of
politics was the extension of the franchise in some
way to at least some sections of the working classes. But an eventual move in that direction formed
part of the consensus idea of progress. There was
more agreement within the consensus on the need for
'cautious gradualism' than there was on the form
such progress had to take. The act of 1867 was the
product of this 'cautious gradualism' - it ensured
that (as Tawney commented) the British working man
would enter the ballot box with cap in hand.7 The
universal manhood suffrage demanded by the Chartists had not been conceded. The vote went to men
with established residential qualification, either
lodger or household tenure, and other proofs of
Victorian responsibility. It reflected the old constitutional principle that the vote was a privilege
attaching to men who had some interest in the main-
tenance of property; it contained elements of that
Victorian view, held by some working men as well as
others, that only a minority of working men could
be considered intelligent and rational human beings
capable of serious thought and judgement. Large
numbers of working men, even in the urban constituencies, did not vote under the act. It demanded
a year's residential qualification; men defined as
lodgers had to register themselves, unlike other
voters who were registered automatically; men who
had accepted poor relief in the previous year were
excluded along with criminals and bankrupts. In
1871, there were about 39,000 adult males in Bradford; in 1874 the electorate numbered 24,331.8

A fundamental change of course had taken place.
In Bradford, the electorate grew from just short of
6,000 in 1866 to 27,000 by 1880 and it became
largely working class in the process. The parties
responded promptly to the new system. Machinery
was quickly created almost everywhere to maintain
control of the vastly augmented vote, (or, as its
creators might have said, to allow democracy to
function effectively). The mechanism of the modern

party system was created. At the social level, Liberal and Conservative clubs appeared, and at the formal political level permanent associations were established. Bradford provided an early model. In 1866, the Conservatives started the Conservative Working Men's Association and in the following year the Bradford Conservative Association.[9] The Liberals drew together into a single organisation almost all their supporters in the town - the moderate Registration Society, the Radical middle-class Reform Union and almost all the members of the Radical working-class Reform League. The new Liberal Electoral Association provided a new base in which Moderate and Radical were united in a pledge to support the same programme and the same candidates[10] It was organised by wards and so provided plenty of opportunity of minor office for its ordinary members. Its principal committee was an executive of 24 members. Only four of them were members of the working class.

Working-class activity was certainly stimulated. A number of working men stood as parliamentary candidates in different parts of the country and one or two of them were elected. But this did not introduce a new element into politics for such men and their supporters remained no more than a section of the Liberal Party with special interests in trade union and working conditions. It was in fact little more than a formal strengthening of arrangements which had existed in a looser form since the 1850s. Sir Titus Salt, commenting on the parliamentary by-election of 1869, gave the situation a good Liberal gloss.[11] Bradford working men had rallied to the support of Edward Miall, the chief propagandist of the Liberation Society and a very orthodox 'laissez-faire' Liberal. It is not easy to see just what working men got out of supporting him. He was perhaps the best available candidate though his opponent, M.W. Thompson, claimed to be as good a democrat and not a kill-joy into the bargain.[12] Miall, however, offered them the dignity of committed Radicalism; he also had the reputation of being a friend to the working man, though he failed to justify it when he had an opportunity to vote on trade-union matters. Salt's comment was revealing. Bradford's working men, he said, had done their duty, as he had always known they would and he was proud of them.[13]

The situation was exposed more starkly in the Bradford election of 1874. James Hardaker, a stone mason and a very prominent member of Bradford's so-

called 'aristocracy of labour', stood for election
with the backing of the local Trades Council. He
was the secretary of the local branch of the Operative Stonemasons' Union, a Sunday School teacher
and a leading member of the working men's teetotal
organisation. His father ran a small building firm,
which he eventually inherited. Although he had
declared his intention to remain independent of
other political organisations, he quickly threw in
his lot with the official Liberal-Radicals once the
election became imminent. He had made little progress in getting together the funds needed to fight
the election. When Alfred Illingworth, Bradford's
Radical leader, offered to finance his campaign and
made promises to cover a parliamentary salary if
Hardaker were to be elected, Hardaker had no hesi-
tation in agreeing to stand as a Radical candidate
in tandem with J.V. Godwin, wealthy wool merchant
and another ex-mayor of Bradford. The election was
dominated by the education issue for the principal
opponent of official Liberal-Radicalism was W.E.
Forster, author of the 1870 Education Act which for
the time being had shattered the unity of the Liberals. Nevertheless, it seems at least odd that
Hardaker should have placed the issue of trade union
legislation last in his list of legislative prior-
ities.[14] The 'people's' government, led by the
'people's' William, which Bradford working men,
earning Salt's praise, had helped to elect, and
which Hardaker now supported, had passed the notor-
ious Criminal Law Amendment Act in 1872. It had
aroused great anger among the local unions who organised one of the most impressive demonstrations in
the country against it and in consequence helped to
re-establish the Bradford and District Trades
Council - the body which had first sponsored Hardaker. We can best suppose that Hardaker was subject
to irresistable pressure on the issue for, middle-
class Radicals had never displayed much affection
for trade unions. It is clear, however, that working-class representation of this sort had not raised
the enthusiasm of Bradford's working men to a level
at which they would face the financial sacrifices
of expenditure on a parliamentary candidate.
    Working men were capable of expressing indepen-
dent views and taking independent action. Even
during the quiet fifties, old Bradford Chartists
like George White, William Angus, Abraham Sharp,
James Wilkinson and George Fletcher hammered away at
the manhood suffrage theme, though most speakers
conceded the need for middle-class support.[15] In

the sixties there was more aggression. In 1864,
for instance, a working men's committee engineered
a demonstration against the Prime Minister, in protest at his well-known opposition to franchise reform, when he came to Bradford to lay the found-
ation stone of the new Wool Exchange. It was an un-
happy experience for the old man; he was reported
as preferring to recall his visit to Saltaire as
the most impressive episode of his visit to Bradford.[16] During the agitations for the Act of 1867,
the Bradford branch of the National Reform League
became one of the two or three most influential in
the country, organising along with the Leeds men,
the two great West Riding demonstrations on Woodhouse Moor in favour of the Act.[17]

There was always a basic element of collabor-
ation with the middle classes and if anything the
spirit of political independence diminished in the
seventies. But there were always elements of uneasy dischord in the situation. The democratic
implications of the 1867 Act led to a number of defections from the Liberal Party; among those in
Bradford were S.C. Lister, M.W. Thompson, H.W.
Ripley and several of the most respected members of
the German community. These elements also underlay
the running dispute between W.E. Forster and his
Radical constituents which went on until his death
in 1886. The trade union issue also was always
likely to provoke controversy and this was particularly the case when trade-union activity began ten-
tatively to penetrate branches of the textile industry untouched by such activities for many years.
Some of Bradford's senior employers were among the
most generous supporters of the National Federation
of Associated Employers formed in 1873 specifici-
cally to combat what they called 'the growing
menace of trade unionism'.[18]

The fragile and uneasy relationship between
the organised working class and the Liberal Party
of Bradford was not so evident elsewhere. It emerges that by the mid-1850s the Chartists were operating as the Advanced Liberal Party in Leeds. The
Labour movement had become absorbed within the
political world of Liberalism. When J. Hales and
S. Brighty visited Leeds in the late 1860s to
assess the state of the Liberal organisation they
reported:

> The increase ... in Leeds is enormous. The
> old register was only, 8,480, whilst the new
> one will be little over 38,000. This extra-

> ordinary addition is principally composed of
> mechanics and factory workers, or as they are
> termed here 'mill hands'. There has been no
> guage taken of their opinion, but they are
> believed to be liberal ... The Trade Societies
> are both numerous and strong, and will be
> useful for working ...[19]

This situation appears to have persisted well into
the 1880s when James Kitson, a large engineering
employer, suggested that Herbert Gladstone, the
son of the Liberal Prime Minister, should stand for
Leeds West, where he had his works and where there
was a strong Co-operative tradition.[20]
   Most other areas of West Yorkshire record a
similar situation to that of Leeds. Liberalism
was preponderant amongst the working classes of
Keighley, Halifax and the vast majority of West
Yorkshire communities where the efforts of organised labour were slight and fitful.

By the 1880s, the way was being prepared for a
more determined assault on the structure of establishment politics. Trade unions took up the political issues much more strongly and the matter of
Labour representation became a regular theme of TUC
debates. The working-class ethic of democracy
evolved more positively with the spread of Socialism and Socialist thought; though its development
owed much to the values of a working-class sub-
culture which had always defied the norms of middle
-class hegemony. For many, John Ruskin confirmed
an opinion that 'a dedication to the great art of
getting on' was not necessarily the best of virtues.[21] Henry George's work provided fresh ammu-
nition for the renewed assault on the sources of
exploitation and deprivation and for forty years
the work of Marx and Engels had been building up a
definition of contemporary Socialism.[22] The
formal organisation of opinion along socialist and
independent labour lines began in 1884 with the establishment of H.M. Hyndman's Social Democratic
Federation, William Morris's Socialist League and
the Fabian Society of Sydney Webb, Bernard Shaw
and Graham Wallas.[23] Both the SDF and the Socialist League drew their inspiration from the work of
Marx and Engels. All were committed to the repla-
cement of nineteenth century Liberal-Capitalism by
more humane forms of social organisation than had
hitherto emerged. And in addition to their understanding of Socialism, working men and women

brought their practical experience of life in industrial society to the development of their democratic institutions - the ILP founded in 1893, the Labour Representation Committee founded in 1900 and the Labour Party which for practical purposes may be dated from 1906 though given formal constitutional basis in 1918.

In West Yorkshire also a new group of working-class leaders was assembling. In Bradford, Samuel Shaftoe, a skep basket maker, one of the founders of the Bradford Trades Council and for many years its leading member had arrived in 1865.[24] Charles Leonard Robinson, a cabinet maker and Bradford's first Independent Labour town councillor, was active in Bradford republican circles by the early 1870s.[25] James Bartley, an Ulsterman from Newry, typographer and journalist, seen by many as the true originator of the Bradford ILP had come in 1872 and W.H. Drew, one of his close associates, was there by the late 1880s.[26] To this emergent Labour leadership may be added many Bradford-born leaders, including Frederick William Jowett, born in 1865, Bradford's first Labour MP, Paul Bland, Jesse Mitchell and George Minty, whom Jowett regarded as Bradford's first Socialists and Joseph Hayhurst, a dyer and Bradford's first Labour Mayor.[27] In Leeds, there was Tom Maguire, Socialism's most passionate advocate in the 1880s, John Lincoln Mahon, a prominent national figure in Morris's Socialist League, and Alfred Mattison, a Leeds engineer.[28] Angus George and Jacob Sanctuary were emerging as Labour leaders in Saltaire, George Garside in the Colne Valley, Ben Turner in Batley, James Beever in Halifax and Allan Gee in Huddersfield.[29] Not all were Socialists and not all were clearly independent Labour men. Some of them maintained a Liberal allegiance all their lives and were engaged in bitter quarrels with Socialists and ILPers. But all contributed to the development of a more aggressive temper in the Labour movement both in the industrial and political field.

The social environment of their activities offered particular advantages. It seems that by the 1880s the working classes were less fragmented than they had ever been. For one thing, the activities of building speculators in the latter part of the century simplified the social geography of the towns and tended to isolate the various classes much more effectively. As we have already suggested, the working-class district of East Bradford was being developed between 1870 and 1890. As it emerged it nurtured the solidarity of working-class people. It was a fruitful base of recruitment for the early Bradford ILP, and many of the leading ILP activists had their homes in the district, often within ten minutes' walk of each other. Growing social and geographical unity amongst the working-classes also began to reduce the social distinctions between the working classes in other West Yorkshire towns as well.

The general weakening of paternalism, as we have already observed, also tended to weaken the identification of the working classes with the employers and provided the opportunity for Socialists and those committed to Independent Labour politics to press forward their gospel. In addition, the onset of trade depressions from the mid-1870s tended to loosen the unquestioning commitment of many working men to the Liberal and Conservative parties.

Some of the disillusionment of working men was given expression after the publication of the evidence given by Bradford businessmen to the Royal Commission on the Depression in Trade and Industry of 1886. Neither Henry Mitchell, the senior Bradford Conservative, nor Jacob Behrens, a prominent Liberal Unionist, had made much of the high levels of unemployment with which the woollen and worsted textile trade was afflicted, though they were clear that there had been a squeeze on profits and prices.[30] Bradford working men were enraged at the one-sided nature of this evidence and complaints both at the monthly meetings of the Trades Council and in the local press were vociferous.[31]

But the most obvious proof came from the spread of trade unionism for the trade union was the most obvious challenge to the paternalistic relationship between master and men. Whatever the accommodation which may have been made with the powerful cotton unions in Lancashire, there can be little doubt that in West Yorkshire many employers saw the trade unions as the enemy. H.W. Ripley, who had dismissed one of his oldest employees in 1869 for voting against him and had long regarded West Bowling as a sort of feudal fief, expressed a fairly general concern when he refused to recognise a dyers' union during the dyers' strike of 1880.[32] Addressing his workpeople he said

> Many of you, grandfathers, fathers, and sons, have worked at Bowling all your lives and this is the first occasion on which you have, during

the long series of years, ever assumed a
hostile attitude. I appeal to you not to
listen to the advances of men who really care
nothing about you, and have not your real
interests at heart.33

During the last quarter of the century, trade
unionism, taking on a new lease of life, spread
more deeply into the semi-skilled and unskilled
trades and practically in Bradford for the first
time since the great strike of 1825, the lower
grades of the textile industry responded. Skilled
men - overlookers, the most highly trained of the
woolsorters, stuffpressers, makers-up and packers -
had been organised for many years though they preferred to think of themselves as friendly societies
rather than trade unions. Their motto, the president of one of these unions said, was 'united to
help, not combined to injure' and continued that
'they had no connection with strikes or trade
unions. They were a class of men whose object was
the benefit of each other in employment and to as-
sist each other in sickness and death'.34 However,
the Bradford-based National Union of Woolsorters,
an organisation of semi-skilled workers ineligible
to join the very exclusive society of highly-skilled
artisans, was started in 1873. It spread quite
rapidly in the textile area and was able in fact to
absorb the exclusive woolsorters' society in 1892.35
The Amalgamated Society of Dyers, refounded in 1878
after a false start in 1872, had 700 members in 1888
and 2,000 in 1892.36 The machine woolcombers, also
failing to establish an organisation in 1872, started the Bradford and District Woolcombers' Society
in 1892 and by 1894 had some 1,200 members.37 The
West Riding Power Loom Weavers' Association, initially formed out of the combination of weavers
unions in Huddersfield and Dewsbury in 1885, opened
its ranks to spinners in 1892, ultimately changing
its name to the General Union of Textile Workers.38
But despite this flourish and the dedication
it implied, the West Yorkshire textile industry
remained weak trade union country. Ben Turner, in
his autobiography, described Bradford 'as the most
heartbreaking district' he could remember, and
Halifax as 'hopeless'.39 Few of the weavers and
spinners, the largest section of the factory workforce, joined the weavers' association in these
towns, although there was more success in Huddersfield, Dewsbury and Batley, as Turner acknowledged.
In Bradford and Halifax the majority of them were

women and young people, not easily organised, and
their proportion of the total workforce had increased as the trade depression had intensified. In
Bradford in the 1850s about half the weavers were
women; by the 1880s the proportion had increased to
two-thirds. In addition, and perhaps more significant than the presence of large numbers of women in
the trades, was the fact that with the collapse of
textile unionism in the Bradford and Leeds area in
1825, no tradition of union organisation had been
able to grow. Equally important, although there
were a number of large firms in existence, a very
large proportion of the textile workers were employed in small businesses. All had their own trade
practices and price lists, and the fixing of piece
rates was a very difficult operation. Indeed, it
was not until 1913 and 1914, respectively, that the
woollen and worsted trades established basic wage
rates, both piece and time, for the district.[40]
Even then, many firms did not pay standard rates to
weavers and spinners. Throughout the late nineteenth and early twentieth centuries small firms continued to 'fine' their workers for alleged poor work,
isolated and discharged 'trouble-makers' and at the
same time offered a sort of 'face-to-face relationship' which generated a sense of loyalty to the
'boss'. It was also in the small firms that hostility to trade unions was greatest, for it was
here that pressure to keep wages as low as possible
was at its highest due to their inability to take
advantage of the economies of scale.
       Trade unionism was naturally more effective
amongst the crafts and in the male-dominated industries. The engineering industry was well unionised
in Leeds, Halifax and Keighley. Engineering was
almost as diversified in West Yorkshire as was
textiles. In Keighley the production centred upon
textile machinery while in Halifax and Leeds the
main line of production was in boilers and railway
engines. The common bond between these districts
was the power and guidance of the large national
craft amalgamations, and particularly the Amalgamated Society of Engineers and the Friendly Society
of Ironfounders. Table 2.1 indicates how successful these two organisations were in Yorkshire as a
whole. Yet it must not be supposed that craft
unions were exceptionally powerful and successful
organisations. Local industrial disputes often
disabused engineers of the view that their position
was invulnerable. As we will indicate, the 1889
engineering dispute in Keighley shook the confidence

Table 2.1: The Membership of Engineering Unions in
Yorkshire between the 1860s and the 1890s

	ASE		FSI	
	1868	1892	1873	1896
Yorkshire Branches	25	53	18	20
Yorkshire Membership	4,400	9,100	3,700	4,300
National Membership	34,000	71,000	12,000	16,000

Source: Details from Parliamentary Papers, Cmnd.
4123, XXXI, 1868-9, Eleventh and Final Report of
the Trade Union Commission, Appendix J; Annual
Report of the ASE, 1892; Annual Reports of the
Friendly Society of Ironfounders.

of engineers in the mastery of their own trade. It
is not without good reason that many of the early
Labour leaders in West Yorkshire were members of
the ASE.[41]
     Elsewhere, craft unionism was not as secure as
it first appeared. Bradford plasterers in 1870
were reported as being able to enforce the rules
vigorously; the master, it was said, was 'not permitted to accept the aid of his nearest relative'
if he was not in the union.[42] One of the by-laws
of the Bradford Bricklayers' Labourers' union was
said to read: 'You are strictly cautioned not to
overstep good rules by doing double work and causing
others to do the same in order to gain a smile from
the master. Such foolhardy and doubtful actions
leave a good portion of good members out of employment'.[43] But what was important was the extent to
which a union could really enforce its rules and
here we have as direct evidence only the records of
the Bradford printers which date from the mid 1860s.
These speak of a constant struggle to establish
their rules rather than of their automatic and
successful employment in the face of every infringe-
ment. Printers, even with their long-established
traditions of chapel organisation, high premiums on
trained skills and superior levels of education did
not control their labour market. In Bradford, as
late as 1892, one-sixth of the printers were not
members of the local branch of the Typographical
Association, and in the villages of the West Riding
there was practically no recruitment at all.[44] The
labour market was always over stocked. Young men
just out of apprenticeship and old men unable to

maintain the speed of work could only find the casual work available at the busy time of the week when the weekly publications were going to press and in the busy time of the year when Bradford firms were producing Christmas cards.[45] A number of employers including the Bradford Daily Telegraph did not recognise the union as yet. The impression that these circumstances were not unique to the printers is confirmed by William Cudworth whose work on the conditions of the industrial working classes of Bradford suggests that few trades had adequate control of such matters as apprenticeship.[46]

But in these unions a good deal of progress was being made by the end of the century, and the printers were among the most notably pugnacious. They had been threatened by technical change at last. In 1889, the Thorne Composing machine was introduced into the offices of the Bradford Observer and its appearance started a series of acrimonious disputes which were not satisfactorily resolved until 1896.[47] By this time all the Bradford men were members of the union and the non-union firms had surrendered. Chapels in the rural districts from Wharfedale to Spen Valley had joined the union. Its policy became extremely aggressive. It complained and threatened when public bodies employed non-union men and started the Fair Contracts movement throughout its area of recruitment. Altogether it was a long way from the occasion in 1867 when the printers, trying to negotiate the first wage increase they had requested in thirty years, assured their masters that they 'did not intend to press their claims arrogantly, nor ... use anything but moral suasion to attain their object'.[48]

The diffusion of trade unionism throughout working-class society in West Yorkshire - even if not a powerful movement - expressed very clearly a growing unity of working-class life. Its particular development created fields of activity for Socialists and independent Labour men to cultivate, for these men saw industrial and political organisation not as separate elements but as two sides of an homogeneous Labour movement. The situation in the textile area was very different from that in the mining areas in South Yorkshire and in the cotton areas of Lancashire. In West Yorkshire there were no large unions able to deliver, en bloc, a working-class vote which would ensure a political majority for the party and candidate they favoured. They could therefore be ignored when they demanded political concessions from the other parties; but the way

lay open for the creation of an independent working-
class party. In the non-unionised trades the 'Independent' men could (and did) contribute to the
beginning of new unions and infiltration of other
unions was easier for the fact that there were no
powerful and successful organisations dominated by
men dedicated to the other parties.

Thus it seems that the time was ripe for the evolution of a comprehensive Labour movement for much
of the fragmentation of the past was being elimin-
ated. Nevertheless, the struggle for an independent Labour party was not merely a struggle with
the upper classes. It was also a fight between men
who supported the existing parties, particularly
the 'old-fashioned' Liberals, on the one hand, and
the new Socialist-Independent men on the other.
   The first public statements of the new spirit
abroad did not appear to arouse much general enthusiasm. In February 1884, William Morris came to
Bradford to lecture on behalf of the Democratic
Federation, soon to become the SDF. He had been
invited by a small committee of local Radicals who
had just started a programme of Sunday lectures
for working men. The committee included such vet-
eran Radicals as James Hanson and T.T. Empsall,
the younger W.P. Byles, part-owner of the Bradford
Observer, as well as Angus George, the manager of
the Tailors shop at Saltaire Co-operative Stores.
The title of Morris's lecture was 'Useful Work v
Useless Toil'. In it, he made a fierce attack on
the supremacy of the middle classes:

> The idea of bettering the existing condition
> of things had taken the form of philanthropy,
> the preaching of thrift, and perhaps in a way
> compelling an economic and social revolution.
> All those plans for the reform of the abuses
> of society were useless because they were all
> founded on the supremacy that was founded on
> the system of Capitalism ... from whence sprang
> the class of victims which formed the found-
> ationstone of our social edifice of luxury and
> well-being. It was that supremacy, on the
> contrary, that Socialism attacked.[49]

Morris's lecture attracted a large audience but
apparently received only a lukewarm reception. The
Bradford Observer commented that 'the audience,
which filled the Temperance Hall, was amused, if
not converted', and Morris himself was disappointed

at the impact he had made: for he referred to Bradford's working men later as a 'sad set of Philis-
tines' content to let their wives and children sup-
plement the household income with wages from the
spinning and weaving departments of the mills.[50]
The second lecture given by a local person, the Rev.
J. Cockson, on 'English Socialism, or the Poor Man's
Politics' was received more willingly. Cockson
accepted much of Morris's denunciation of extremes
of poverty and wealth, but his solution was more to
the taste of an audience composed principally of
the 'aristocrats of labour'. If only men were good!
The revolution was needed rather in men's hearts
than in the institutions of society.

Parliamentary reform in 1884 and 1885 caused
some activity. The Act of 1884, extending the
principle of the 1867 Act to male householders outside the parliamentary boroughs, gave the vote to
the majority of working men living in the West Riding rural areas of the Calder, Spen, Colne and Aire
Valleys. Well attended meetings were held throughout the area and by early 1885 the Liberals and
the Tories had set up political organisations to
take over from the county associations.[51] In the
parliamentary boroughs there were more positive
signs of political interest amongst the working
classes. Samuel Shaftoe stood as a trade union
candidate at a municipal election at East Bowling
in Bradford. He was defeated by 672 votes to 513
to the regret of the Bradford Observer, a Liberal
paper, which was actively supporting the working-
man's cause.[52]

The re-distribution of seats also strengthened
the cry for working-class representation. In place
of the two members, both elected by a poll of the
whole vote, Bradford was to have three constituencies, each with its own MP. Given the social
geography of the town this meant that in one constituency at least, East Bradford, the working-class
vote would easily predominate. Working-class leaders thought that this should naturally be a working
-class seat and started, in February 1885, the process of securing a Labour candidate. At the beginning of March the Bradford Observer published an
article from S. Neil, of the Northumberland Miners'
Union, in which the point was made that so far
working men had been little more than voting mach-
ines manipulated by the party organisations. They
needed to be represented by men who spoke for them,
like them and with them as did their companions in
the pits. The same issue contained a letter from a

Bradford working man making the same plea: 'What
advantage will it be to the working men of Bradford
when we have three instead of two members if the
interests of all three clash with those who elect
them'. He went on to suggest that with men like
Abraham Sharp to call on - men who had devoted their
lives to the political battle and had held their own
with the greatest in the land - Bradford need not
fear that intelligent and forceful representation
might not be found.[53]

The committee, set up to explore the situation
in the new East division, were much more concerned
that the 'fiasco of 1874' (Hardaker's contest) should not be repeated and emphasised in their public
statements that their candidate would keep clear
of all party connections. They had thus to find out
to what extent working men were prepared to support
a candidate financially, and circulated trade unionists for information. The answers were disappointing. The reply of the printers was typical. The
Typographical Society replied that the question of
a Labour candidate for Bradford 'was inopportune'
and reluctantly the committee stood down.[54] In
other parts of West Yorkshire similar events were
taking place. The Leeds Trades Council proposed to
ask Henry Broadhurst to stand as their candidate
but nothing came of it and in the Colne Valley discussion went no further than the question of financial obligation.[55]

Later in the year the Bradford Trades Council
tried a less-ambitious project. It asked the Liberal Executive Council to nominate one working man
in their list for the forthcoming School Board elections. Although the proposed candidate was John
Hollings, president of the Trades Council and a much
respected life-long Liberal, the idea was rejected
with some contempt.[56]

Other sources of inspiration and activity were
however developing. By 1886 there were two small
branches of Morris's Socialist League in existence
in Bradford and Leeds; a good many of their members
were among the founders of the National ILP in 1893.
In Leeds they included Tom Maguire, E. Connell, J.
Flinn, Tom Paylor and Alfred Mattison; in Bradford,
Fred Pickles, Paul Bland and Fred Jowett and a number about whom we have little more than tantalising
hints - among them Karl Heuze and Karl Burlauf,
German political refugees and G.A. Gaskell a local
artist.[57] By 1887 both groups were pursuing policies
which had been given the stamp of approval by
H.H. Champion and the heirs of Marx - Engels,

Aveling and Eleanor Marx - and which led them away
from the anti-parliamentarianism of the Socialist
League and led them directly into the working-class
struggle. Their efforts were to be aimed at winning
the trade unions and to the formation of a united
Labour movement with its own political party and its
trade union movement.

In Leeds the prominent figures in this political movement were Tom Maguire and John Lincoln
Mahon. Maguire, who has been the subject of some
detailed study, was a Leeds-Irish photographic
assistant who appears to have turned towards Socialism in about 1883.[58] By 1885, after some determined
propaganda work in Leeds, he had mustered sufficient
supporters to form the Leeds branch of the Socialist
League, a body of about 15 to 20 members, many of
them of Irish and East European descent, which provided the pioneering spirit of Socialism not only in
Leeds but throughout West Yorkshire.[59] From the
early days, Maguire and the Leeds Socialist League
became increasingly characterised by their commitment to winning support from within the working
class, and particularly amongst trade unions. In
this endeavour they were helped by John Lincoln
Mahon, a national figure in the Socialist League who
became a close personal friend of Maguire. Mahon
came to Leeds, as National Secretary of the Socialist League, in 1885 to help establish the branch in
Leeds and was a frequent visitor to Leeds before
settling there between 1890 and 1894.[60]

Mahon had been prominent within Socialist
League ranks in trying to get the national leadership to drop its disdain of working with working-
class organisations, a move which eventually took
him, Maguire and others from the anti-parliamentary
attitude of Morris to the pro-parliamentary attitude
of the ILP. In 1887, Mahon put forward a resolution
to the annual conference of the Socialist League
demanding that

> every effort be made to penetrate the existing
> political organisations with Socialism; that
> all possible help be given to such movements
> as trades-unionism, co-operation, national and
> international labour federations, etc. by
> which the working classes are trying to better
> their condition; that Parliament, municipal
> and other local-government bodies, and the con-
> tests for the election of members to them, be
> taken advantage of for spreading the principle
> of Socialism and organising the people into

> a Socialist Labour Party ... tho' complete
> emancipation can only be achieved by the tran-
> sformation of society into a co-op common-
> wealth.61

The anti-parliamentarians defeated the resolution;
nevertheless, it embodied the sort of policy which
the Leeds and Bradford branches of the Socialist
League were to pursue as they, and their members,
embraced the challenge of winning political support
which was to lead their main activists into the ILP.
    Maguire and Mahon shared their views with
other Socialist and independent Labour men throughout West Yorkshire. In July 1887, James Bartley
had a series of letters published in the Bradford
Observer. He pointed to the injustices of a
system organised to ensure that Labour always played second fiddle to Capital and called for a
'practical means of giving expression to working-
class needs'. Something beyond simple trade union
organisation was needed, for except in very rare
circumstances he could not see how pure-and-simple
trade unionism could exert direct political influ-
ence.62 Certainly the few trade union MPs there
were had made little impact upon the House of Commons. Bartley called for a new party freed from
all other political influences, avoiding the extremes of theorising Socialism and the errors of
capitalistic Liberalism, for 'Socialist propaganda
was not sufficiently belligerent to make much headway and no true help could be expected from the
Liberals in their existing organisations'. He
offered the new party a tentative programme - mild-
ly Socialist, though much of it was simple radicalism - adult suffrage, reform of local government,
disestablishment of the Anglican Church, abolition
of the House of Lords, land law reform, nationalis-
ation of railways and payment of MPs. This had to
be a working-class party, supporting its activities
from its own financial resources and represented at
every level by working men who thought like them.

> And the party must not be composed of men who
> are ashamed to wear as their headgear the
> billycock of their class. There must be no
> chimney pots in the new party. Its members
> must be men who are sufficiently courageous to
> defy caste and all that caste means. They
> must be the sworn enemies of that feeling
> which has done so much to keep the workers
> enslaved - the feeling of artificial respect

for class power.[63]

He had recently attended a conference in London of
like-minded men and he had returned convinced of
the need for a big national conference supported by
immediate local initiative.

Fred Jowett and G.A. Gaskell joined Bartley
in the discussion. There was nothing to expect from
the parties, said Jowett, for their concern was
merely to protect the 'sacred rights of capitalism.
If we ask the Tories for social change, they answer
confiscation. If Liberal leaders be approached the
times are said to be inopportune for such change'.[64]
Gaskell said it was obvious that a new party was
coming into existence. It would, he said, represent
men and not 'hands'. It would discard the 'servil-
ity of the present slave-labour representatives' -
and he was particularly scathing about the activities of the trade-union MP Thomas Burt who, he said,
offered no challenge to anybody. Meanwhile wages
were low and unemployment high - working men would
have to be much more militant if they were to get
anywhere.

The Socialism of these men is not easy to de-
fine. Bartley, in particular, gives the impression
that he was basically an Independent Labour man.
All of them would have defined Socialism as a way
of approaching the problem of fundamental social reform, of fulfilling Labour's aspirations, rather
than of a scientific analysis of the nature of society. But all understood the implications of the
class struggle and were prepared to fight it. The
Bradford 'independents' differed from the Leeds
Socialists in that they were not much concerned
with the need for a missionary campaign to make con-
verts to Socialism. The emphasis of their programme was placed on the need for a separate party
through which they could act - the party's activities would make Socialists for them.

Another stimulus to activity was provided by
the trade union Liberals. At the beginning of 1887,
trade unionists met in Bradford to discuss the creation of a wider Labour interest on the political
field. It was attended by most of the leaders of
the Bradford Trades Council. As a result of its
deliberations a Bradford branch of the Labour Electoral Association was established, to fight parliamentary and local elections.[65] They were as committed as the Independent-Socialists to the need for
working-class representation for the working class.
Shaftoe had declared angrily after the Liberals had

rejected John Holling's request to be nominated for
election to the School Board that 'If the political
parties ignore the cause of labour as they have done
in the past, then Labour must run its own men, whatever political party may suffer or political chief-
tain be disappointed'.[66]
     The fundamental lack of agreement between the
Liberal trade unionists and the Independent-Socialist group was quickly revealed. The Liberal trade
unionists really demanded little more than Hardaker
in the Bradford parliamentary election of 1874 - a
separate labour interest within the embrace of the
existing Liberal organisation. They held firm to
the Liberal creed of individualism and a minimum of
state activity in the economic and social concerns
of the people. This was understandable; men like
Shaftoe had spent a political lifetime in the Liberal Party and had achieved a measure of success
and some local prestige.[67] Since they were the
most important members of the existing trade unions,
it was inevitable that the 'independent' men should
regard them as the principal barrier to the creation of an homogeneous Labour movement with its
own political party.
     Yet it should not be assumed that even at this
early stage the embryonic Independent-Socialist
movement in West Yorkshire was exclusively working-
class in its orientation. It is clear that in West
Yorkshire, as well as in the country at large,
there were many middle-class people who were being
drawn to Socialism. In Bradford there were, amongst
those who were to become prominent later, E.R.
Hartley, a butcher; Willie Leach, a textile merchant
and manufacturer; Arthur Priestman, a Quaker textile
businessman of some substance, and many Congregational ministers, such as the Rev. T. Rhondda Williams
and the Rev. R. Roberts. In Leeds, there were the
Ford sisters, particularly Isabella and Bessie,
members of a well-established Quaker family. In
addition there were Congregationalists, such as the
Rev. Westrope, and A.R. Orage, a school teacher who
later moved from the ILP to Guild Socialism while
editing in London the literary and political paper
the New Age. In Halifax there was John Lister, a
well-to-do landowner who later became the first
Treasurer of the National ILP; Montague Blatchford,
the brother of Robert Blatchford; and the Rev.
Bryan Dale, a Congregational minister. In Colne
Valley there were a number of small manufacturers
emerging into early Labour movement, most particularly France Littlewood who also, like John Lister,

became the Treasurer of the National ILP.[68]

Although these people, and many of their type, were drawn to the Independent-Socialist movement for a variety of reasons- the Ford sisters were involved by virtue of their work in trying to improve the conditions of tailoresses in the Leeds tailoresses strike of late 1889 and Willie Leach was drawn in through his friendship with Fred Jowett - it is clear that many were won to the movement by the flood of Fabian literature which emerged during the late 1880s and by the book Fabian Essays. By the end of 1892 there were Fabian societies at Batley, Bradford, Copley (near Halifax), Halifax, Huddersfield, Leeds and Sowerby Bridge. A branch was also formed at Dewsbury before May 1893.[69] There may not have been the overwhelming middle-class presence in these branches which characterised the Fabian organisation in London, but it is clear that there was a strong middle-class presence in some of these provincial branches and that Fabian 'gradualism' helped ease many members of the middle class into the ILP.

Although the records of West Yorkshire Fabian activities are sketchy the middle-class nature of much of their support is provided by the surviving details of the Halifax Fabian Society. It was formed by John Lister, the Rev. Bryan Dale and a number of small manufacturers and businessmen, although there were some prominent trade unionists, such as James Beever, who figured prominently in the early history of the Halifax ILP and was Halifax's first Labour agent, who were prominent in the branch activities. John Lister's account of the early days of the Labour movement make it clear that the Halifax Fabian Society was formed by middle-class people such as himself and that, with the Halifax Trades Council, it was responsible for the formation of the Halifax Labour Union, the forerunner of the Halifax ILP. Lister also makes clear that the Fabian Society did much propaganda work in West Yorkshire in the late 1880s and early 1890s.[70]

This middle-class presence within the early West Yorkshire Labour movement offered both advantages and disadvantages. The main advantages were that it provided the emergent ILP with financial and propaganda help. The Halifax ILP did not manage to clear the financial debt it had built up with Lister, though he wrote much of it off, until 1900. Also by the mid 1890s most of the West Yorkshire Fabian societies had become submerged within

the local ILP branches. The main disadvantages,
however, related to the suspicion in which middle-
class support was often held by the working-class
representatives. This did not always break the
surface of equanimity which the early ILP built up
but was all too evident in the Mahon-Lister conflict
of 1893, when Mahon, objecting to the radical-demo-
cratic demands of Lister in the Halifax parliamentary by-election of 1893, advised the Halifax working men not to vote for Lister. The rumpus which
this created is examined in more detail in chapter
three and it is evident that Mahon's views were
shared by others. Tom Maguire felt that if
the Leeds ILP was to avoid the mistakes of the past
it must 'fall more closely into touch with the
humbler wants of the people ... It must relinquish
the delight of manipulating Fabian statistics and
come a little nearer to the unfamiliar weekly wage
question ...'71

It would be wrong to underestimate the influence of the work of Marx in the formulation of individual ideas. But on the whole the Socialism of
the movement was not one based on a scientific
analysis of society. Socialism for most was the
fulfilment of a Labour dream, the completion of a
homogeneous movement - in which the trade unions
organised men and women for industry, the co-operative movement organised them for the provision
of their daily needs and the Labour Union organised
them for democratic political action. Socialism
was the expression of working class need in politics. As such, a programme of fundamental social
reform could be presented which took a great deal
from the Liberal radicalism which most of them had
left behind - a programme which left available a
bridge for others of the Liberal Party. Thus the
name itself was significant. Many of the most important pioneers of the movement had been members
of the Socialist League, most of the members were
proud to call themselves Socialists. Nevertheless
the movement started as a movement of Labour
Unions.

NOTES

1. George Lichtheim, The Origins of Socialism
(Weidenfeld and Nicolson, London, 1968).
2. Bradford Observer, 8 Jun. 1852, 19 Apr.
1865, 15 Mar. 1868; J. James, Continuation and
Additions to the History of Bradford (Longman Green,
Bradford 18-6), p. 117; Parliamentary Papers, 1866,

lvii, p. 747.
    3. J. Reynold, The Great Paternalist, Titus
Salt and the Growth of Nineteenth Century Bradford
(Temple Smith, London, 1983), chapter four.
    4. Ibid., p. 202.
    5. Ibid., p. 206.
    6. Ibid., p. 39.
    7. Ross Terrill, R.H. Tawney and His Times:
Socialism and Fellowship (Andre Deutsch, London,
1973), p. 173.
    8. Parliamentary Papers, Census of England
and Wales, 1871.
    9. Bradford Observer, 4, 6 Oct, 22 Nov. 1866.
    10. Ibid., 16 Jan. 1868.
    11. Ibid., 12 Feb. to 12 Mar. 1869.
    12. Ibid.
    13. Ibid.
    14. D.G. Wright, 'The Bradford Election of
1874' in J.A. Jowitt and R.K.S. Taylor (eds.)
Nineteenth Century Bradford Elections (Bradford
Centre Occasional Papers No. 1, University of Leeds,
Department of Adult Education, Leeds, 1979); pp. 62,
64, 66; Bradford Observer Budget, 7 Sep. 1889.
    15. Bradford Observer, 22 Apr. 1852, 21, 28
Jan. 1858.
    16. Ibid., 21 Jul., 4, 14 Aug. 1864; Reynold's
Newspaper, 14 Aug. 1964.
    17. Ibid., 16 Jan. 1868, Feb. 1874, passim.
    18. Capital and Labour, 31 Dec. 1873.
    19. T. Woodhouse, 'The working class' in D.
Fraser (ed.), A History of Modern Leeds (Manchester
University Press, Manchester, 1980), p. 356.
    20. Ibid., p. 357.
    21. J. Ruskin, The Crown of Wild Olives (George
Allen, London, 1886, 1906 ed.) pp. 105-6.
    22. D. McLellan, Karl Marx: His Life and
Thought (Macmillan, London, 1978).
    23. A.M. McBriar, Fabian Socialism and English
Politics, 1884-1918 (Cambridge University Press,
London, 1966).
    24. Mary Ashraf, Bradford Trades Council, 1872-
1972 (Bradford Trades Council, Bradford, 1972).
    25. K. Laybourn and J. Saville, 'Charles
Leonard Robinson 1845-1911' in J. Bellamy and
J. Saville, Dictionary of Labour Biography, vol. 3
(Macmillan, London, 1976), Vol. 3, pp. 155-6.
    26. K. Laybourn and J. Saville, 'W.H. Drew
1854-1933', in J. Bellamy and J. Saville, Dictionary
of Labour Biography, Vol. 4 (Macmillan, London,
1977), pp. 75-7.
    27. Brockway, Socialism over Sixty Years,

pp. 29-30.
28. E.P. Thompson, 'Homage to Tom Maguire', in
A. Briggs and J. Saville, Essays in Labour History
(Macmillan, London, 1960, 1967), pp. 276-316.
29. K. Laybourn, 'The Attitude of Yorkshire
Trade Unions to the Economic and Social Problems
of the Great Depression, 1873-1896', unpublished
PhD thesis, University of Lancaster, 1973, biographical sketches, pp. 478-85.
30. Reynolds and Laybourn, 'The Emergence of
the Independent Labour Party in Bradford', p. 322.
31. Ibid.
32. S.C. Kell, 'The Political Attitude of our
Law-Making Classes to the Unenfranchised',
Bradford Review, also issued as a pamphlet in
Bradford, 1861; Bradford Observer, 28 Mar. 1870.
33. Bradford Observer, 7 Feb. 1880.
34. Ibid., 6 Feb. 1868, 31 Jan. 1870.
35. Laybourn, 'The Attitude of Yorkshire Trade
Unions', chapter three; Reynolds and Laybourn, 'The
Emergence of the Independent Labour Party in Bradford', p. 321.
36. Reynolds and Laybourn, 'The Emergence of
the Independent Labour Party in Bradford', p. 321.
37. Bradford Observer, 8 Mar. 1872.
38. Laybourn, 'Yorkshire Trade Unions',
chapter three.
39. B. Turner, About Myself (Toulmin, London,
1930); B. Turner, A Short History of the General
Union of Textile Workers (Yorkshire Factory Times,
Heckmondwyke, 1920), pp. 124, 153-6.
40. J.A. Jowitt and K. Laybourn, 'The Wool
Textile Dispute of 1925', Journal of Local Studies,
Vol. 2, No. 1 (Spring, 1982), p. 11. The details
are presented in an article by Ben Turner entitled
'Textile Workers at Bay', Yorkshire Factory Times,
6 Aug. 1925.
41. Laybourn, 'The Attitude of Yorkshire Trade
Unions', chapter three.
42. W.T. Thornton, On Labour, Its Wrongful
Claims and Rightful Dues: Its Actual, Present and
Possible Future (London, 1869, 1870 edition), pp.
206-7.
43. Ibid.
44. J. Reynolds, The Letter Press Printers of
Bradford (Bradford Graphical Society, Bradford,
1972), pp. 19-26.
45. Ibid., p. 6.
46. W. Cudworth, The Condition of the Industrial Working Classes of Bradford and District
(Byles, Bradford, 1887).

47.   Reynolds, Letter Press Printers.
48.   Letter of Bradford Letter Press Printers to employers, 23 Nov. 1867, at front of Minutes of Letter Press Printers now deposited in the J.B. Priestley Library, University of Bradford.
49.   Bradford Oberserver Budget, 23 Feb. 1884.
50.   Philip Henderson (ed.) The Letters of William Morris to his Family and Friends (Longmans, Green & Co., London, 1950). letter dated 25 Feb. 1885.
51.   Bradford Observer Budget, 6, 20 Mar. 1885.
52.   Ibid., 6 Mar. 1885.
53.   Ibid.
54.   Ibid., 27 Feb, 17 Mar., 2 Apr. 1885; Bradford Typographical Society, Minutes, Mar. 1885.
55.   Bradford Observer Budget, 3 Apr. 1885.
56.   Reynolds and Laybourn, 'The Emergence of the Independent Labour Party in Bradford', p. 314.
57.   Brockway, Socialism over Sixty Years, p. 30.
58.   Thompson, 'Homage to Tom Maguire', pp. 292-3.
59.   Ibid., pp. 292-302.
60.   Ibid., passim.
61.   E.P. Thompson, William Morris: Romantic to Revolutionary (Merlin Press, London, 1955, 1977 edition), p. 452.
62.   Bradford Observer, 12, 20, 27 Jul. 1887.
63.   Ibid., 2 Aug. 1887.
64.   Ibid., 18 Aug. 1887.
65.   Reynolds and Laybourn, 'The Emergence of the Independent Labour Party in Bradford', p. 322.
66.   Bradford Observer, 25 Sep. 1885.
67.   K. Laybourn and J. Saville, 'Samuel Shaftoe 1841-1911', in J. Bellamy and J. Saville (eds.), Dictionary of Labour Biography, Vol. 3, pp. 158-60.
68.   H.J.O. Drake, 'John Lister of Shibden Hall, 1847-1933', unpublished Ph.D thesis, University of Bradford, 1973.
69.   Thompson, 'Homage to Tom Maguire', p. 302.
70.   Drake, 'John Lister of Shibden Hall', passim.
71.   Quoted by T. Woodhouse, 'Trade Unions and Independent Labour Politics in Leeds 1885-1894', unpublished paper, p. 33.

Chapter Three

TRADE UNIONS AND THE INDEPENDENT LABOUR PARTY: THE
GENESIS OF THE ILP IN WEST YORKSHIRE

Even as late as 1890 the Labour movement in West
Yorkshire was a weak vehicle for the political aspirations of the working class. Trade unionism was
patchy, Labour's political organisation was fitful,
flimsy and embryonic, and the trades councils of the
West Riding were only just beginning to emerge and
become effective in protecting the economic interests of working men. In truth, the Liberal Party
had little to worry about and was confident in its
estimation that at least two-thirds of the working-
class voters would continue to vote Liberal in
future. It was this almost endemic weakness of
Labour organisations which deluded the Liberal Party
into thinking that it could stand still in the face
of the 'little breezes' of discontent that occasionally emerged.[1] What local Liberal parties failed
to appreciate was the seething discontent which had
erupted amongst trade unionists as a result of the
Manningham Mills strike of 1890 and 1891. This neglect combined with working-class anger and frustration to produce an Independent Labour movement
which eventually made significant inroads into the
existing two-party political system. Between 1890
and 1895 the genesis of a viable ILP occurred in
West Yorkshire.

What transformed the small Socialist societies of
the 1880s into a burgeoning Labour movement was the
support which came from trade unions and trades
councils. For a variety of reasons an increasing
proportion of trade unionists became frustrated at
the obduracy of Liberalism in the face of rising
working-class expectations. The fact that many
leading Liberals were prominent employers in the
engineering and textile industries and also formed
the local political oligarchy meant that economic

40

issues could be readily translated into political
ones. A Socialist presence in a climate of industrial conflict helped to unite the frustrations of
trade unionists and channel their rising energies
towards Socialist and Independent Labour activities.
This was most readily apparent in Keighley and Bradford.

In Keighley, normally the most sedate of towns,
the engineering strike of August and September 1889
united skilled, semi-skilled and unskilled engineering workers together in the demand for a wage
increase. This dispute exposed the genuine griev-
ances of the working classes in Keighley who had
been unfairly treated under the old system.[2] A
speaker at a strike meeting reflected the new, less
compliant, spirit of the workforce:

> Keighley was known throughout the country for
> two things. In the first place it was famous
> for science and art and technical education,
> and in the second place ... it was notorious,
> not famous, for low wages. He wanted to put
> the two together and he wanted to ask them
> seriously what was the benefit of science and
> art and technical education unless they put
> more money in their pockets.[3]

The men were also warned to 'see that no mischief
was done, that they do not run themselves into the
police court or into the hands of the magistrates,
for they would find as a rule that those men were
not on the side of Labour'.[4] In the wake of this
dispute a Trades Council was formed, which was closely associated with the Keighley ILP in the early
1890s.

Of more lasting and pervasive influence was
the Manningham Mills strike of 1890 and 1891. It
was the product of the attempt by Samuel Cunliffe
Lister and the shareholders of Manningham Mills to
reduce the wages of their silk and plush weavers by
amounts varying from 15 per cent to 33 per cent of
their wages. During the course of the dispute the
entire workforce, of several thousands, struck or
were forced out of work, the Weavers' Association
became embroiled in the dispute, the issue of free
speech was raised, violence occurred and the riot
act was read.[5] This dispute has been scrutinised by
many historians, most notably E.P. Thompson.[6] They
have demonstrated how vital it was to the political
education of the working classes of West Yorkshire.
Much contemporary evidence, and most recent inter-

pretations, have stressed the way in which the political consensus between the Liberals and the working classes was destroyed and replaced by a sense of deep injustice amongst a significant proportion of the working classes in Bradford and West Yorkshire. The Bradford Observer reported that 'The struggle took on the character of a general dispute between capital and labour since it is well known that a large number of prominent Bradford employers agreed with the action Mr. Lister had taken'.[7] The strike evoked a remarkable display of local working-class solidarity, so much so that the Yorkshire Factory Times, the weekly newspaper which served the textile workers, announced the end of the strike with the prophetic statement that 'Labour has so associated itself that even defeat must be victory'.[8]

Indeed the Manningham Mills strike acted as a catalyst for many of those trade unionists and individuals who had begun to doubt both the impartiality of the Liberal Party and its willingness to represent their interests. The Yorkshire Factory Times was correct in its estimation of the impact of the strike for the process of disengagement from Liberalism had already begun before the end of the dispute. In April 1891, at a strike meeting at Peckover Walks a famous open-air meeting place in Bradford, speaker after speaker pinpointed the lessons of the strike. Charlie Glyde summed up the frustrations of many when he reflected that 'We have had two parties in the past, the can'ts and the won'ts and it is time that we had a party that will'.[9]

The 'party that will' was officially formed about six weeks later at Firth's Temperance Hotel, formerly Laycock's, in East Parade, Bradford. A meeting was called for Thursday 30 April. Very few attended; those present, however, included W.H. Drew, James Bartley, E.W. Roche, Edwin Tolson and George Minty, men who were to become prominent in the Bradford Labour movement. A small committee was set up and a further meeting was arranged at Firth's Temperance Hall for 25 May 1891. At this meeting the Bradford and District Labour Union was formed to 'further the cause of direct Labour representation on Local Bodies and in Parliament'.[10]

The formation of the Bradford Labour Union presaged the rapid formation of others. The Colne Valley Labour Union was formed on 21 July 1891, and others were formed soon afterwards. By early January 1893 there were at least eight Labour unions, or similar organisations, in the West

Riding textile belt. Indeed Yorkshire was the best
represented county at the Independent Labour Party's
Inaugural Conference in January 1893. Of the 120
delegates present, 48 came from Yorkshire and of
these, West Yorkshire sent the largest number. The
Bradford Labour Union was represented by 20 delegates, Leeds ILP sent three, Halifax three, Batley
one and Huddersfield six. In addition, although the
Colne Valley Labour Union did not send a delegate it
was effectively represented by two men, Edward
Hoskins, of Slaithwaite Labour Club, and France
Littlewood.[11] In total, then, 35 of the 120 delegates in Bradford were drawn from the woollen district of Yorkshire.

Table 3.1 Labour Unions/ILP branches in West Yorkshire, 1891-5

Organisation	Formed
Bradford Labour Union	28 May 1891
Colne Valley Labour Union	21 July 1891
Huddersfield Labour Union	14 September 1891
Halifax Labour Union	July 1892
Keighley Labour Union	October 1892
Leeds ILP	November 1892
Batley ILP	1893
Dewsbury ILP	1893
Shipley ILP	1895

Sources: Yorkshire Factory Times, 29 May 1891, 25
September 1891; Colne Valley Labour Union, Minutes,
21 July 1891; Keighley News, 8 October 1892 and the
accounts of the National ILP Conference of 1893
which appear in several newspapers.

The prominence of West Yorkshire is further
demonstrated by the national figures of branch
affiliation. In 1895, for instance, 102 of the 305
ILP branches were to be found in Yorkshire, compared with 73 in Lancashire and Cheshire, 41 in Scotland, 29 in London, 23 in the Midlands, 18 in the
North-East, 8 in Kent, four in the Eastern Counties,
three in Ireland, three in Southern England and one
in Wales.[12] Although many branches collapsed over
the next five years it is clear that the North, as
E.P. Thompson suggested many years ago, was the real
home of the ILP and that the West Yorkshire textile

district was its heartland.13 It is hardly surprising then that Bradford ILP members, in particular, should constantly echo their justifiable pride
in the fact that the National ILP was formed in
Bradford, and that W.H. Drew, a member of the Bradford ILP and the Bradford Trades Council, should
remind J. Ramsay MacDonald, shortly before the
Labour Representation Conference held in Bradford
in 1904, that Bradford was the 'Birthplace of the
political Labour movement'.14

The early Labour breakthrough in Bradford and
the woollen district was largely based upon the
fact that the Labour Union/ILP organisations were
quick to capture the support of some local trade
unions and trade councils, many of which had only
emerged in the late 1880s and early 1890s. Indeed
the late emergence of a well-organised trade union
movement in West Yorkshire might well account for
the slowness of Socialist and ILP politics to
develop before 1890 and its rapid growth therafter.

Until 1885 there were only two trades councils
in West Yorkshire, at Leeds and Bradford. By the
end of 1890 there were seven, and by 1895 the number had increased to 14. Apart from Leeds and
Bradford, the majority of the trades councils were
relatively small, although there was significant
expansion at Halifax and Huddersfield in the early
1890s. The membership of the Leeds and Bradford councils fluctuated around 10,000 members each in the
mid 1890s; Huddersfield had 2,000 members in 1893
and about 3,300 by 1899; Halifax fluctuated between
about 3,000 and 4,000 members in the 1890s;
Keighley claimed to represent 1,302 members in 1895;
Batley had 3,000 members by the late 1890s; and
other trades councils appear to have had fewer than
1,000 members in their early years.15

The relative weakness of most of these trades
councils was a reflection of the weakness of trade
unionism in West Yorkshire as a whole. We have
already noted that textile trade unionism was weak
in this region and the Webbs emphasised this in
their estimate of the strength of trade unionism in
1892. According to them there were only 141,140
trade unionists in the county out of a total population of 2,464,415. Since about 55,000 of these
were members of the Yorkshire Miners' Association,
and several thousand were metal workers in Sheff-
ield, it is evident that only about three per cent
of the West Yorkshire population was unionised in
the early 1890s.16

Indeed, there was little semblance of trade-

Table 3.2 Trades Councils in the West Yorkshire
Textile District up to 1895

Organisation	Formed
Leeds Trades Council	1860, reformed in 1865
Bradford Trades Council	1868, reformed in 1872
Huddersfield Trades Council	1885
Shipley Friendly and Trades Societies	1887
Halifax Trades Council	1889
Keighley Trades Council	1890
Morley Trades Council	1890
Dewsbury and Batley Trades Council	1891
Brighouse and District Trades and Labour Council	1891
Wakefield Federated Trades Council	1891
Spen Valley Trades Council	1892
Todmorden Trades Council	1892
Batley Trades Council	formed about 1895

Source: K. Laybourn, 'The Attitudes of Yorkshire
Trade Unions to the Economic and Social Problems of
the Great Depression, 1873-1896', unpublished PhD
thesis, University of Lancaster, 1973, particularly
chapters three and ten.

union unity or effective organisation in the woollen
and worsted industry before the First World War.
Many unions were formed during the nineteenth century but they were, invariably, small combinations
of skilled men with a propensity to collapse when
employers applied the least pressure.[17]
  The great difficulty faced by the wool textile
unionists was that the woollen and worsted industry
was so diverse that it made it almost impossible
for large unions to emerge and represent a wide
variety of interests. Some areas produced woollen
dress fabrics whilst others produced worsted coat-
ings. Huddersfield produced heavy woollens on a
one-loom system, whilst Bradford weavers, largely
female in contrast to the more male-dominated weaving sections in Huddersfield, worked two or more

looms.[18] Other areas, such as Dewsbury, produced
'shoddy cloth' from the wool recovered from used
garments. The industrial diversity of local industry, local customs, and the power and independent
action of many employers who wished to determine
wage rates directly with their workers made it difficult for wool textile unions to attract wide support.

The fact that the Bradford, Leeds and Halifax
trade union movements, and their trades councils,
were reasonably powerful in the 1890s is due largely
to the fact that the craft unions, and particularly
the engineering unions, in these districts were
well established and powerful in their own trade.
The fact is that woollen and worsted textile trade
unionism was never able to carry influence in the
West Yorkshire trade union movement which was at
all commensurate with the importance of the industry
within the area.

Faced with this weakness of trade unionism the
local Liberal parties practically ignored the demands of trade unions and trades councils during the
1880s. It was only the rapid emergence of trade
unionism and trades council organisations during the
late 1880s and early 1890s which led local Liberal
parties to make political approaches to the trades
councils, by which time the vast majority of these
bodies had allied themselves with the emerging ILP
organisations.

E.P. Thompson has rightly pointed out that
trades councils formed around 1890 were quickly committed to the Socialist cause. He argued that 'In
almost every case, they were formed by socialists
and new unionists with the direct aim of promoting
independent political action; in some cases, the
Trades Council formed the local I.L.P. as its political arm'. He also noted that 'The Trades Councils, even more than the Labour Unions, were the
organisational units upon which the West Yorkshire
ILP was based'.[19] Certainly those trades councils
formed in West Yorkshire after 1889 fitted this bill,
though many of their early progenitors would hardly
have described themselves as Socialists.

Between 1890 and 1892 the leaders of the Bradford
ILP, acting through their supportive unions
took control of the Bradford Trades Council, ousting
from its executive almost all the representatives of
the hitherto dominant Lib-Lab group. The subsequent resentments, which almost led Liberal trade
unionists to leave the Trades Council and form their

own body, subsided and were eventually, and apparently successfully, contained with the creation of the Workers' Municipal Election Committee in 1901, soon to become the Workers' Municipal Federation.[20] The value of the organisational strength thus obtained is incalculable.

In an earlier publication we outlined the major reasons for the growth of the Bradford ILP. The gist of our argument was that 'strong trade-union support proved to be an essential corollary of effective independent working-class action'.[21] Because of the Bradford Liberal Association's contemptuous rejection of the Bradford Trades Council's attempt to secure working-class School Board candidates in the 1880s Liberal support in the Council began to be eroded.[22] The dissatisfaction thus engendered was translated into political action by the formation of the Bradford branch of the Labour Electoral Association in 1887. This body was formed in February 1887, following a conference at Bradford in which the Parliamentary Committee of the TUC convinced men like John Hollings (tailor), president of the Trades Council, Samuel Shaftoe (skip maker), secretary, and John Sewell (tailor), treasurer, of the need for positive action on the question of labour representation. They were not, however, so convinced of the need for independent political action - preferring, as we have argued, to act as a Labour group within the Liberal Party. Shaftoe, particularly, had made his career within the Liberal Party. He was a member of the Bradford Liberal Six Hundred, on the Executive Committee of the Eastern Division of the Bradford Liberal Association, and he stood for East Bowling as a Liberal in the municipal elections of 1884. Like many of his type, he saw nothing incompatible between his membership of the Bradford Labour Electoral Association and his connection with the Liberal Party.

Other working-class political activists were of a different opinion. Fred Jowett, C.L. Robinson and James Bartley objected to the alliance with Liberalism. Bartley could write in 1887: 'I believe it to be extremely undesirable to mix trade union-ism with politics'.23 Two years later, he led an attack on the dominant Lib-Lab faction in the Bradford Trades Council. In 1891, Robinson, elected unopposed at a by-election for Manningham Ward, became Bradford's first ILP councillor. The alliance between Socialism and trade unionism in Bradford had laid its roots. As a first step towards independence, the Socialists and their allies joined the

Bradford branch of the Labour Electoral Association.
Like its parent body, the National Labour Electoral
Association, the Bradford branch was divided into
two camps from the start - the Liberals led by
Shaftoe and the Socialists led by Jowett and
Bartley.

It was the latter camp which began to win support on the Trades Council between 1888 and 1892.
A number of issues, but most importantly the actions of Shaftoe, lost the Liberal Party much of its
support on the Trades Council. Shaftoe became embroiled in conflict by his criticism of the typo-
graphers over the delay in printing the congress
reports in connection with the TUC Conference which
was being held at Bradford in 1888.[24] Shaftoe's
action in supporting an 'unfair printer' in the
School Board elections of November 1888, and the
bitter debate which surrounded this affair drove the
Bradford Typographical Society and other trade societies towards Bartley and the Socialist camp.[25]
From 1888 to 1893, Trades Council meetings were dominated by conflict between Bartley and Shaftoe, and
the Socialist contingent gained increasing support
from both the old craft societies and the new societies of unskilled and semi-skilled which flooded
into the Trades Council.[26]

The Manningham Mills strike of 1890 and 1891
helped push the Trades Council more firmly in the
direction of Socialism and political independence,
but the switch of political power on the Trades
Council did not come until the summer months of
1892. The formation in the Bradford Labour Union,
in May 1891, and its decision to support Ben Tillett's candidature of the West Bradford parliamentary constituency in the 1892 general election were
vital events in the conversion of the Trades Council. The formation of a Labour Union, whose club
membership rose swiftly in 1891 and 1892, provided
a focus for agitation against trade-union support
for the Liberal Party; the majority of its support
being drawn from the ranks of trade unionism.[27]
The Tillett election campaign of 1892, a product of
the formation of the Bradford Labour Union, forced
the Trades Council to decide whether to support
Tillett or Illingworth, the Liberal candidate and
sitting MP.[28]

Matters came to a head at the Trades Council
meeting in June, a month before the General Election. There had been a majority in favour of the
policy of the Labour Union for some time - as the
election of George Cowgill, of the Amalgamated

Society of Engineers, as president had indicated.
Nevertheless, the Tillett issue was bound to be di-
visive. The Bradford Observer, 18 June 1892 reported that

> The proceedings of Tuesday's meeting of the
> Trades Council were very lively. The Labour
> union members were determined to get a general
> vote in favour of Tillett ... They have had a
> majority on the Trades Council for some time
> ... they managed to get their vote but only
> after heated discussion.

In the vote which followed, 47 delegates supported
Tillett and 33 opposed him. The Labour Union won,
but, as Walter Sugden, a staunch Lib-Lab pointed
out, the victory was not an overwhelming one.
Voting revealed 'that very strong differences of opinion existed within the ranks of the Trades Council
itself. Some bodies have even gone to the length of
publicly expressing their disapprobation - such as
the overlookers, the stuffpressers and the amalgamated boot and shoe makers'. Sugden continued:
'May I assure Mr. Tillett that his candidature in
West Bradford has driven a knife into every labour
organisation in town, the realities of which will be
felt dramatically in the year to come'.[29] It proved
an accurate prediction. The political balance of
the Trades Council was clearly altered - but the
Labour Electoral Association and Liberal supporters
had not been thoroughly routed and continued to
fight a rearguard action for more than a year.
Yet the Labour Union went from strength to
strength. Tillett's impressive performance in the
1892 general election, despite coming third, did
much to enhance the support for the Labour Union.
Trade unionists joined the Labour Union in increasing numbers, and a large number of clubs, connected
with the Labour Union, had been formed by the end
of 1892.[30]
Meanwhile the LEA was becoming isolated from
the mainstream of trade-union activity. Shaftoe
was its only representative in the higher echelons
of Bradford trade unionism and its only municipal
representative, having been elected for West Bowling
in 1891. C.L. Robinson referred to the LEA 'as fast
becoming an extinct volcano'.[31] George Cowgill was
later to call it 'a Liberal association for the
defence of blacklegs',[32] and its leaders were left
in no doubt that they were seen to have betrayed
their class during the Tillett election. Shaftoe,

as secretary of the Trades Council, was the obvious
target for hostility. In the election of officials
held in January 1893 he was opposed by George Cowgill, a leading figure in the Labour Union and the
former president of the Trades Council, and defeated. Shaftoe was defeated by 48 votes to 38, and
the Bradford Observer referred indignantly to the
'cliquism' which now dominated the affairs of the
Trades Council, reporting that 'no fewer than 17
delegates of the Dyers' Society attended and voted
as a man for Cowgill'.33
    There was no doubt at all that in future the
weight of the Bradford Trades Council would be
thrown behind the ILP. Shaftoe had been ousted on
the 4 January 1893, and within two weeks the Bradford ILP had strengthened its position. On 8 January the Labour Church and Institute was opened in
Peckover Street, and the first National Independent
Labour Party Conference was held in Bradford on 13
and 14 January. The success of the Bradford Labour
Union/ILP was complete. The new balance of power
was clearly established. By 1896, J. Sewell was
the only member of the nine-member executive of the
Trades Council who was not a member of the ILP.34
    It is fair to assume that by the mid 1890s the
Bradford Labour Union/ILP had established its firm
control over the Trades Council and that it derived
much benefit from this relationship. W.H. Drew, a
prominent member of the ILP a trade unionist, and
the leading organiser in the Manningham Mills strike, was emphatic:

> I do say without the slightest hesitation that,
> at the inception of the Bradford Labour Union
> (from which body, of course, sprang the present
> Bradford ILP), it was the avowed intention of
> members of the union that it should be an essen-
> tially trade-union organisation.35

Although there was some dissent from this opinion in
1895, some middle-class members of the ILP objecting
to the predominance of trade-union opinion within
the ILP, it is clear that an elemental connection
had been forged between the ILP and the Trades
Council.36
    The Bradford Trades Council formally dropped
its apolitical stance in 1895 by adopting the Dyers'
resolution, introduced by Joseph Hayhurst: 'That
no person be accepted by the Council as a candidate
for an elective body who is not pledged to support
the collective ownership of the instruments of

production, distribution and exchange'.37 By this
resolution the Trades Council formalised a relationship which had existed since 1892, although the
Trades Council, with the support of many of its ILP
members, was later to change the basis of that arrangement in order that Liberal and Tory trade unionists might be drawn into Labour politics.38

In some cases, particularly amongst the newer trades
councils the situation was not one in which the
local Socialist and ILP organisations had to win the
support of the local trades council but rather one
in which the trades councils formed the first Labour
union or ILP organisations. Two particular examples stand out - those of the Keighley and Halifax
trades councils.

It was the engineers' strike in Keighley during
1889 which caused the formation of the Keighley
Trades Council in 1890. Because of the comparative
weakness of trade unionism in Keighley the Trades
Council founded the Labour Union in 1892 in order to
widen its base.39 In the mid 1890s the two organisations pulled apart. A similar type of situation
occurred in Halifax where the Trades Council was
formed in 1889. Though the Council drew widely from
the whole political spectrum of trade union opinion
it very quickly gravitated towards Labour policies.
It did so for two main reasons. In the first place
it was a recently formed organisation, with no established ties with the Liberal or Conservative
parties. Secondly, the dismissals of James Beever
and James Tattersall, both prominent members of the
Trades Council, by a firm whose directors were well-
known Liberals made it difficult for trade unionists
to side openly with the Liberal party.

Beever was dismissed from his employment in
April 1892, after serving his employer as a silk
spinner for seventeen years. An indignation meeting
was held soon afterwards, and the local press acknowledged that

> The Labour Party has been very much in evidence
> during the past week, much more so in fact than
> it has been before. On Saturday evening the
> working class crowded the Mechanics' Hall to
> contemplate the position which Mr. Beever, Pre-
> sident of the Trades and Labour Council, now
> occupies, forced from the services of Messrs.
> Clayton, Murgatroyd and Co. He is to be the
> first Labour Agent for the Labour Party in
> Halifax.

James Tattersall was also dismissed about two
months later. Testimonials were arranged for the
two Labour martyrs and, in August 1892, they were
presented with funds which permitted them both to
enter business on their own account.[41]
     Beever and Tattersall were victimised because
of their prominence in Socialist circles. Beever
was President of the Trades Council, was a member
of the Halifax Fabian Society from 1891 and the
President of the Yorkshire Federation of Fabian Societies when it was formed in January 1892. At ap-
proximately the same time he left the Liberal Party,
and soon afterwards the Trades Council 'asserted in
the most unqualified manner that they would have no
political connection with the Liberal party'.[42] It
would appear that the spite of the Halifax Liberal
Four Hundred, the policy making body within Halifax
Liberalism, led to the dismissal of Beever. In
Tattersall's case there may have been personal mo-
tives involved in his dismissal for during the 1880s
he became the Secretary of the Boothtown Liberal
Club in Halifax.[43] He ditched Liberalism and pro-
claimed himself in favour of Labour independence in
1890, representing the latter view on the Halifax
School Board from November 1891.
     In July 1892, in the wake of the Beever and
Tattersall dismissals, the Halifax Labour Union was
formed. The political reaction of Halifax Trades
Council to the victimisation of some of its members
was the decision to separate its trade functions
from its political functions. As Councillor J.W.
Crossland, a member of the Trades Council, later
acknowledged:

> Some time ago the political element was separ-
> ated from this organisation and the money
> which had been collected or contributed for
> political and electioneering purposes was taken
> over, and the Labour Union was formed for the
> purpose, so as to leave the Council untramelled
> to deal purely and simply with trade and lab-
> our topics. I voted strongly against it at the
> time but it was passed.[44]

However, the Halifax Trades Council found it difficult to separate industrial and political activities
and formally re-established the connection with the
Halifax Labour Union, by now the ILP, in September
1894.
     As Thompson suggests then, trades councils and
ILP branches worked in close harmony, even to the
52

point of trades councils forming Labour Unions. Yet
it is also true that the older trades councils
could sometimes take some persuading to join the ILP
cause, as was the case of Leeds Trades Council.

The Leeds Trades Council was slow to respond to the
socialist pressures. It was not until the early
twentieth century that the Leeds ILP and the Leeds
Labour Representation Committee became influential
within the Trades Council, and even then relations
were often sticky.[45] Part of the problem may well
have been that some of the leading Socialists came
from outside Leeds and clashed with local trade
union leaders in their presentation of their demands for Labour representation. Yet as Thompson has
suggested, Leeds-based Socialists acted as the mis-
sionaries for the rest of the woollen textile area,
attending meetings, organising labourers into the
Gasworkers and General Labourers' Union, and encouraging Socialist groups in the district.[46] From
the late 1880s Tom Paylor, William Cockayne, Peter
Curran and J.L. Mahon took an active part in promoting the joint causes of Socialism and trade
unionism. Whilst they succeeded well in the textile district they were much less successful in
Leeds. The problem they faced was that Leeds was a
multi-industry town, unlike many West Riding textile towns which were dominated by one industry.
Therefore, Leeds was never likely to suffer the
same level of economic dislocation experienced in
some towns, for whilst some industries experienced
economic depression others remained prosperous.
This industrial diversity reduced the likelihood
that economic factors alone would stimulate support
for the ILP.
     The Socialist challenge in Leeds began in the
mid 1880s, with the formation of the Leeds branch
of the Socialist League, but effectively dates
from the formation of the Leeds branch of the Gasworkers' Union in October 1889.[47] Within months
the gas workers had won a bloodless victory against
the Leeds Gas Committee, obtaining reduced working
hours and improved working arrangements.[48] This
victory underlined the value of having full-time
officials organising the district. William Cockayne
acted as district secretary and Tom Paylor was
district organiser. Both men had been involved in
London Socialism and brought their experience to
bear in organising the Union's Leeds District.
Membership increased rapidly and was further stimulated by the victory of the Leeds gasworkers in

53

the four-day lock-out imposed by the Gas Committee
in June 1890.[49] This famous, and bloody, victory
increased membership and led to the opening of new
branches. By the end of 1891 the Leeds District
had organised more than 8,000 workers into 29 branches, representing 15 different trades. Twelve of
these branches, and more than half of the members,
were located in Leeds.[50]

This increase of membership altered the balance of Leeds trade unionism in three ways. In
the first place, it brought a new section of workers into Leeds trade unionism which, although less
stable, rivalled the membership of the Leeds craft
unions. Secondly, it introduced militancy into
Leeds trade unionism. Thirdly, it helped to neu-
tralise the Liberals on the Leeds Trades Council,
thus allowing the 'anti-political' faction to control the Council during the early 1890s.

All three factors were interrelated, and represented a progressive deepening and widening of
Socialist activities. By 1889 and 1890 almost
every unorganised Leeds workforce was attempting to
establish its own union. In November 1889 the
Wholesale Clothiers Operatives' Union was formed to
unite male workers in the wholesale tailoring
trade.[51] This was followed by an attempt to form a
tailoresses' union following the strike of 900 tailoresses at Messrs. Arthur & Co.[52] The Leeds tram-
way men held organisational meetings on a night.[53]
The Jewish tailors, pressers, and machinists, formed three separate branches of the Gas Workers'
Union. Public meetings were held regularly on
Sunday afternoons and invited speakers included Tom
Mann, Ben Tillett and Will Thorne.

The 'outside' Socialists who had fuelled the
surge of Socialist and trade-union agitation in
1889 and 1890 gathered around them a mixed body of
locally-established trade unionists, writers and
middle-class philanthropists, including Tom
Maguire, Alf Mattison, John Brotherton, Isabello O.
Ford and J.H. Sweeney.[54] As a group they challenged
the precepts of established trade unions.

The activities of these Socialists were, at
first, strongly opposed by the craft unions of the
Trades Council. It is important to remember that,
in 1890, William Marston, John Bune and Sergeant
Ellis, president, secretary and treasurer of the
Trades Council, respectively, were all Liberals.
John Bune in fact was a ward treasurer for the
Liberal Party and became a Liberal councillor in
1893. Only John Judge, the vice-president of the

Trades Council, of the leading officials was not a
Liberal - regarding himself as an independent.
Thus it is hardly surprising that the attempts of
the Socialists to organise the unskilled and semi-
skilled workers into unions were not supported by
the Trades Council. Indeed, the Trades Council
appears to have made a deliberate decision to stay
out of the activities surrounding the famous Leeds
Gas Strike of 1890, when the Liberal-dominated Gas
Committee of the City Council attempted to win back
the wage concessions and improved working conditions it had been forced to concede to the gasworkers in the previous year.

Relations between the Socialists and the Trade
Council were, understandably, poor. The Socialist
activists of the Gasworkers and General Labourers'
Union formed the Yorkshire Labour League in early
1890, intending it to highlight their opposition to
the Trades Council.[55] In the wake of the successful Gas Strike of 1890, there was an ill-fated
attempt to bring the two sides together when the
Labour Electoral League was formed in July 1890,
with Tom Maguire as chairman and John Judge as president. But it foundered with the unsuccessful
attempt to find a suitable municipal candidate in
the autumn of 1890. Also, in May 1891 the Leeds
Trades Council refused to be represented at the
massive May-Day demonstration which was held in
Leeds.[56]

The antipathy between the two bodies was obviously fuelled by a variety of political and economic eddies, many of which actually fragmented
the Trades Council response to the Socialists. The
traditional links with Liberalism had obviously
enhanced the political careers of some of the
Trades Council officials who were reluctant to have
their good fortune impaired. Many of the leaders
of craft unions were also sensitive to the Gasworkers and General Labourers' Union organising the
semi-skilled workers in their industries which they
had hitherto ignored. Some delegates to the Trades
Council were clearly of the view that it should not
attach itself to any political group.

Yet between 1891 and 1895 the hostility of the
Trades Council to the Socialists did begin to
falter. This was partly due to the fact that the
Gasworkers and General Labourers' Union joined the
Trades Council in the autumn of 1890, and that
Mahon became one of its representatives. The fight
was taken into the Trades Council. In the
conflict which ensued the Trades Council produced

some odd and inconsistent decisions. Yet there were
signs of change. The conflict between the Socialists and Liberals on the Trades Council did permit
the neutral, anti-political, independent and Conser-
vative-minded factions to emerge. These various
factions were led by John Judge, John Demaine and
J.H. Maundrill. It was Demaine, of the Leeds Typographical Society, who had originally maintained the
need for the Council to be represented on the Leeds
City Council independently of the other political
parties in 1887, and had revived the idea in 1891.
John Judge supported this suggestion soon after his
trial for intimidation in October and November 1887,
which appears to have hastened his departure from
the Liberal Party.[58] Together, they directed the
Council on a rather precarious course to political
neutrality, the first signs of which appeared at the
municipal elections of November 1891, when the
Trades Council supported James Leach, an independent
candidate who was incidentally the President of the
Co-operative Society. Subsequently, when Mahon attempted to contest the School Board elections of
1891 it opposed Mahon's candidature and supported
the Conservative sponsorship of John Demaine, who
was duly elected. On a later occasion, Mahon's desire for School Board honours was rejected because
the Trades Council 'did not wish to become involved
in party politics'.[59] At the municipal elections of
1891, the Trades Council supported three of its own
candidates - Cockayne (Socialist), Childerson (Liberal) and Maundrill (ex-Liberal independent).
During the early 1890s the Leeds Trades Council
struggled to give the impression that it was not attached to any particular political party but that it
supported trade unionists in politics because they
were trade unionists. Political neutrality was to
be its watchword.

In May 1892 the Leeds Trades Council acted to
establish a Labour Electoral Union, a body consisting of two-thirds Trades Council members and one-
third Socialist members. But it withdrew from this
political organisation in October 1892, maintaining
that industrial and political matters should be kept
separate, though it advised its affiliated unions to
join separately.[60]

The Trades Council's reluctance to join with
the Socialists direct was partly conditioned by the
bitter conflict which occurred between J.L. Mahon
and John Judge. Mahon decided to settle in Leeds
in 1890 and take up the leadership of the local
Socialist movement.[61] Judge had first come to Leeds

in 1877, was an active figure in the Leeds branch
of the Rivetters and Finishers (Boot and Shoe
Makers), had twice been found guilty of offences under the Conspiracy and Protection of Property Act
and had been found guilty of slander his £300 lia-
bility being partly met by the Leeds trade unionists.[62] His martyrdom in the cause of trade unionism made him an attractive and popular leader.
Judge's support for an independent, rather than Socialist, line made him an obvious target for Socialist propaganda. His uncompromising trade-union
stance led him to criticise Mahan, who he felt was
not a genuine trade unionist and who he accused of
having deserted the London Postman's Union after
having led them into strike activity in 1890. Mahon
threatened to sue Judge, but in the end the affair
was settled by an arbitration committee composed of
the societies involved in the dispute.[63]

The weakness of the Leeds Socialists was fully
exposed by the Mahon-Judge affair. They had little
support amongst the Trades Council delegates, which
is why Mahon became a delegate to the Trades Council
in January 1892.[64] Despite, or perhaps because of,
Mahon's efforts Socialism remained weak in Leeds.
The Trades Council continued its uncompromising policy of independence, and when the relationship
between it and the Leeds ILP was discussed in May
1894 the minutes reveal that 13 delegates spoke against the suggestion that the Council should unite
politically with the ILP.

Yet such a policy proved difficult to sustain
in the face of mounting unemployment. Between the
autumn of 1894 and the spring of 1895 the Trades
Council and the ILP came closer together in their
attempts to offer solutions to rising unemployment.
At this time it was varyingly estimated that between 5,000 and 10,000 workmen were unemployed 'in
the worst year that the West Riding had known'.[65]
Inevitably, both organisations were drawn into the
unemployment agitation that occurred in Leeds, and
throughout the West Riding textile district, and
both were united in committee work designed to find
a solution to the problem, an action which culmin-
ated in the joint publication of a pamphlet entitled
The Unemployed: A Discussion of Causes and Remedies
for securing of Employment - Special Reference to
Leeds (Leeds, 1895), which advocated the introduction of the eight-hour day to all industries - a policy which the Trades Council would not have enter-
tained in 1891 or 1892.

Mere agreement on one issue was not, however,

sufficient to cement an alliance between the Trades
Council and the ILP. Indeed that alliance seemed
increasingly remote in the mid 1890s. The Mahon-
Judge affair and Mahon's criticism of John Lister in
the Halifax parliamentary by-election of 1893 had
worsened relations. The Socialist delegates on the
Trades Council were reduced by the Gasworkers' Union
failing to pay its subscription and Paylor, Cockayne
and Mahon all disappeared from the Council. And
William Marston, the long-serving president of the
Trades Council, led the Liberal group in a staunch
resistance to the Socialist and ILP challenge. Yet
the threat of unemployment did produce a Leeds trade
union movement which became more pugnacious and inclined to the left, and some of the new Trades Council leaders were equivocal in their relationship to
Liberalism and Socialism. For instance, Owen Connellan, secretary from 1892 until the early twentieth century, was returned to East Ward in the municipal elections of 1895, with Liberal support,
but sought the Labour candidature of the East Leeds
parliamentary constituency, following the Leeds
Trades Council's affiliation to the LRC in 1900.66
By 1900 the Leeds Trades Council was prepared to
give its political support to the Labour Representation Committee, the non-Socialist Labour Party,
though not to the Socialist ILP.

The support of trade unions and trades councils was
clearly vital in explaining the growth, or lack of
growth, of the embryonic ILP in West Yorkshire. It
is obvious that the newer trades councils became
quickly committed to the Socialist cause. It is
equally obvious that the longer-established trades
councils, such as Leeds and Bradford, gravitated
more slowly to the ILP and the Labour Party. Yet
the winning of trade-council support was not of itself a guarantee of local political success for the
local ILP branch. Only where trade unionism was
well organised by the relatively lowly standards of
West Yorkshire was the local ILP or Labour Union
likely to make a political impact.
    Of those ILP branches which had trades-council
support in the 1890s the most important were clearly
Bradford and Halifax. With about 10,000 trade
unions members affiliated to the Bradford Trades
Council in the mid 1890s it is hardly surprising
that the Bradford ILP could muster something in the
region of about 2,000 members. The Halifax Trades
Council with more than 3,000 members supported an
ILP organisation which fluctuated between 600 and

700 members.67 Together, Bradford and Halifax
provided more than half the paid-up ILP membership
in West Yorkshire in 1895. Indeed, Paul Bland, a
leading member of the Bradford ILP, claimed that in
1895 the Bradford ILP was providing one-thirteenth
of the National Administrative Council of the ILP's
entire income and one-sixth of its affiliation
fees.68

In Keighley, which had a fairly sizeable ILP
branch of 120 members throughout the 1890s, the
Trades Council was far too weak and vacillating to
carry it to much local political success, and it
was unable to mount an effective parliamentary challenge to the Liberal Party through the ILP branch
it supported. In other areas, such as Dewsbury and
Huddersfield, a modestly successful trades council
supported a modestly effective ILP. In those areas
where the membership and funds of the trades councils were low, as in Brighouse, Elland, Sowerby
Bridge, Todmorden and Spen Valley, the local ILP
branches offered very little challenge to Liberalism - though there was some fitful success in
Brighouse.

It is our contention that the support of an
exuberant trade union movement was essential to the
successes which the ILP and Labour Party achieved
in West Yorkshire during the 1890s and early twentieth century. Where trade unionism was relatively
ineffective political success was limited. Yet,
it is argued, that there is at least one major
exception to these observations. In his book
Colne Valley: Radicalism to Socialism, David Clark
has argued that trade unionism was not 'an essential
pre-requisite for Socialism', by which he means
the success of an ILP candidate.69 He has argued
that Tom Mann was unable to enhance the claims of
the local ILP organisation, the Colne Valley Labour
Union, to political control in the area because the
message he put forward, in his An Appeal to the
Yorkshire Textile Workers, was the collective one
of advising them to join their unions.70 The fact
is that trade unionism was weak in Colne Valley,
there being only 1,545 trade union members in 1895
and only 867 by 1905.71 It is hardly surprising,
Clark maintains, that Tom Mann was unsuccessful in
contesting Colne Valley in the 1895 General Election. What transformed Mann's defeat in 1895 into
Victor Grayson's parliamentary by-election victory
in 1907 was the continuance of Labour clubs which
underpinned the rising Labour optimism of the early
twentieth century, the increasing support of

Anglican priests and Nonconformist ministers, and
the sustained propaganda work which went on between
1905 and 1907. The whole was topped off with the
selection of a charismatic ILP candidate, Victor
Grayson, who touched the right ethical and individ-
ualistic nerve of the Colne Valley community. Moral
suasion sustained by a thriving club life was therefore responsible for converting Liberals into Socialists and Liberal voters into ILP voters.

We will deal with the Grayson saga in a later
chapter. At this point we merely seek to suggest
that in emphasising the ethical appeal of Socialism,
which clearly did attract many small businessmen
into the Colne Valley Labour leadership, David
Clark has neglected to emphasise the importance of
the trade union contribution to Grayson's success.

There was nothing particularly unusual in a
West Yorkshire ILP organisation being sustained by
the moral indignation of those who objected to the
economic and social inequalities of Capitalist
society. John Lister, the Halifax landowner, and
Arthur Priestman, the Bradford businessman, were
sustained by such an outlook. There was nothing
unusual in ILP and Socialist clubs sustaining the
movement throughout its difficult periods. There
were nine local Labour clubs in Colne Valley in
1893, reducing to a core of three between 1895 and
1905; there were 29 ILP clubs or groups in Bradford
by 1895, reduced to about 10 by 1900; and the
Halifax ILP had at least 8 clubs in 1895.[72] Labour
clubs were not inimical to trade unionism, and the
majority of members in Bradford and Halifax were
clearly drawn from the trade unions. One suspects
that the situation must have been similar in Colne
Valley.

Trade unionists also played an important part
in the Colne Valley Labour movement. The Colne
Valley Labour Union, formed on 21 July 1891, was
largely achieved at the instigation of trade unionists.[73] The inaugural meeting was the result of a
prior meeting of the Amalgamated Society of Railway
Servants and was strongly advocated by George
Garside, of the Amalgamated Society of Engineers.
It was dominated by the representatives of the
Weavers' Association and the outside speakers included James Bartley, the Bradford typographer who had
been instrumental in the formation of the Bradford
Labour Union, Allan Gee and Ben Turner of the
Weavers' Association. Of the ten members who were
elected as the first officials only one, a local
millowner named George William Haigh, appears not

to have been a member of a trade union.[74] Many of
these officials remained within the CVLU throughout
their lifetimes and, though there was no trades
council in Colne Valley, they drew support from the
nearby Huddersfield Trades Council.

We are not disputing the sterling work which
David Clark has undertaken on Colne Valley, we are
merely suggesting that the emphasis is misleading.
Clearly there was something beyond mere trade unionism which contributed to Grayson's success in 1907,
but just as clearly Mann's defeat in 1895 could have
been the result of the national swing against the
ILP or the failure of the CVLU, for a variety of
reasons, to win wider support in Colne Valley;
just as Grayson's defeat in the 1910 General Election may well have been due to the lack of a large
and firm trade-union base in Colne Valley.

Despite the fact that Labour clubs emerged,
that in towns like Bradford and Leeds there were
thriving Labour Church organisations, it is clear
that strong trade-union support proved to be an
essential corollary of effective independent working-class political action in the West Yorkshire
textile district. In the woollen textile district
progress had already been made to capturing trade-
union support to the ILP well before Alderman Ben
Tillett made his prophetic ambitions clear to the
National ILP Conference at Bradford in 1893:

> ... in spite of all that had been said about
> the Socialists, he thought English trade union-
> ism was the best sort of Socialism and Labour-
> ism ... He wished to capture the trade union-
> ists of this country, a body of men well organ-
> ised, who paid their money, and were Socialists
> at their work every day, and not merely on this
> platform; who did not shout for blood-red
> revolution, and, when it comes to revolution,
> sneak under the nearest bed.[75]

Weak as trade unionism was in the West Riding
textile district it had committed itself to the
cause of independent Labour with verve and zeal in
the early 1890s, and had been responsible for ILP
branches winning significant political support in
the textile district. It is true that the parliamentary impact of West Yorkshire ILP branches was
not great - Ben Tillett failing in his two West
Bradford contests, John Lister being defeated in his
two parliamentary contests in Halifax, and Tom Mann
being defeated in the Colne Valley parliamentary

Table 3.3: The Membership of West Yorkshire ILP
organisations in the 1890s

Constituency	Branch	1893	1895	1899
Bradford (three seats)	Bradford	2,000	2,000	1,000
Colne Valley	Delph			6
	Golcar			18
	Honley			44
	Meltham			24
	Milnsbridge			50
	Mossley			45
	Netherton			12
	Slaithwaite			36
		300–400	300	235
Dewsbury	Batley		300	
	Dewsbury		500	
	Thornhill Lees			120
Elland	Brighouse		60	60
	Elland			9
Halifax (two seats)	Eight clubs	500	600	591
Huddersfield	Huddersfield	300–400	120	84
	Lindley	30–60	defunct	defunct
	Lockwood	60–90	17	defunct
	Longwood	50	45	27
	Milnsbridge	130	33	59
	Paddock	50–70	defunct	defunct
	Salford	80	defunct	defunct
		780–880	215	170
Keighley	Cowling			20
	Keighley	30+	100	120
Leeds (five seats)	Armley			29
	Birstall			18
	Central			100
	Hunslet – East			30
	– West			25
	Middleton			40
	North			25
				267

Table 3.3 (cont'd)

Constituency	Branch	1893	1895	1899
Pudsey	Farsley			42
	Pudsey			
	Tong			9
	Yeadon			27
Shipley	Shipley			60
Sowerby	Hebden Bridge			14
	Sowerby Bridge			18
	Todmorden			
Spen Valley	Cleckheaton			54
	Heckmondwike			60
	Spen Colliery			25

Details for Holmfirth, Morley, Otley and Wakefield are not available.

Sources: ILP News, May, Jun. 1898, Feb., Mar. 1899; Labour Union Journal, for 1891 and 1892; Bradford Daily Telegraph, 27 Nov. 1893; Bradford Labour Echo, 17 Nov. 1897; D. Clark, Colne Valley: Radicalism to Socialism. The Portrait of a Northern Constituency in the formative years of the Labour Party 1890-1910 (Longman, London, 1981), pp. 109-12; R.B. Perks, 'Trade Unionism and the Emergence of the Labour Party in Huddersfield', forthcoming article in J.L. Halstead and W. Lancaster, (eds) Socialist Studies (Harvester, Brighton, 1984).

contest in the 1895 General Election - but a start had been made, and the ILP was beginning to make inroads into Liberal domination at the local level.

The most immediate evidence of a burgeoning ILP was the proliferation of branches and the initially rapid growth of membership before the difficult years of the late 1890s. Whatever the outward re-action of the Liberal leaders they must have been shocked by Labour's swift political progress. By 1893 there were probably about 4,500 or so ILP members in West Yorkshire, a number which remained fairly stable until the loss of support following

the disappointments of the 1895 General Election.
Even then, and despite the difficulties of obtaining
accurate membership figures, there were probably
about 3,250 members in 1899. Thereafter, ILP membership increased until the First World War and was
added to by an enormous rise in Labour Party membership.

The ILP's impact had, of course, been immensely
variable. Bradford and Halifax were centres of ILP
activity, whilst Leeds, Huddersfield, Dewsbury and
Colne Valley showed some fitful potential of being
ILP strongholds. Keighley, many of the smaller
towns and some outlying districts were much less
promising. In many of these areas membership figures were in the tens rather than in the hundreds
and in some areas, such as Wakefield there was no
ILP branch in the 1890s: 'It was barren territory
which contained not one known I.L.P. supporter. The
trade unions were weak and there was no local trades
council'.[76]

This patchiness of ILP support is further reflected in the municipal and local political successes
of the ILP. The municipal successes of the ILP were
confined to six West Yorkshire towns up to the mid
1890s, and there were only twelve municipal representatives in West Yorkshire in 1895, and 19 in 1900.
Yet there were successes in other local political
elections. George Garside was returned for Slaithwaite in the West Riding County Council elections
of 1892 and sat as a county councillor until his
death in 1907.[77] In addition there were some successes in the urban district council elections in
Colne Valley and elsewhere, to which might be added
the successes in School Board and Guardian elections.
The overwhelming evidence suggests that Labour was
making steady, if unspectacular, progress in the
municipal and local elections in West Yorkshire; not
enough to worry the Liberal Party in the district as
a whole but sufficient to embarrass them in Bradford
and foreshadow the great growth in Labour's municipal support which occurred in the twentieth century.

The 1890s saw the National ILP rise to political
importance in local elections. In 1896 a 'suggestive
figure revealed that it had at least 181 representatives on local bodies, a figure which rose to over
400 by 1905.[78] A detailed breakdown of its 247 local
representatives in 1900 indicated that there were at
least 63 town, four county, 36 urban district, three
rural-district and 16 parish councillors; plus
eight citizen auditors, 51 members of board
of guardians and 66 members of school boards

Table 3.4: The Municipal Successes of the ILP in four West Yorkshire textile towns, 1891-1900.

Year	Number of Municipal Representatives				
	Bradford	Halifax	Huddersfield	Keighley	Total
1891	2				2
1892	2	3	1		6
1893	4	3	1		8
1894	4	1	1	1	7
1895	6	0	1	1	8
1896	4	0	1	1	6
1897	5	1	1	2	9
1898	5	1	1	4	11
1899	5	2	1	5	13
1900	6	2	1	5	14

Note: a. The Bradford figures for 1891 are composed of C.L. Robinson who was returned unopposed in a municipal by-election and C. Woods who was returned as a Conservative working man at the November elections, though he subsequently associated himself with the ILP.
Sources: These figures have been largely compiled from the November issues of the Labour Leader, ILP News, Labour Union Journal, Bradford Observer, Huddersfield Examiner, Halifax Guardian, Halifax Courier and Keighley News.

Table 3.5: The Number of ILP Representatives in West Yorkshire, 1891-1900

Year	Municipal	CC,UDC,RDC PC,LB	Board of Guardians	School Board	Total
1891	4			2	6
1892	7	2		4	13
1893	10	2		4	16
1894	10	2		5	17
1895	12	2		7	21
1896	11	2		7	20
1897	14	10		11	35
1898	15	9	3	15	42
1899	19	10	3	18	50
1900	19	10	3	21	53

Note: a. This list includes the details of the County Council, urban-district councils, rural-district councils, parish councils and local boards. These details are not always fully presented in the Labour press and should therefore be taken as the minimum numbers. It may well be that the particular columns, and thus the total number of ILP representatives have been underestimated.

Sources: These figures have been taken from the March, April, May and November editions of the Labour Leader, ILP News, Bradford Observer, Labour Union Journal, Bradford Telegraph, Halifax Guardian, Halifax Courier and Keighley News.

representing the ILP throughout the country.[79] Of these totals it is clear that at least 20 representatives were to be found in West Yorkshire in 1896 and 53 in 1900. In other words, West Yorkshire ILP representation had increased from eleven per cent of the total national ILP local representatives in 1896 to about 13 per cent by 1900. West Yorkshire was clearly becoming a major political centre for the ILP.

Yet whilst such local successes broke the mould of the two-party system in some Yorkshire textile communities, one should not expect the ILP's political successes to exert much impact upon the pattern of local political events. ILP representatives were still isolated voices in the political wilderness in the 1890s, and the real breakthrough in a local political sense did not occur until after 1906. Although ILP councillors had a vision of a collectivist society in which the municipality would be responsible for ensuring that poverty was tackled and employment guaranteed through municipal action, it is clear that in these early days they were able to do little more than register their political presence. They remained overwhelmingly outnumbered on local political bodies and were unable to do much about the rising problems of unemployment which afflicted most Yorkshire textile towns in the early and mid 1890s. ILP councillors were unable to move the local authorities to action despite the fact that one survey, in 1894, indicated that 27.1 per cent of the population of Bradford, 57,558 people, were affected by unemployment and that other less detailed surveys suggested that a similar situation pertained in Leeds, Huddersfield and other towns in West Yorkshire.[80] Boards of Guardians protested that unemployment was no more than 'average'. Town Councils did little more than set up temporary un-

employment registers to help the unemployed, and the
numerous Labour protest meetings remained largely
ignored. The Yorkshire Labour Movement Conference,
held at the Labour Institute, Bradford, in November
1893 brought together 70 delegates representing
6,000 ILP members and trade unionists. This mass
meeting of ILP opinion offered the eight-hour day,
public works and land colonies as the trio of policies which the Yorkshire labour movement was to
pursue.[81] But none of these policies had the sli-
ghtest chance of being accepted in the 1890s, or of
offering a solution to unemployment. A solution to
unemployment was well beyond the scope of local
effort; it was a national problem which required
national solutions, although the Yorkshire ILP branches did not appear to realise this until after
1906.

Yet whilst the big problem eluded the influence
of the ILP, the smaller issues fell within their
compass. Many local authorities - town councils,
school boards and boards of guardians - had come to
accept the need for some type of 'fair wages' or
'fair contracts' resolution by the mid 1890s, although the implimentation of such resolutions,
whereby contracts were only given to firms paying
trade-union wage rates, often necessitated great
vigilance on the behalf of ILP representatives and
trade union officials. In both Bradford and Leeds,
the Liberals appear to have taken fright at the ILP
challenges and offered more 'progressive' policies
at the municipal elections in 1894. In Leeds this
included a range of measures to cleanse the River
Aire, to cheapen the cost of travelling by tram,
and to extend the provision of public baths. The
Leeds Mercury reflected that 'From the appearance
of the Liberal Programme last year we shall come to
date a new era in the history of the civic life of
Leeds'.[82] In Bradford, J.W. Jarratt, an advanced
Liberal, helped to formulate a progressive municipal
programme for the Bradford Liberal Association,
which included a commitment to introduce an eight-
hour day and a forty-eight hour week for Corporation
workers, Corporation control of nightsoil clearance
and tramways, and the introduction of fair contracts. Jarratt maintained that if the Liberal
Party adopted a progressive policy 'they could cut
the ground from under the feet of the Independent
Labour Party'.[83] The very fact that Liberals were
persuaded to discuss the possibility of introducing
progressive measures at this early stage is clear
evidence that the ILP was exerting an impact upon

local politics.

With a rapidly growing membership, at least before
1895, a measurable impact upon local elections and
a modest influence upon the operation of municipal
corporations, it is clear that the ILP organisations
in West Yorkshire were exerting some pressure on the
local Liberal organisations. The ILP was taking its
first steps to political viability. Yet, despite
its rapid growth in a very short period of time, the
ILP was still a comparatively rudimentary and un-
tried organisation. In the enthusiasm of youth it
pushed forward to contest parliamentary elections,
often without the administrative infrastructure,
including funds and full-time local agents, which
the Liberals and Tories deemed to be essential in
such contests. Without adequate funds and full-time
agents, the ILP organisations lacked the essential
pre-requisites for winning political support amongst
enfranchised working men. Notwithstanding such
disadvantages, and mindful of the fact that it was
not until 1906 that the ILP won its first parliamentary seats in West Yorkshire, it is clear that parliamentary contests between 1892 and 1895 indicated
that the ILP had much to look forward to, despite
some local difficulties.
      The Bradford Labour Union, as we have seen, had
been founded on a refusal to work within the Liberal
Party. It was this sentiment which promoted the
candidature of Ben Tillett, first suggested for
Bradford East. The shift to Bradford West was above
all a blow struck deep into the heart of the Lib-
Lab alliance, for here was the domain of Alfred
Illingworth. Tillett's refusal to accept the Liberal offer of a straightforward run in Bradford East
in order to leave Illingworth's alliance with the
LEA intact was probably decisive in confirming the
split between the LEA and the ILP, the former emphasising the need to concentrate upon local action
whilst the latter was prepared to risk a parliamentary contest.
      In the early months of 1892, Katherine St.
John Conway, Enid Stacey, Bernard Shaw, Tom
McCarthy, and many other national Labour figures, came to Bradford and helped to keep the parliamentary ambitions of the Labour Union at fever
pitch. As already seen, Tillett's candidature was
an essential ingredient in converting the Trades
Council to the ILP cause. In this respect the impact of a parliamentary candidate had proved decid-
edly helpful to the Labour Union cause at the local

68

level. When the 1892 General Election was called it was clear that the Irish vote would be against him, largely on the grounds that he put social reform on a par with Home Rule, and that Bradford Nonconformity was with Illingworth rather than, the also Nonconformist, Tillett.[84] Despite the redoutable opposition, Tillett pressed forward with his demands for an Eight-Hour Bill, old-age pensions, and a whole range of Socialist policies. In the event, he lost the election, coming third, but indicated that the fledgling Labour Union (later ILP) was a political force to be reckoned with. Tillett obtained more than 30 per cent of the vote. Although his second contest in the 1895 General Election was disappointing, he philosophically reflected that the ILP was down to its hard-core support.

Whilst Tillett might have held modest ambitions of winning Bradford West in the 1890s it is equally clear that the ILP's entry into other contests was less optimistic, largely borne of a desire to register an ILP presence, to challenge Liberalism in its parliamentary strongholds and to give working-class voters an alternative to the established political parties. As a result, John Lister contested the Halifax by-election, shortly after becoming the treasurer of the National ILP at the Bradford Conference in January 1893, exceeding wildest expectations by obtaining 25.4 per cent of the vote.

Yet, although the ILP could do well in the odd isolated contest, where many of the ILP branches in the region would help out, it was patently obvious that its fragile political structure was not capable of finding the funds, organising the voters, and mustering the level of propaganda activity which was necessary for a more sizeable onslaught upon West Yorkshire Liberalism. This became obvious in the 1895 General Election in which the ILP contested six West Yorkshire constituencies, being badly defeated in four and doing modestly in two.

Table 3.6: West Yorkshire Parliamentary Contests fought by the ILP, 1892-5

Constituency	Date	Candidate	Votes Cast	Labour % of the poll
Bradford West	1892	B.Tillett	2,749	30.2
Halifax	1893	J.Lister	3,028	25.4
Bradford West	1895	B.Tillett	2,264	23.4
Colne Valley	1895	T.Mann	1,245	13.4
Dewsbury	1895	E.R.Hartley	1,080	10.5

Table 3.6 (cont'd)

Constituency	Date	Candidate	Votes Cast	Labour % of the poll
Halifax	1895	J.Lister	3,818	20.5
Huddersfield	1895	H.R.Smart	1,594	11.2
Leeds South	1895	A.Shaw	622	6.4

Source: F.W.S. Craig, British Parliamentary Election Results 1885-1918, (Macmillan, London, 1974).

Although the 1895 General Election was the nadir of the ILP growth it is clear that the confidence of the movement engendered the need to make a dramatic breakthrough into parliamentary politics. That this did not occur, and that the ILP temporarily declined is obvious, but it must be equally obvious that Liberalism did not escape unscathed. At the national level, the Conservative Party returned to office in place of the Liberals, and in the Yorkshire textile district the Liberal dominance was significantly eroded. In 1892 20 Liberals and three Conservatives were returned to the district. In the 1895 General Election, and indeed the 1900 General Election, 14 Liberals and nine Conservatives were returned to Parliament. The Liberals lost all three seats in Bradford, one seat in Halifax, one seat in Otley, one seat in Shipley, and regained the Huddersfield seat lost at a by-election in 1893. Although there had been a national swing against the Liberals, it did not go unnoticed that some of the most significant local losses occurred in areas where the Labour challenge was strong and where Labour candidates were either contesting seats or where Labour voters were refusing to vote for the other two candidates, operating their personal claim to the 'Manchester Fourth Clause' which so dominated the discussion at early National ILP conferences.85

It is clear that ILP candidates were often being put forward simply in order to demonstrate their independence by an open challenge to Liberalism. Ben Tillett had had the opportunity of a straight run against the Conservatives in Bradford East during the 1892 General Election but had opted to fight the more difficult seat of Bradford West

in which Alfred Illingworth, the doyen of Bradford
Liberalism, was the sitting MP. Similarly, Tom
Mann, in giving his reasons for contesting Colne
Valley in 1895 suggested that one of his reasons was
'that the sitting member was a prominent Liberal
capitalist, the head of a well-known engineering
firm in Leeds, Mr. James Kitson, afterwards Sir
James'.86
    It is hardly surprising that, given such tac-
tics, the Liberal parties in the textile district
began to fear the loss of some of the traditional
working-class Liberal vote, and began to view the
Labour challenge as a plot to let the Tories in.
The 1895 General Election appeared to confirm these
fears.

What then had the ILP organisations of West Yorkshire achieved by the mid 1890s. Although local
electoral successes were modest, and parliamentary
success was non-existent, the embryonic ILP organisations had demonstrated that they were committed
to political independence and posed a threat to the
traditional working-class support for Liberalism.
Above all, they wrested control of the local trades
councils, and thus the trade union movement, from
the Liberal Party. Propelled forward by the intransigence of local Liberalism and fuelled by the political support which emanated from industrial conflicts, such as the Manningham Mills strike, local
ILP organisations became almost synonymous with
trade unionism. Many ILP members would have sub-
scribed to the vociferous comment of Councillor C.
L. Robinson, the first ILP councillor in Bradford:

> an ILP man cannot be a true Labour man unless
> he favours the principle of trade unionism,
> and that the position of a trade unionist is a
> very anomolous one when he be not also an
> I.L.P. man, or at any rate perfectly indepen-
> dent - that is, prepared to steer clear of
> Liberal and Tory alike. Yes, I certainly think
> that the "trade unionist" and the "I.L.P.ers"
> ought to be absolutely synonymous terms.87

By the mid 1890s this was largely the situation in
West Yorkshire. Most trades councils were attached
to the ILP and most members of the ILP were also
trade unionists, although many trade unionists still
needed to be won from Liberalism. By 1895 the ILP
was prepared to act as the representative of trade
unionism and the vehicle for working-class

aspirations. It was already posing a threat to
Liberalism and the Liberal Party in West Yorkshire
had to decide how to react.

NOTES

1. _Bradford Observer_, 9 Dec. 1891. The comment
was made by Alfred Illingworth, Liberal MP for
Bradford West.

2. D. James, 'The Emergence of the Keighley
Independent Labour Party', unpublished MA dissertation, Huddersfield Polytechnic, 1980, chapter
three.

3. _Keighley News_, 7 Sep. 1889.

4. Ibid., 31 Aug. 1889.

5. K. Laybourn, 'The Manningham Mills Strike:
Its importance in Bradford History', pp. 7-35;
Reynolds and Laybourn, 'The Emergence of the Inde-
pendent Labour Party in Bradford', pp. 327-31.

6. Thompson, 'Homage to Tom Maguire', pp.
305-7.

7. _Bradford Observer_, 28 Apr. 1891.

8. _Yorkshire Factory Times_, 1 May 1891.

9. _Bradford Observer Budget_, 25 Apr. 1891.

10. _Yorkshire Factory Times_, 29 May 1891.

11. A.W. Roberts, 'The Liberal Party in West
Yorkshire, 1885-1895', unpublished PhD thesis, University of Leeds, 1979, p. 255.

12. Ibid., p. 256.

13. Thompson, 'Homage to Tom Maguire', p. 277.

14. Labour Party Archive, Labour Representation Committee, 11/69.

15. Laybourn, 'Yorkshire Trade Unions',
particularly chapters three and ten; Board of Trade
Reports on Trade Unions, 1896 (c. 8644), 1900 (cd.
773); James, 'Emergence of Keighley Independent
Labour Party', p. 64; Labour Representation Committee 14/5, Leicester Trades Council Balance Sheet for
1902 and Directory of Trades Councils.

16. Sydney and Beatrice Webb, _The History of
Trade Unions_ (Longman, Green, 1920 edition), pp.
427-33.

17. J.A. Jowitt and K. Laybourn, 'The Wool
Textile Dispute of 1925', _The Journal of Local
Studies_, Vol. 2, No. 1, Spring 1982, pp. 11-12.

18. K. Laybourn, 'Yorkshire Trade Unions',
chapter one.

19. Thompson, 'Homage to Tom Maguire', p. 309.

20. Bradford Trades and Labour Council, _Year-
book 1912_ (Bradford Trades Council, Bradford, 1912),
pp. 21-2.

21. Reynolds and Laybourn, 'The Emergence of the Independent Labour Party in Bradford', p. 313.
22. Ibid., 324-5.
23. Bradford Observer, 16 Jul. 1887.
24. Reynolds and Laybourn, 'The Emergence of the Independent Labour Party in Bradford', p. 324.
25. Ibid., p. 325.
26. Ibid., pp. 336-7.
27. Ibid., pp. 337-40.
28. Ibid., pp. 331-4.
29. Bradford Observer, 24 Jun. 1892.
30. There were between 19 and 21 ILP clubs by the end of 1892, and 29 by 1895, before a decline to about ten by the late 1890s.
31. Bradford Observer, 11 Jul. 1892.
32. Bradford Observer Budget, 2 Nov. 1893.
33. Bradford Observer, 6 Jan. 1893.
34. Bradford Trades Council, Minutes, Jan. and Feb. 1896.
35. Bradford Labour Echo, 1 Jun. 1895.
36. Reynolds and Laybourn, 'The Emergence of the Independent Labour Party in Bradford', pp. 337-40.
37. Bradford Labour Echo, 22 Jun. 1895.
38. Bradford Observer, 18 Jun. 1892.
39. James, 'Keighley Independent Labour Party' pp. 67-8.
40. John Lister, 'The Early History of the ILP Movement in Halifax', MSS. copy in the Archives Collection, Calderdale Library Services.
41. Beever was presented with £157 and became a coal merchant and Tattersall was presented with £130 and became a tobacconist and confectioner.
42. Lister, 'The Early History of the ILP Movement in Halifax'.
43. Yorkshire Factory Times, 27, 29 Apr., 11, 22 Jul. 1892.
44. Halifax Guardian, 29 Sep. 1892.
45. Thompson, 'Homage to Tom Maguire', p. 302.
46. Ibid., p. 294.
47. Yorkshire Factory Times, 13 Dec. 1889.
48. Thompson, 'Homage to Tom Maguire', p. 299.
49. Ibid., pp. 299-301; Yorkshire Factory Times, 4 Jul. 1890; Second Annual Report of the Gasworkers and General Labourers of Great Britain and Ireland (Gasworkers and General Labourers, London, 1891), p. 11.
50. Gasworkers, Second Annual Report, pp. 25-6.
51. Yorkshire Factory Times, 6 Dec. 1889.
52. Ibid.
53. Ibid., 1 Nov. 1889.

54. Mattison was a member of the Amalgamated
Society of Engineers, and his personal letters and
diaries are in the Brotherton Library, University of
Leeds.

55. Thompson, 'Homage to Tom Maguire', p. 298
refers to the formation of a Yorkshire Socialist
Federation in July 1889, though this appears to have
given way to the Yorkshire Labour League in February
1890.

56. Yorkshire Factory Times, 8 May 1891.

57. The Leeds Typographical Circular produced
by the Leeds Graphical Society in the late 1880s
and 1890s provides extensive details on Demaine. It
is still in the hands of the Leeds Graphical Society.

58. Yorkshire Factory Times, 1 Jul. 1892.

59. Leeds Trades Council, Minutes, 26 Apr. 1893.

60. Ibid., 14 Apr. 1892.

61. Thompson, William Morris: Romatic to
Revolutionary, p. 563.

62. Leeds Trades Council, Minutes, 6 Apr. 1887,
10 Aug. 1887; Yorkshire Factory Times, 1 Jul. 1892.

63. Leeds Trades Council, Minutes, 22 Jan.
1892; Yorkshire Factory Times, 1 Jul. 1892.

64. Leeds Trades Council, Minutes, 22 Jan. 1892.

65. Ibid., 6, 12 Feb, 6 Apr. 1895; Yorkshire
Factory Times, 1 Jul. 1892.

66. There is extensive correspondence between
the Leeds Trades Council and the Labour Representation Committee in the Labour Party Archive, LRC
Correspondence boxes. Although the Leeds Trades
Council joined the national LRC in 1900 it was not
immediately affiliated to the Leeds Labour Representation Committee, which caused some local
political difficulties. See particularly Owen Connellan's letter to MacDonald, LRC/13/367. Connellan was the secretary of the Trades Council and had
been nominated to stand for the East Leeds constituency by the Trades Council despite the Leeds LRC
giving its support to O'Grady.

67. Annual Report of the Halifax ILP, 1897, for
1896; ILP News, May and Jun. 1898.

68. Reynolds and Laybourn, 'The Emergence of
the Independent Labour Party in Bradford'. p. 315.

69. Clark, Colne Valley: Radicalism to Socialism, chapters four and nine.

70. Ibid., p. 195. There are copies of this
particular document in the Webb Collection, the
British Library of Political Sciences and in the
G.H. Wood Collection, the Polytechnic Library,
Huddersfield.

71. Clark, Colne Valley, Radicalism to

Socialism, chapter four.

72. I.L.P. Directory of 1895 (ILP, London, 1895) indicated that there were 29 branches or clubs in Bradford, eleven in Colne Valley, nine in Spen Valley, eight in Leeds, eight in Halifax, eight in Huddersfield and five in Dewsbury.

73. Clark, Colne Valley: Radicalism to Socialism, pp. 7-19; Colne Valley Labour Union, Minutes, 21 Jul. 1891.

74. Ibid.

75. Bradford Observer, 14 Jan. 1893.

76. Colin Cross, Philip Snowden (Barrie & Rockliffe, London, 1966), p. 55.

77. Clark, Colne Valley: Radicalism to Socialism.

78. Bradford Labour Echo, 11 Apr. 1896; Forward, 10 Jun. 1905.

79. R. Moore, The Emergence of the Labour Party 1880-1924 (Macmillan, London, 1978), p. 60.

80. K. Laybourn, '"The Defence of the Bottom Dog": The Independent Labour Party in Local Politics' in D.G. Wright and J.A. Jowitt (eds), Victorian Bradford (City of Bradford Metropolitan Council, Libraries Division, Bradford, 1982), pp. 229-33.

81. Yorkshire Factory Times, 1 Dec. 1893.

82. Leeds Mercury, 27 Oct. 1894.

83. Bradford Observer, 11 Oct. 1894.

84. Reynolds and Laybourn, 'The Emergence of the Independent Labour Party in Bradford', p. 332; Bradford Observer, 4 Aug. 1891, 21 Apr. 1892.

85. The 'Manchester Fourth Clause' was pushed forward by Robert Blatchford and the Manchester ILP members who felt that, if there was no Labour candidate standing at an election, the ILP voters ought to abstain.

86. Tom Mann, Memoirs (Labour Publishing Company, Lond, 1923), p. 95.

87. Bradford Labour Echo, 15 Jun. 1895.

Chapter Four

LIBERAL RESPONSES AND LABOUR DIFFICULTIES IN THE
1890S

The Liberal Party organisations were supreme in the
local and parliamentary politics of West Yorkshire
during the late 1880s and early 1890s. The Home
Rule crisis had tended to consolidate Liberalism
behind a small number of Liberal-Nonconformist mill-
owners rather than to divide and weaken it. Self-
confident and well-organised, West Yorkshire Liberalism tended to regard Socialist and Independent
groups, such as the Independent Labour Party, as a
mere irritation rather than a serious threat to its
political dominance of the region. Indeed, Alfred
Illingworth probably summed up the preponderant mood
of West Yorkshire Liberalism when he described the
Bradford Labour Union as 'one of the little breezes
which occasionally crosses Bradford'.[1] Disdainful
of the ILP challenge, and almost contemptuous of the
power of local trade unionism, the leading West
Yorkshire Liberals made few concessions to the working classes, were unwilling to allow working-class
Liberals to stand in local elections and offered
little in the way of progressive social policies at
the local level. The Newcastle Programme of 1891
might have meant a lot to the Liberal Party's national leaders but was largely ignored by the Liberal
millocracy of West Yorkshire. It was not until the
1895 General Election that the Liberals became aware
of the serious nature of the Labour challenge, which
some felt had cost them seats to the Conservative
Party. But even then the West Yorkshire Liberal
organisations began to see their main opposition as
a revived Conservative Party rather than an embarrassing, and probably spent, ILP. In short, the
Liberal Party ignored the ILP before 1895, and was
too preoccupied with the Conservative challenge to
give much thought to the ILP therafter. The problems which ILP organisations faced in the late 1890s

tended to strengthen the resolve of Liberals that they should challenge Conservatism rather than confront the ILP. This led the Liberal Party to shore up its middle-class support rather than to cater to the interests of the working classes and trade unions.

The confidence which the West Yorkshire Liberal organisation revealed in the face of mounting Labour opposition was hardly surprising given the parliamentary and local electoral successes of the Party. Liberalism dominated the parliamentary representation of West Yorkshire and was overwhelmingly in control of most of the school boards in West Yorkshire and the municipal authorities. It was not until about 1895 that its political position began to slip and given that the main challenge appeared to come from the Conservatives it is hardly surprising that Liberal anxiety focused upon the Conservative, rather than the Labour, challenge.

Table 4.1: The Parliamentary Representatives for West Yorkshire, 1886-1900[a]

General Election	Liberals	Conservatives	Total
1886	19	4	23
1892	20	3	23
1895	14	9	23
1900	14	9	23

Note: a. A list of the constituencies is provided in note 7 of chapter one.
Source: W.F.S. Craig, British Parliamentary Election Results 1885-1918 (Macmillan, London, 1977).

Table 4.2: The Municipal Balance of Power in Bradford, Leeds and Huddersfield, 1890-1900

Year	Bradford				Huddersfield				Leeds	
	L	C	ILP	O	L	C	ILP	O	L	C
1890	42	17		1	37	19		3	46	18
1891	36	23		1	38	19		3	40	24
1892	32	27	2		39	18	1	2	43	21
1893	30	26	4		38	18	1	3	40	24

Table 4.2 (cont'd)

Year	Bradford				Huddersfield				Leeds	
	L	C	ILP	O	L	C	ILP	O	L	Ca
1894	29	27	4		38	18	1	3	36	28
1895	28	26	5	1	38	17	1	3	26	38
1896	28	27	4	1	37	17	1	5	30	34
1897	28	26	5	1	38	16	1	5	30	34
1898	26	29	5		39	15	1	5	26	38
1899	27	44	5	8	28	16	1	5	26	38
1900	28	42	6	8	37	19	1	3	27	37

Note: a. The abbreviations are L for Liberal, C for
Conservative, ILP for the Independent Labour Party
and O for Others.
Sources: Bradford Observer, Huddersfield Examiner
Nov. issues; T. Woodhouse, 'The working class', in
Derek Fraser (ed.), A History of Modern Leeds
(Manchester University Press, Manchester, 1980), p.
363.

The Liberal Party clearly had control of the
progressive vote in West Yorkshire and it is perhaps
not surprising that local Liberalism was aggressive,
abrasive and unwilling to compromise with Labour.
The Huddersfield Examiner, the organ of the Huddersfield Liberal Association, attacked the programme of
the Socialist Party as 'so impractical that Liberals
and Radicals easily recognise how foolish it would
be to take up the bulk of it ...'[2] Liberals in
Bradford tended to dismiss the formation of the Labour Union as being an irrelevance and W.B. Priestley,
who was to become the Liberal MP for Bradford East
in 1906, summed up this attitude when he said that
'Liberals believed that the I.L.P. were thoroughly
honest in their intentions but they were a little
too previous'.[3]
    Not surprisingly, the West Yorkshire Liberals
tended to dismiss the growth of an independent Labour movement as either unnecessary, since the Liberals were effectively representing the interests of
the working classes, or as a Tory plot to undermine
the progressive vote and return Tories to public office. The Huddersfield Examiner declaimed that
'Every working man in the Liberal ranks knows that a
vote given to the Socialists is in effect a vote
given to the Tories, and that every alienation is a

means of weakening the cause of progress'.[4]

Yet the West Yorkshire Liberals did little to endear themselves to the working-class electorate. After the parliamentary victories of 1892, and despite the good showing of Ben Tillett in Bradford West, the Liberal Party did not attempt to heal the rifts that were opening up between Liberalism and the working classes. The Tillett contest, indeed, had revealed how reactionary was the Liberal candidate, Alfred Illingworth, who favoured the continuance of the half-time system and opposed the eight-hour day for miners. Two parliamentary by-elections in early 1893 revealed further evidence of the continued intransigence of Liberalism. The Halifax parliamentary by-election of February 1893 saw a bitter contest in which John Lister, a local land-owner, member of the Halifax Labour Union and treasurer of the newly formed National ILP, obtained a promising vote of more than 3,000 for Labour. Although the Huddersfield parliamentary by-election of February 1893 contained no ILP candidate, it too added to the increasing tensions between the Liberal Party and the working classes. The narrowly defeated Liberal candidate, J. Woodhead, the owner and editor of the Huddersfield Examiner, was firmly opposed to trade unionism and had run a non-union shop for more than 30 years. The Huddersfield Chronicle, maintained

In Huddersfield not only have the Liberals ignored the Labour Party but they have literally courted destruction by flying in the face of the Labour Party by selecting a candidate who is chiefly known throughout Yorkshire by his hostility to the Labour movement; a man who has said ... that he would rather lose the election than vote for the Eight Hours Bill for miners ....[5]

The local Liberal parties also compounded their sins by victimising leading Labour Union and trade-union officials. It was such action which had given rise to the Halifax Labour Union in 1892.[6] The Keighley Labour Journal, the organ of the Keighley ILP, also reflected that

It is not so long since a prominent Liberal candidate told a defeated Labour candidate "it was a good job for him that he had not won the election as if he had his whole future career would have been blasted". Nor is it

> very long since a son of one of our so-called
> Liberal employers told another with respect to
> a Labour candidate, that "they would not have
> such a man about the place" and this ...
> simply because of his political opinion.[7]

G.F. Wardle, who edited the Keighley Labour
Journal, was also placed under considerable pressure
to give up his political activities. He explained
how

> Some of the employers in Keighley ... had per-
> secuted him because he dared to have an opin-
> ion of his own ... he was brought to the
> headquarters (of the Midland Railway Company)
> and made to sign an agreement not to take part
> in any public meeting belonging to the Inde-
> pendent Labour Party. ... He signed for the
> sake of his wife and children.[8]

Similar pressure was applied to many ILP members and some of their religious supporters. The
Rev. J. Goldsack, a Keighley Nonconformist minister
and confessed Socialist, was forced to resign his
pastorate. 'What is the reason for this', asked
the Keighley Labour Journal, 'Can it be that there
are some members of his flock who prefer the old
darkness to the new light'.[9] The Rev. R. Roberts,
a leading ILP figure from the mid 1890s until 1903
and on the eve of the First World War, was forced to
leave Frizinghall Congregational Chapel for Brown-
royd Congregational Chapel, largely because of his
political beliefs.[10] Similarly, the Rev. W.B.
Graham, a Church of England Minister who had been
active in the Bradford and Colne Valley labour movements during the early twentieth century, found himself victimised in Colne Valley.[11]
Liberal organisations still tended to be dominated by a few, intermarried, Nonconformist woollen
and worsted manufacturing families, as they had been
in the mid 1880s, and, despite the rise of the ILP
challenge, the working classes had little active
involvement in the organisation of the Liberal associations. Samuel Shaftoe, secretary of the Bradford
Trades Council throughout the 1880s and up to 1893,
was one of a small handful of working men in the
Bradford Six Hundred, the policy-making body for
Bradford Liberalism as a whole.[12] Given the difficulty of winning support for the return of working-
class delegates to Liberal organisations it is hardly surprising that many working-class activists

drifted into the ILP.

There appears to have been relatively little support either for Lib-Labism or the new Liberalism in West Yorkshire. Samuel Shaftoe and Walter Sugden, both Bradford Lib-Labbers, were active in the national Labour Electoral Association but, as previously suggested, they found it difficult to sustain the movement in the face of obvious Liberal opposition to their aim of supporting the candidature of working men in local and parliamentary elections.[13] New Liberalism, in the sense that it offered a positive set of social policies to benefit the working classes, was also thinly represented in West Yorkshire. It was only in Leeds that Lib-Labism made any positive showing and only in Shipley that there was anything like a success for the Lib-Labs and new Liberals. In both areas, it was the work of William Pollard Byles, sometime editor of the Bradford Observer, which encouraged a new more progressive Liberalism to emerge - although only briefly.

The established political consensus between old Liberalism and the working classes in the Shipley constituency had been largely based upon Sir Titus Salt, Saltaire and the continuing influence of the 'Salt Ideal', which had as its basis notions of responsibility to employer, deference, and a working class prepared to follow the political lead of the Liberal middle class.[14] The death of Salt in the mid 1870s had done much to undermine the perpetuation of working-class deference in Shipley. Neither his sons nor his fellow directors carried the same influence amongst the workforce, or the same interest in the firm. In 1892 a new company took over the firm, and the loyalty of the workforce to the firm declined with the removal of family control and the increasing remoteness of decision-making.[15] Even though the new company left W.C. Stead, a former fellow director of Sir Titus, in charge the administration remained aloof and remote. Stead had become one of Titus Salt's partners in 1852 and, in various capacities, maintained his position in the firm until his death in 1897. It was Stead who was the President of the Shipley Liberal Association in the late 1880s and early 1890s, and it was Stead who emerged as the chief opponent to the idea that working men might be allowed to choose the Liberal candidate, and thus the MP, for Shipley.

In 1891 J. Craven, the Liberal MP for Shipley, declared his intention of retiring at the next

election. The Shipley Liberal Association therefore
made its intention clear that it wished Alfred E.
Hutton, a young man connected with a highly-esteemed
business family, and a Congregationalist, to be the
new Liberal candidate. Stead, managing director of
Salts mills, pressed forward Hutton's name to the
Liberal Two Hundred in Shipley. From the start,
however, the intentions of Stead, and his supporters, were challenged by one member of the Shipley
Liberal Two Hundred, W.P. Byles, one of the proprietors of the Bradford Observer.

Byles was the son of William Byles, who had
founded the Bradford Observer in the 1830s, and was
involved with the paper as owner and editor. Byles
also had financial interests in other firms and was
a shareholder at Lister's Manningham Mills. This
situation permitted him to make representations on
the behalf of the workforce during the Manningham
Mills strike.[16] He and his wife suggested that a
lower dividend would enable the firm to forego the
imposition of wage reductions. From this time onwards, Byles became identified with the cause of
improving the lot of working men.

Byles was a formidable adversary to Stead and
the leading Shipley Liberals, for he could use the
power of the press to illuminate the trenchant opposition of old, established, Liberalism to the de-
sires of working men. In an extremely bitter conflict he used his political prestige and the power
of the press to put forward his own claim for the
Liberal candidature of Shipley in opposition to
Hutton. Although the details of the conflict of
opinion are very complex, it is clear that Byles
put his name forward on the basis that the existing
Shipley Liberal Two Hundred was coming to the end
of its existence and that the issue of the new Liberal candidate should be left to the newly-elected
body.[17] As a result, the selection of new delegates for the Shipley Liberal Two Hundred became
fiercely contested as Liberal clubs in Shipley,
Bradford, and other areas where Shipley voters were
organised, selected their candidates.[18] Throughout
January 1892 Liberal club after Liberal club selected its delegates, in the heady atmosphere of internecine conflict between the Byles and Hutton
factions.[19] In February 1892 the new Shipley
Divisional Liberal Association, the Shipley Two
Hundred, was formed. It consisted of 142 delegates,
59 who supported Hutton, 72 who supported Byles or
were opposed to Hutton, and 11 who were members by
virtue of their £5 annual subscription to the

Shipley Liberal Association. Of these, 133 attended
the annual meeting and it is clear, from the voting
that Byles had a majority of about six delegates,
although voting on some official positions was sometimes narrower. The delegates decided, by 68 votes
to 62, to reject Hutton's candidature, which had
been approved by the previous body in August 1891.[20]
Seth Bentley, manager of the Saltaire washhouse,
replaced Charles Stead, the managing director at
Salts, as president, and most of the other positions, of nine vice-presidents, treasurer, secretary
and 20 Executive Committee members, were filled by
Byles's supporters. By the end of March 1892,
Byles was formally adopted as the Liberal candidate
for Shipley and a month later Hutton decided to
withdraw his name and to stand for the Morley Division.[21]

What is particularly interesting about this
conflict is that organised labour supported Byles
to defeat the representative of Liberal millocracy.
In effect, what had happened was that the Lib-Labs
had captured a Liberal Association. The Shipley
Trades Council supported Byles and helped form the
Shipley Labour Electoral Association towards the
end of February 1892. James Tiplady, a prominent
member of the Bradford LEA and a Shipley man, reflected upon what had been achieved at Shipley, and
the chairman of the meeting stated that

> He was glad to say, however, that in Shipley
> the Labour Party was thoroughly united, and
> that the great bulk of the workers were work-
> ing for the Liberal party. The workers in
> that district were not going in for an inde-
> pendent position, but they had taken a very
> unusual course. A good deal of hard work had
> been given by workers with the object of get-
> ting hold of the machinery of the Liberal
> party in the division, and the attempt had been
> successful. They had selected the Liberal
> Executive altogether, and most of the dele-
> gates to the Two Hundred were with them. This
> was, he thought, the right way in which the
> labour question should be advanced.[22]

Such sentiments had already been expressed more
than a month earlier, whilst the Hutton and Byles
contest was still in progress. A public meeting,
organised by Byles's supporters, including James
Tiplady, Isaac and J. Sanctuary, members of a
prominent working-class Saltaire family, found the

chairman reflecting that

> It had also been said that Mr. Byles and his
> friends were setting class against class. The
> Executive did not give them the opportunity of
> doing this. They set themselves against Mr.
> Byles and his friends from the very first, and
> the charge of setting class against class
> could only be brought against those who made
> it.23

Working-class Liberals certainly felt that their
interests had been neglected by the previous Shipley
Liberal Two Hundred and that they were justified in
fighting for their interests within the Liberal
Party. This is what they had done, and they had
won.

By the early 1890s, then, W.P. Byles had already set course on his career of supporting Lib-
Labism, with its political connotations of an alliance between Liberalism and working men, and the
new Liberalism, with its desire to promote legislation to improve the conditions of the working
classes. He was adamant that Liberal and Labour
interests were identical and stated that

> I myself and my supporters, who form a very
> large party in the division, as you will all
> admit, say that a Labour candidate and a Lib-
> eral candidate ought to be one and the same
> thing (hear, hear). I say that it ought to be
> an absurd question to ask whether a man is a
> Liberal candidate or a Labour candidate.
> There are Liberals, it is true, who are trying
> to drive the Labour section of the Liberal
> party out of the Liberal party. There are
> Labour men, it is also true, for instance, the
> Labour Union in Bradford, who are trying to
> drive Liberals out of the party. But I and
> Mr. Bentley and Mr. Watson and my supporters
> are trying to keep the two together.24

Yet it is obvious that Byles blatantly failed
to keep Labour and Liberalism together. The Bradford ILP was ambivalant towards him, at once criticising his ultimate ambition whilst offering him
political support. George Cowgill, President, and
later Secretary, of the Bradford Trades Council,
and a prominent member of the ILP, supported Byles's
candidature in the 1892 General Election, informing
an audience that 'They had come to look upon

Mr. Byles as one of the best friends of the working
man (cheers)'.[25]   The supporters of the previous
Shipley Liberal executive were less undecided; they
appear to have gone over to support Theo Peel,
Byles's Unionist opponent. The Bradford Observer
noted:

> All along Mr. Byles's supporters had felt that
> they were fighting three parties, and as one of
> those parties, whatever its size, was a section
> of the Liberal party, it lent to the contest
> all the keenness of internecine warfare. As
> one went about the division on Saturday the
> magnitude of the forces opposed to Mr. Byles
> was most apparent. The bill-posting places
> were deluged with hostile blue, white and yel-
> low literature, and yellow cards bearing on
> them the words "Vote for Peel and the backbone
> of the Liberal party".[26]

Despite such opposition, Byles won the seat by 282
votes, with 5,746 votes to Theo Peel's 5,464, much
less than the 2,197 majority which had been recorded
by Craven at the last contested parliamentary election in 1885.
    Byles represented the Shipley constituency in
the House of Commons between 1892 and 1895 but was
narrowly defeated in the 1895 General Election when
J. Fortescue Flannery (Liberal Unionist) obtained
5,999 votes to Byles's 5,921. Although Joseph
Craven, the first Liberal MP for Shipley, and Charles
Stead gave Byles their official support it is clear
that many old Liberals remained hostile to Byles,
and some, such as A.E. Hutton, were to be found supporting the Liberal Unionist opponent.[27]
    Therafter, some of the Labour supporters of
Byles began to drift towards the ILP, and a Shipley
branch of the ILP was formed in 1895 with Jacob
Sanctuary to the fore. In 1898 there were 61 members of the Shipley branch of the ILP.[28] But the ILP
and the Labour Party were never to be significant
forces in Shipley until after the First World War.
    Byles, on the other hand, continued to develop
his Lib-Lab and new-Liberal ideas. His election
address, published for the 1892 General Election,
indicated how progressive a Liberal he was. Whilst
he recognised that the main issue of the 1892 General
Election was 'the treatment of Ireland' he regarded
the second great issue to be 'the condition of the
people'.[29] Under this second heading he indicated
that he was more than a Lib-Lab, wishing to extend

the franchise, the abolition of plural voting and
the payment of MPs, but that he wanted to see a co-
herent social policy presented by the Liberal Party.
Having referred to the issue of land nationisation
and other issues which many Liberals would have
agreed upon he concluded that

> Beyond these things I hope it may be found that
> social reforms will take legislative shape.
> Owing to the complexity of modern society, and
> to the development of the industrial system,
> there are many thousands of men and women who
> can only earn their livelihood at the will of
> another. This state of things appears to me to
> impose on society increased duties towards
> those members of it who are unemployed, over-
> worked, or underpaid, as well as towards the
> young, sick, and the aged poor. I am ready to
> support just and reasonable proposals which
> are designed to overtake such responsibilities,
> and to increase the comfort, the health, the
> leisure, and the education of the people.[30]

Byles's position on these issues had, if anything,
hardened by 1895 and once he was out of Parliament
he began to explore the possibilities of working
more closely with the ILP.
    Byles's first direct approach to the ILP was,
however, a tempetuous one. Having been defeated in
the Shipley parliamentary election of 1895 he began
to search out future possible seats. That was not
easy. Byles, although he was reasonably wealthy
was not rich enough to be able to pay the expenses
of elections, of election agents, and the contri-
butions to numerous societies, which most Liberal
Associations favoured. However, an opportunity
presented itself in 1896 when Byron Reed, the Conservative MP for Bradford East, died. For a while,
the Liberals were unable to find a candidate and it
appeared that Keir Hardie, the ILP candidate, would
have a straight fight with the Conservative candidate. But it was obvious that Alfred Illingworth
was looking for a suitable Liberal candidate and
Byles hoped to presume himself on to the Liberal
Party and the ILP alike as a compromise figure.
Byles's suit was unsuccessful, but his exchange of
letters with Hardie reflects the extent of his
personal commitment to the new Liberalism. Byles
wrote:

> When you say I vacillate between two opinions

and do not choose between Liberalism and Labour, you absolutely misunderstand my position.
I will explain: you and I hold practically the
same opinions. These opinions have led you to
disbelieve in the Lib. party as an engine
for the reforms you seek, and therefore to leave it and form a separate party. The same opinions have not led me to the same conclusions.
Bad and reactionary as many Liberals are, I
believe that salvation must come thro the
Liberal party wh. still contains more friends
of Labour than can be found outside it, and
the destruction of which (if it were possible
wh. it isn't) would set back the Labour clock
a generation.31

By the end of the 1890s, having sold his shares in
the Bradford Observer and having asked Charles W.
Dilke to intervene on his behalf with Hardie, Byles
stood as a Labour candidate for Leeds East, obtaining 1,266 votes or 20.1 per cent of the vote.
      The circumstances of Byles's labour candida-
ture in Leeds East were unusual and confused. There
was extensive correspondence on Byles between the
Leeds Trades Council and the Labour Representation
Committee, or, more precisely, between Owen Connellan, Secretary of the Trades Council, and MacDon-
ald.32 The gist of the correspondence was that
Byles's candidature had been sought by the East
Leeds branch of the United Irish League which had
approached the Trades Council with a view to getting
Byles accepted as a Labour and Home Rule candidate.
The Trades Council endorsed Byles's candidature in
September 1900 and it was clearly hoped that the
Liberal Party would be persuaded to accept Byles as
the Liberal candidate as well. These events were
clearly deplored by a number of local Labour activists who considered the 'Byles business' to be 'dis-
graceful'.33 Owen Connellan, who hoped to be selected as Labour candidate for Leeds East, was Byles's
bitterest opponent. Reflecting that the Labour Representation Committee ought to have been rather
broader in its political approach, and selected its
own Liberal-Labour man, Connellan trenchantly, but
accurately, summed up the situation by suggesting
that it would have been better than'to see the
Trades Council, ILP and Socialist influence used for
the purpose of forcing an unpopular man upon his own
party. And I believe it would have been easier to
induce the Liberal party to accept a Labour man than
to swallow Mr. Byles'.34 Byles soon returned to the

Liberal fold, left Bradford, and successfully sought
his political fortune in Lancashire where his new-
Liberal ideas appear to have gone down well. But he
does not appear to have created much of a following
in West Yorkshire. The old Liberal millocracy suspected him, and were positively opposed to him in
Shipley, Bradford and Leeds. On the other hand, the
ILP and Labour Representation Committee leaders were
equally dubious of Byles and, urging him to join the
ILP, one political commentator reflected that 'As a
Liberal fighting on a Liberal platform, he is very
little more to us than the rest of the plutocrats
who are beguiling and misleading the workers'.[35]

There were very few victories for Lib-Labism
and the new Liberalism in West Yorkshire throughout
the 1890s. There is evidence of initiatives by the
new Liberals. J.W. Jarratt, an advanced Liberal,
helped to formulate a progressive municipal programme for the Bradford Liberal Association in 1894,
which contained commitments to introducing an eight-
hour day and forty-eight hour week for Corporation
workers, Corporation control of nightsoil clearance
and tramways, and the introduction of fair contracts,
but it does not appear to have stemmed the flow to
the ILP.[36] When this policy failed to achieve the
desired result the Liberals began to make overtures
to the ILP, and there were meetings between leading
Liberals and ILP members in April 1897, orchestrated
by W.P. Byles.[37] The opprobrious reaction within
ILP circles quickly ended the initiative, though the
Bradford Observer was proud to report that the Joint
Committee of the Trades Council and the ILP after
having put three test questions to all municipal
candidates in 1898 had recommended 'working men to
support Liberal candidates in all wards in which no
Labour candidate had appeared'.[38] In 1899 the
Bradford Labour Echo speculated that the feud betwe-
en the 'Radical Socialists' in the Liberal Party and
'old-time Liberalism' could only end 'in the disap-
pearance of old Liberalism'.[39] There was much optimism within some sections of Liberalism when
W.E.B. Priestley's secret mission to H. Gladstone
led to Jarratt's standing down from Bradford West,
thus permitting Fred Jowett a straight fight with
the conservative candidate in the 1900 General Election. But, in the end, the old Liberalism prevailed,
a fact testified to by Byles's eventual departure
from Bradford politics in 1903, for the more politically agreeable air of Manchester and Salford.[40]

Apart from Byles, there is little evidence of
prominent Liberal politicians from West Yorkshire

exhibiting much interest in the Liberal ideas of
the 1890s. C.P. Trevelyan was only returned for the
Elland constituency in the parliamentary by-election
of March 1899 and there is little evidence that he
was inclined to new Liberalism before 1906.[41] Old
Liberalism, dominated by a Nonconformist textile
millocracy remained dominant in West Yorkshire throughout the 1890s and remained almost impervious to
the demands being put forward by advanced and new
Liberals such as Byles. In the early 1890s old Liberalism refused to acknowledge the seriousness of
the Labour challenge, and from 1895 onwards became
increasingly preoccupied with the rise of Conservative fortunes which had reduced the parliamentary
strength of Liberalism in West Yorkshire and removed
it completely in Bradford.[42] In many respects this
concern to meet the challenge of Conservatism was
most sensible, given the problems which the ILP
faced in West Yorkshire during the late 1890s.

The previous chapter suggested that ILP membership
in West Yorkshire declined substantially after the
1895 General Election which pricked the bubble of
support which had welled up for the ILP between 1893
and 1895.[43] Membership fell from about 2,000 to
1,000 in Bradford between 1895 and 1896, and many
small ILP branches began to collapse throughout West
Yorkshire. This situation was worsened by the internecine conflict which emerged within the Halifax
ILP, one of the most powerful ILP branches in the
country.
    In its early years, the three leading political
figures in the Halifax Labour Union had been John
Lister, James Beever and James Tattersall. John
Lister was the owner of the Shibden Hall estate, on
the outskirts of Halifax, had been educated at
Oxford, where he was greatly influenced by the
writings of John Ruskin and William Morris, and was
drawn into Fabianism in 1891. By 1892 he had joined the Labour Union and in January 1893 he had become the Treasurer of the National ILP, a post which
he retained until he left the ILP in 1895.[44] Beever
and Tattersall, on the other hand, had been drawn
into the ILP by their trade union activities. As
previously suggested, both had been victimised by
their employer in 1892, and it was out of the indignation which followed that the Halifax Labour Union
was formed.[45] Beever was an active Fabian, became
President of the Halifax Trades Council, and effectively became the 'first Labour agent' for Halifax.
Tattersall became the first president of the

Halifax Labour Union in 1892.

In a traumatic train of events all three were gradually forced out of the ILP between 1894 and 1895. The internal squabbles of the Halifax Labour Union were widely reported in the local and national press, doing much damage to the cause of independent Labour. They began in May 1894 when Lister, Beever and Tattersall, the ILP's three town council representatives, divided over the issue of the reorganization of the Town Clerk's Office. Lister voted in favour, and Beever and Tattersall against the motion for reorganization. Although this division appeared to be an isolated incident, the June meeting of the Halifax Labour Union, chaired by Montague Blatchford, decided that in 'future councillors were to confer with the Union' before voting on any item of the Council agenda.[46] Although the possibility of conflict appeared to subside, it is clear, from a letter which Henry Backhouse sent to Keir Hardie, that there was much indignation that the three representatives were divided. Discussing the rising political level of activities in anticipation of Town Council, School Board and Guardian elections, Backhouse reflected that 'Everything hinges on, whether these men (three) can be persuaded to fall into line to practice the teachings of socialism – to submit to the great heart of the people and to esteem it and honour it ...'[47]

Local tensions subsided until the 23 October 1894, the day before the municipal nomination deadline, when Lister sent a letter to Tattersall, and the Labour Union, asking for his nomination for Central Ward to be withdrawn. In a fit of pique, Lister informed Tattersall that

> I can't attend to the duties properly and I don't like the job. Moreover, I feel that I have not given satisfaction to the Labour Union during my term of stewardship, and I am not prepared to accept the new conditions that the Union has imposed upon its representatives. I cannot submit to having my opinion, even in matters of detail, cut and dried for me.[48]

During the next twenty-four hours the Halifax Labour Union attempted to find a suitable substitute candidate for Lister. None was forthcoming, although Beever intimated his willingness to contest Central Ward if some type of political arrangement could be made with the Tories. The Labour Union declined to accept the suggestion but, to its

consternation, found out on 24th October that
Lister's name had been put down for the North Ward
and that Beever's name had been put forward for
Central Ward. Beever was immediately asked to withdraw his nomination from Central Ward, but refused
to do so and Lister re-entered the affair with three
telegrams on 25th October, at first declaring his
intention to stand for Council but then indicating
his decision to retire from municipal work.[49] There
was a strong feeling amongst the Labour Union members that the Liberal Party was connected with the
fact that Beever had been nominated for Central as
well as Southowram Ward, and a meeting was held
that night, chaired by Alderman Tattersall, which
repudiated Beever's candidature by 88 votes to 68.
Beever still contested Southowram however, with the
support of the Southowram Labour Club.

When the November municipal elections occurred
Central Ward was uncontested, the three Labour
candidates, including Beever were defeated, and
only Alderman Tattersall was left on the Council.
Retribution was swift. Beever was expelled from the
Halifax Labour Union for 'insubordination' and
Lister was forced to make his apologies to the Coun-
cil of the Halifax Labour Union.[50]

The matter might have rested there had it not
been for the Clarion taking the issue as an opportunity to strike at the ILP executive in general,
and Keir Hardie in particular. Lister was the treasurer of the ILP and a friend of Hardie. Neither
Robert Blatchford nor Montague Blatchford cared for
either, there being differences of opinion over ILP
tactics, municipal policy and Socialist unity.
Robert Blatchford condemned Lister and Beever through the Clarion, pronouncing that

> In a Democratic body the rule of the majority
> must be obeyed. If the ruling of the majority
> is disobeyed, the fact that the rebel holds a
> high position in the party is the strongest
> argument in favour of his condign punishment.
> Socialism without Democracy would be an abom-
> inable tyranny.[51]

Whilst Blatchford emphasised the need for a
democratic body to have control over its members,
and argued that the Halifax affair had proved the
quality of democracy within the ILP, others begged
to differ. Edward Carpenter, the Sheffield-based
Socialist, was critical of what he called the
'dancing-doll delegate ... You know what I mean.

The constituents (or is it not more often a caucus of the constituents?) pull the string; the delegate holds up his hand. They slacken and he drops it'.[52] John Burns felt that 'It is necessary to compromise in non-essential methods in order to achieve the essential things they were after'. Hardie felt that 'There is a spirit of distrust and suspicion abroad in our movement ... distrust and suspicion which is the reverse of our real purpose'.[53]

The petulant nature of this affair continued when, in mid-November 1894, James Beever was returned as a School Board candidate, whilst the Labour Union candidates, Montague Blatchford, Tattersall and Marsden, were all defeated.[54] The N.A.C. of the ILP requested that the Halifax Labour Union should consider reinstating Mr. Beever, but it declined to do so.[55] In addition, several of the local ILP clubs such as Southowram, Siddal and Caddy Field opposed the Labour Union, and the Caddy Field club informed the N.A.C. of the ILP that 'payment of affiliation fees would be paid direct to the treasurer' as it was 'now not part of the Halifax Labour Union'.[56]

Relations deteriorated in December 1894 when Montague Blatchford, and some of his supporters, demanded that Lister should be censured and stripped of his ILP parliamentary candidature for Halifax; he had stood in the parliamentary by-election of January 1893. Lister was in no hurry to attend a censure meeting and the threat to humble him before the Labour Union provoked fierce responses on both sides.

Lister wrote to Hardie explaining his actions and threatening to resign from the party rather than face a second meeting.[57] As the National ILP was in debt to Lister to the tune of about £135, and as Hardie expressed his personal obligation to pay off some of this debt, it is hardly surprising that Hardie was unwilling to lose the Treasurer of the ILP and its financial benefactor in one fell swoop. On Christmas Day 1894 he wrote to Lister giving him his support, suggesting that the Blatchford request was insulting, advising him to join another branch of the ILP, and noting that

> It might be as well to write to Tom Mann as secretary protesting against the Resolution already passed, and appealing to the N.A.C. against being condemned unheard. The upshot will probably be the severance of the Halifax Labour Union from the I.L.P. and for the present I see nothing better that could happen. If the

spirit of the Halifax Labour Union became general in the movement, I for one would clear out.[58]

The animus created by the Halifax events flowed over into the national movement. Hardie was criticised by Robert Blatchford and many local Halifax men for his public support of Lister in the Labour Leader. Robert Blatchford's relatively restrained letters to Hardie were laced with references to Lister being 'a weak man' and a 'wrong un'.[59] Others were less diplomatic. Robert Morley, a local engineering trade unionist who was subsequently to become closely involved in the formation of Tom Mann's Workers' Union,[60] criticised Hardie's 'one-eyed approach', and concluded one lengthy letter, in which he outlined the whole affair as he saw it, in the following manner: '"A score of sound honest men are better than 20,000 unreliable" so said Hardie in Halifax last June. We believe it still & are therefore safe. Hoping a similar judgement may possess you, & a less prejudiced position be assumed towards us'.[61]

In the event, Lister faced the second censure meeting on 3 January 1895. Despite strong criticism, and a 'lively discussion', Lister remained a member of the Halifax Labour Union, was not censured and remained the Labour Union's parliamentary candidate for Halifax.[62] Within a few weeks he was campaigning for the Halifax seat and in July 1895 he made a spirited attempt to win the seat for the ILP.[63] He subsequently contested the municipal elections in November 1895, but then quickly drifted out of the local and the National ILP.[64] Beever briefly returned to the Labour fold, to speak in favour of Lister at the 1895 General Election, but then re-established his Liberal credentials.

Alderman Tattersall also left the ILP, in November 1895. In 1892 Tattersall had been supported by the Conservatives who pushed for him to be raised to the aldermanic bench in preference to Beever who was favoured by the Liberals.[65] On the town council, Tattersall found that he gained most support from Alderman Whittaker, the Conservative party boss in Halifax, and maintained that 'so far as industrial legislation is concerned I am quite convinced that the Labour Party has more to hope for from the Conservative Government than they can possible get from a Liberal Administration'.[66] During the 1895 General Election, when he was the ILP candidate for Preston, he despatched An Appeal to the working men

of Halifax in which he advised Labour voters to cast
their second vote, Halifax being a two-seat constituency, 'against the most illiberal set of men in
Halifax and the nominees of the so-called Liberal
Association'.[67]   The implication was that Labour
voters should use their second vote to support the
Conservative candidate. He also stressed that the
split votes indicated that 1,351 Conservatives voted
for Lister in the 1895 General Election whilst only
700 Liberals had done the same.[68]   Eventually, in
November 1895, Tattersall was drummed out of the
Halifax Labour Union by the overwhelming majority of
75 votes to 15.[69]   Soon afterwards he became a full-
time agent for the Halifax Conservative Party.[70]
    The Liberal Party and the nation's press made
much sport out of the open conflict which had emerged between the factions of the Halifax Labour Union
and the National ILP. Such internecine conflict was
not the best way to approach a general election, and
was obviously a contributory factor in the disappointing results achieved by the ILP in 1895.

The 1895 General Election was, indeed, a great set-
back for the national movement. The loss of Hardie's West Ham seat, the defeat of 35 ILP candidates,
who could only muster 50,000 votes between them -
about 15 per cent of the vote in what were considered to be improving seats for the ILP - told dis-
astrously on the national movement. Membership
slipped away following this political defeat for
the party was not as yet established to fight on a
comparatively large scale. Despite the relative
strength of the ILP in West Yorkshire, Labour leaders were desperately sifting through the possibilities of reviving the movement. Stephen Yeo has
suggested that it was at about this stage that the
'Cause' began to lose its sense of Socialist purpose and to concentrate its efforts upon improving
its electoral performance. Yeo feels that at this
stage the pursuit of electoral success began to
undermine the Socialist purpose of the 'Cause'. The
Socialist movement neglected its original aim of
winning ground for Socialism and offering a Socialist way of life.[71] However, what is clear in West
Yorkshire is that the spiritual and religious side
of the movement continued to flourish at the same
time as the movement became increasingly dominated
by trade unions. Indeed, the Socialist Sunday
school movement was only just beginning to get under
way, the real growth occurring from 1899 onwards
with the formation of the Central Socialist Sunday

school in Bradford and the formation of the Yorkshire Socialist Sunday School Union.[72] Therafter
the movement continued to grow until the First World
War winning an increasing number of children, and
their parents, to the pursuance of a Socialist way
of life. And although the Leeds Labour Church was
experiencing some difficulties, the Bradford Labour
Church continued to act as an inspirational force in
the Bradford Labour movement by providing lectures:
'Sunday after Sunday it brings to the town speakers
of the first rank, and in many ways help to keep
the goodwork going'.[73] It is clear that the various objectives of the independent movement were not
so much countervailing as complementary in West
Yorkshire. Out of the hardships of the late 1890s
was forged a much more unified, realistic and toler-
and independent Labour movement.

The ILP contested six of the 23 seats in West
Yorkshire during the 1895 General Election, and
came bottom of the poll in all these contests.[74]
The Bradford East by-election of November 1896, in
which Keir Hardie stood for the ILP, and the Halifax
by-election of 1897, in which Tom Mann stood for the
ILP, did little to improve the prospects of the ILP,
both candidates also coming firmly at the bottom of
the polls.[75] Despite the growing unity of the working classes there was still enough fragmentations to
make victory in a constituency like Bradford East
difficult. There was undoubtedly a working-class
enclave at the centre of the constituency - but this
was surrounded by an equally numerous area of middle
class and lower middle-class housing and flanked on
the south by the Irish community whose voters still
voted Liberal. Local election results were little
better, though there were a few local and municipal
successes. But these disappointments did not so
much discourage the ILP as spur it on to examine
ways of extending its support.

In essence, the West Yorkshire Labour movement
was faced with three possibilities. It could rejoin
the Liberal fold, seek to establish a Socialist
party uniting all Socialist and Labour groups throughout West Yorkshire or, as it finally did, strengthen its connections with trade unionism. The semi-
autonomous nature of ILP branches could have mili-
tated against an effective attempt to tackle the
problems of the ILP. The events in Halifax had demonstrated the dangers of the NAC of the ILP inter-
fering in local matters. In the case of West Yorkshire, however, it is clear that the national and
local leadership were moving in the same direction

Neither were seriously prepared to examine the possibilities of an alliance with Liberalism or the
establishment of Socialist unity. In the case of a
projected Liberal-Labour alliance, it is clear that
the Liberal leadership had, in general, set its face
against such a possibility. In the case of the
issue of Socialist unity it is clear that the West
Yorkshire ILP organisations were largely opposed to
it, as was Keir Hardie, on the grounds that they
could not see the advantage of such an alliance and
felt that it would lose them support. They appear
to have been in tune with Hardie's sentiments, expressed in the pages of the Labour Leader and the
I.L.P. News, which saw an alliance with the SDF, in
particular, as an anathama to ILP success. Hardie
expressed the view that 'Rigidity is fatal to growth
as I think our S.D.F. friends are finding out', and
reflected upon the possible loss of trade-union support for the two organisations if they merged.[76]
His attitude was neatly presented in the I.L.P. News:

> It may be that there is something in the meth-
> ods of propaganda, if not in the principles of
> the S.D.F. that not only renders it somewhat
> antipathetic to our members, but out of touch
> and harmony with the feelings and ideals of
> the mass of the people. If, too, it be the
> case that the S.D.F., even if not decaying, is
> not growing in membership, the indication would
> seem to be that it has not proceeded on the
> lines of British industrial evolution. It
> might be, therefore, that the introduction of
> its spirit and methods of attack would check
> rather than help forward our movement.

This view was strongly upheld by most of the ILP
branches in West Yorkshire during the national debate which occurred between the ILP and SDF over the
issue of Socialist unity in 1896, 1897 and 1898.
Keir Hardie and the national leadership of the ILP
opposed fusion with the SDF and it is clear that
they obtained much support.
    In Bradford the rejection of Socialist unity
was very evident. In September and October 1897
there was almost total indifference to the issue
when the national debate was at its height. Attempts to re-organise the Bradford ILP clubs in 1898,
which followed the appointment of Sam Hemsley as the
local agent in 1897, also clearly veered away from
any implication that a Socialist unity group would
be established. It is obvious that during the

96

Why Socialism does not succeed in GB

discussions various local Socialist societies had
misinterpreted the intentions of the Bradford ILP.
The General Council of the Bradford ILP had decided
to meet with a committee of 15 'outsiders', in the
hope of widening support for the ILP. Their action
was misunderstood. As the Bradford Labour Echo
reflected:

> They the outsiders endeavoured to ignore the
> fact that the meeting was an ILP branch meet-
> ing, and proceeded to treat the gathering as
> one specially called to bring into being an en-
> tirely new Socialist party. Some of the out-
> siders who proposed to serve on the committee
> withdrew their names, when the meeting passed
> the following resolution: "That the fifteen
> members elected from the meeting should declare
> themselves Socialists who are willing to become
> members of the I.L.P. under the reconstituted
> constitution". Carried by an overwhelming
> majority.[78]

The Bradford Observer report, contained in the same
issue of the Bradford Labour Echo, was even more
direct: 'One fact made quite clear was that no fusion of Socialist sections is intended. The representatives of various smaller Socialist bodies attended, and did their best to turn the discussion
into this groove, but entirely without avail'.
    The Halifax ILP assumed a similar stance to the
Bradford ILP. The July 1898 issue of the Record,
organ of the Halifax Independent Labour Party, did
refer to the 'One Socialist Party' campaign being
conducted in Bradford but played down its importance, doubting its 'practical superiority' to the
existing situation. It was suggested that the term
'fusion' indicated a tightening and hardening of
Socialist policies which did not fit the more general approach favoured by the membership of the Halifax ILP. Also most ILP members spent a working week
protected by trade union surveillance, and weekends
attending Labour Church activities, glee club meetings and rambles. Satisfied with their achievements
they were not inclined to join forces with the SDF,
which had little influence in Halifax and which
played down the value of trade unionism. On the
whole one is left with the impression that Socialist unity barely merited serious consideration in
the new ILP strongholds of Bradford and Halifax.
There only appears to have been marginal support for
the notion in Keighley and perhaps some fitful

support for it in the Huddersfield area.[79]
This situation is not wholly unexpected given the numerical support of the ILP over other Social-ist parties in the West Riding. The ILP was broad-ly and firmly based, whilst the SDF carried little weight. Indeed, there was no active branch of the SDF in Halifax during the mid 1890s and only one small branch in Bradford. The Bradford branch had been formed in 1894 with six members. In 1896 it had reached a peak of 28 members, before collapsing in 1898.[80] It was not revived until 1902. The only figures of real stature in the SDF, though neither appears to have been actively involved in local branch activities, were Charles A. Glyde and Edward Robertshaw Hartley. Glyde had been a member of the SDF since 1887 but was also active in the ILP and a trade-union organiser for the Gasworkers and General Labourers' Union.[81] Hartley was an ILP member who joined the SDF about 1902. He was also the secre-tary of the Clarion Van movement in the early twen-tieth century.[82] Neither of these local political figures was able to bridge the gap between the Bradford ILP and the Bradford branch of the SDF. The simple fact is that the ILP in Bradford, and throughout West Yorkshire, outnumbered the SDF mem-bers by more than 30 to 1 and, understandably, saw no advantage in uniting with an almost non-existent party.
The hopes and aspirations of achieving Social-ist unity therefore remained unfulfilled. Some measure of unity was established with the formation of the Labour Representation Committee in 1900, to which the ILP and the SDF, temporarily, affiliated. But this was a federation of Socialist and trade-union bodies, not a Socialist party, and the SDF soon withdrew.

As indicated in chapter three, the ILP branches of West Yorkshire were closely interlinked with the local trade union movements. The formation of the Labour Representation Committee in 1900 was thus welcomed by West Yorkshire ILP branches, who had already gone some way in identifying with trade un-ions and their demands. With the local Liberal or-ganisations showing remarkable indifference to the rising political challenge of Labour in the 1890s, it is hardly surprising that Yorkshire ILP branches continued to tap the sustaining power of trade uni-onism. It was this support which permitted the ILP to weather the parliamentary disasters of the 1895 General Election and the bout of internecine conflict within the Halifax ILP and between it and the leadership of the National ILP. It was also this support which proved inimical to the campaign for Socialist unity and paved the way for a revival of ILP fortunes at the turn of the century.

NOTES

1. Bradford Observer, 9 Dec. 1891.
2. Huddersfield Examiner, 13 Jul. 1895.
3. Bradford Observer, 4 Dec. 1896.
4. Huddersfield Examiner, 13 Jul. 1895.
5. Huddersfield Chronicle, 21 Jan. 1893.
6. Lister, 'The Early History of the ILP Movement in Halifax'.
7. Keighley Labour Journal, 8 Mar. 1896.
8. Ibid., 26 Mar. 1898.
9. Ibid., 20 Mar. 1897.
10. ILP News, Dec. 1902.
11. Clark, Colne Valley: Radicalism to Socialism, p. 149.
12. The Bradford Liberal organisation was divided into three Liberal Two Hundreds, which consisted of about 200 elected delegates and life members, one for each of the three Bradford constituencies. The three together formed the supreme policy-making body, the Liberal Six Hundred, which elected the Executive of the Bradford Liberal Association.
13. Reynolds and Laybourn, 'The Emergence of the Independent Labour Party in Bradford', pp. 314-5; Bradford Observer, 25 Sep. 1895.
14. Jack Reynolds, Saltaire: An Introduction to the Village of Sir Titus Salt (Bradford Art Galleries and Museums, City Trail No 2, Bradford, 1976), pp. 10, 28.
15. K. Laybourn, 'The Emergence of Working-Class Independence and the rejection of the Salt Ideal', a lecture delivered at the Victoria Institute, Saltaire, 7 Mar. 1979, copies of which are to be found in Bradford Central Library and various branch libraries in the Shipley and Saltaire districts.
16. Laybourn, 'The Manningham Mills Strike: its importance in Bradford history', p. 16.
17. Bradford Observer, 16 Oct. 1891.
18. Ibid., 6, 8, 9, 14, 15, 18, 19, 23 Jan. 1892.
19. Ibid., 2, 18 Feb. 1892.
20. Ibid., 22 Feb. 1892.
21. Ibid., 28 Mar, 21 Apr. 1892.
22. Ibid., 29 Feb. 1892.

23. Ibid., 15 Jan. 1892.
24. Ibid., 9 Jan. 1892.
25. Ibid., 9 Jul. 1892.
26. Ibid., 18 Jul. 1892.
27. Ibid., 28 Mar., 18 Jul. 1892.
28. ILP News, May and June 1898.
29. Mr. Byles's Address to the Electors: General Election, 1892, Shipley Parliamentary Division, Bradford Archives Collection, 40D78/150.
30. Ibid., p. 3.
31. ILP Archive, Francis Johnson Collection, 1896/84, letter from James Keir Hardie, dated 21 Nov. 1896.
32. Labour Party Archive, Labour Representation Committee, 1/224, 2/192.
33. Ibid., 2/17.
34. Ibid., 2/192.
35. Bradford Labour Echo, 25 Sep. 1897.
36. Bradford Observer, 11 Oct. 1894.
37. Bradford Labour Echo, 17 Apr., 1 May 1897. Meetings took place at the Gladstone Liberal Club and the house of Rev. R. Roberts.
38. Bradford Observer., 2 Nov. 1894.
39. Bradford Labour Echo, 4 Feb. 1899.
40. Bradford Daily Telegraph, 31 Mar. 1903.
41. A.J.A. Morris, C.P. Trevelyan, 1870-1958: Portrait of a Radical (Blackstaff Press, Belfast, 1977).
42. See Table 4.1.
43. ILP Archive, Francis Johnson Collection, 1895/105, F.W. Jowett to J.K. Hardie, 6 Jul. 1896 suggests that the Bradford ILP's financial membership had declined to 1,600.
44. H.J.O. Drake, 'John Lister of Shibden Hall, 1847-1933'.
45. Lister, 'The Early History of the ILP Movement in Halifax'.
46. Drake, 'John Lister of Shibden Hall', pp. 448-9.
47. ILP Archive, Francis Johnson Collection, 1894/116.
48. Halifax Guardian, 27 Oct. 1894.
49. Drake, 'John Lister of Shibden Hall', pp. 449-51; Bradford Observer, 27, 30 Oct. 1894.
50. Drake, 'John Lister of Shibden Hall', pp. 453-4; Bradford Observer, 17 Nov. 1894.
51. Clarion, 2 Nov. 1894.
52. Drake, 'John Lister of Shibden Hall', p. 456; Clarion, 24 Nov. 1894.
53. Labour Leader, 3 Nov. 1894.
54. Bradford Observer, 13 Nov. 1894.

55. National Administrative Council of the
ILP, Minutes, 4 Dec. 1894.
56. Ibid.
57. ILP Archive, Francis Johnson Collection,
1894/212.
58. Ibid., 1894/213.
59. Ibid., 1894/214.
60. R. Hyman, The Workers Union (Clarendon
Press, Oxford, 1972).
61. ILP Archive, Francis Johnson Collection,
1895/2.
62. Drake, 'John Lister of Shibden Hall', p.
464.
63. Lister won 20.5 per cent of the vote, in
this two-seated constituency, compared with the
29.3 per cent and 27.2 per cent of the Conservative
and Liberal victors, respectively. He obtained
3,818 votes, 790 more than at the by-election in
1893.
64. Drake, 'John Lister of Shibden Hall', pp.
470-4.
65. Lister, 'The Early History of the ILP
Movement in Halifax'.
66. Halifax Guardian, 19 Oct. 1895.
67. Drake, 'John Lister of Shibden Hall',
p. 466.
68. Halifax Guardian, 20 Jan. 1895.
69. Ibid., 23 Nov. 1895.
70. Drake, 'John Lister of Shibden Hall', p.
470.
71. Stephen Yeo, 'A New Life: The Religion of
Socialism in Britain 1883-1896', History Workshop,
issue 4, autumn 1977.
72. Bradford Labour Echo, 24 Jun. 1899,
Forward, 14, 21 Jul., 22 Sep. 1906.
73. Bradford Labour Echo, 1 Feb. 1896.
74. Labour candidates were defeated in Bradford West, Colne Valley, Dewsbury, Halifax, Huddersfield and Leeds South.
75. Hardie obtained 1,953 votes, or 17.1 per
cent of the poll and Tom Mann obtained 2,000 votes,
or 15.5 per cent of the poll.
76. Labour Leader, 4, 18, 25 Sep., 2 Oct. 1897.
77. ILP News, Aug. 1897.
78. Bradford Labour Echo, 20 Aug. 1898.
79. I am indebted to David James, the Bradford
Archivist, for this information on Keighley, and to
Robert Perks, until recently a Research Assistant
in the Humanities Department of Huddersfield Polytechnic.
80. Justice, 8 Feb. 1896.

81. M. Cahill, 'C.A. Glyde' in J. Bellamy and
J. Saville (eds.),Dictionary of Labour Biography,
vol. 6 (Macmillan, London, 1982).
82. K. Laybourn and J. Saville, 'Edward Hartley
1855-1918', in J. Bellamy and J. Saville (eds.),
Dictionary of Labour Biography, vol. 3 (Macmillan,
London, 1976).

Chapter Five

LABOUR RESURGENCE 1900-6

The formation of the Labour Representation Committee
in 1900 was to quickly transform the sagging fortunes of the West Yorkshire Labour movement. Whilst
it brought the ILP and other political labour organisations more closely into line with each other its
greatest benefit was that it encouraged the involvement of non-Socialist trade unionists in the demand
for an independent political voice for the working
classes. Labour representation committees were
quickly formed in Leeds, Wakefield, and in other
West Yorkshire towns.[1] Most of the leading West
Yorkshire trades councils joined the LRC and there
was a proliferation of intermediary bodies, such as
the Workers' Municipal Federation in Bradford and
the Halifax Workers' Election Committee, which fac-
ilitated the alliance between trade unions and
Labour's independent political organisations.[2] What
was impressive about the West Yorkshire Labour movement in the early years of the twentieth century was
the immense energy it exerted in its urgent task of
widening the appeal of Labour. Encouraged by the
missionary work being conducted by members of the
ILP and the LRC, trade unions were constantly joining the LRC, or declaring their intention to join
once their financial conditions permitted. Even the
relatively supine Keighley and District Trades and
Labour Council reflected the new strident tone in
Labour circles when, in April 1901, it announched
'That in the opinion of our Council the time has arrived when our new democratic party should be formed
in the House of Commons to give national expression
to the democratic ideals among the labouring masses'.[3] The fact that the West Yorkshire Labour movement moved quickly, and that Liberalism failed
to rise to the challenge this posed to its working-
class electorate, has led one writer to conclude that

103

'The evidence suggests that, notwithstanding its
success in the General Election of 1906, the Liberal
Party in West Yorkshire was in a state of irrevers-
able decline by the outbreak of the First World
War'.[4] This is a view with which we concur. But it
is clear that the seeds of Liberal decline and Labour resurgence in West Yorkshire were sown between
1900 and 1907.

For more than 50 years historians have attempted to
explain how the Labour Party was able to break the
two-party system in the early years of the twentieth
century whilst its forbears made only fitful headway
in that direction during the 1880s and 1890s. A
variety of explanations have been offered. Some
historians have suggested that the growth of social
control in the second half of the nineteenth century,
whether in the form of better wages for some skilled
workers or in the growth of leisure and sporting activities, had an enervating effect upon Socialist
and Independent Labour movements.[5] Patrick Joyce
provided a regional variant of this social control
argument in his work on factory politics in Lancashire.[6] What he suggests is that between the 1850s
and the 1890s a few large mill-owning families were
able - owing to their economic power, their exploitation of a deferential relationship between master
and operative, and their involvement in the politics
of their local community - to impose the culture of
the factory upon their workers and submerge demands
for political independence. As a supplementary to
this argument, and by way of contrast, Joyce has
suggested that the later arrival of mechanisation
to the woollen and worsted, as opposed to the cotton, industry permitted the independent-craftsman
tradition to persist in Yorkshire until the late
1880s when the radicalism it portended flowed into
the ILP and Socialist movements at the end of the
century. Only in a few areas, such as Keighley did
the influence of factory politics appear to exert
the same degree of influence which existed in some
Lancashire textile towns.
    The most common explanation of the ILP's halt-
ing growth in the 1890s is that it lacked trade-
union support.[7] The failure of ILP candidates in
the 1895 General Election, the Bradford East by-election defeat of 1896, the disastrous Barnsley by-
election of 1897, and many other political disappointments convinced Keir Hardie, and other ILP
leaders, that it was the lack of trade-union support
which was responsible for the failure of the ILP to

become a mass political party.

But these checks on Labour's political growth appear to have dissipated within less than a decade. During the period between about 1895 and 1905, factory politics began to be extinguished, for a variety of reasons, and trade unions were won over to the idea of independent working-class politics by a flurry of industrial disputes and court decisions which undermined the old attachments to the two-party system in general, and Liberalism in particular. Serious attention has been paid to the Taff Vale Decision of June 1901 as a catalyst in this change of political emphasis within trade unionism.[8]

These general and particular observations on the rise of Labour are partly reflected in the events that occurred in West Yorkshire. Whilst the pervasiveness of social control and factory politics is difficult to measure, just as much as is the independent and radical spirit which survived between the Chartist period and the Socialist revival, it is equally evident that the Taff Vale decision did convert many trade unionists to the ILP and LRC. But it is clear that in West Yorkshire, at least, the process of accretion to the Labour movement had begun before the Taff Vale decision was announced.

The formation of the Labour Representation Committee at Memorial Hall, London, on 27 February 1900 may not have attracted the interest and attention it deserved but it was certainly of vital importance to the continued development of the Labour movement in West Yorkshire. A large number of West Yorkshire delegates attended on the behalf of trade union and ILP branches. Allan Gee, Secretary of the General Union of Textile Workers and an active figure in Huddersfield Labour politics, became a trade-union member of the National Executive of the LRC and James Parker, an engineering warehouseman, trade unionist and a leading figure in the Halifax ILP, became, with Keir Hardie, one of the two ILP representatives on the National Executive.

This early interest is, perhaps, best reflected in the fact that the Bradford and Leeds trades councils had affiliated to the LRC within a few months of its formation. In April 1900, W.H. Drew, Secretary of the Bradford Trades and Labour Council, wrote to Ramsay MacDonald, stating that 'an an individual member of it (Bradford Trades Council),I shall have pleasure in doing all that lays in my power to induce the Council to affiliate'.[9] His efforts were clearly successful for in May 1900 he wrote again

to MacDonald informing of his Trades Council's decision to affiliate.[10] In April 1900 Owen Connellan,
secretary of the Leeds Trades and Labour Council,
wrote to MacDonald on the advisability of contesting
the Leeds East constituency in the forthcoming general election, although the Trades Council does not
appear to have officially joined the LRC until July
1900.[11] In May 1900 the Huddersfield Trades Council
contacted MacDonald, seeking clarification about
whether or not it was eligible to join the LRC, though it did not affiliate for some time afterwards.[12]
In the first two or three years of the LRC's existence then it was through the trades councils rather
than through the creation of separate local LRCs
that it extended its influence in West Yorkshire.
The basis of that approach had been firmly laid down
before the end of 1900.

Table 5.1: West Yorkshire Trades Councils affiliated
to the Labour Representation Committee

Trades Council	Affiliation date	
Bradford Trades Council[a]	May	1900
Leeds Trades Council	July	1900
Todmorden Trades Council	4 May	1901
Halifax Trades Council	23 June	1902
Wakefield Trades Council	August	1902
Keighley Trades Council	19 February	1903
Dewsbury, Batley Trades Council	March	1903
Huddersfield Trades Council	March	1904
Shipley Trades Council	between 1902 and 1904	

Note: a. Only the brief title of the various trade
councils is given. In most cases the full title
includes 'and Labour' or 'and District'.
Source: Details have been extracted from the Labour
Party Archive, Labour Representation Committee
Correspondence, boxes 1-31.

Notwithstanding this early domination by the
West Yorkshire trades councils, many unions began
to affiliate to the LRC in their own right, and most
of the leading Yorkshire textile unions were affiliated to the LRC by early 1903.[13] Imposed upon this
structure of affiliation was a further layer of organisation - the local LRCs. According to the national constitution of the LRC, local LRCs could only

be formed by trade unions and Socialist societies in
districts where there was no trades council affiliated to the LRC or where an affiliated trades council had been consulted and was agreeable to a local
LRC being formed. Not surprisingly the local LRCs
were formed in the wake of the earlier activity of
the trades councils and trade unions. The first in
West Yorkshire appears to have been formed at Leeds
in October 1902, quickly to be followed by the
Batley LRC in December 1902. Within three years
most of the West Yorkshire towns had their own LRC
branch, although no unifying body appears to have
been established for Bradford. Some organisations,
such as the Leeds LRC, appear to have spawned many
district organisations within their town or city
borders.

Table 5.2: Local Labour Representation Committees
in West Yorkshire

Organisation	Formed	
Huddersfield LRC	November	1900
Leeds LRC (also Central)	September	1902
District LRCs		
East Hunslet LRC	March	1905
Armley & Wortley LRC	May	1905
New Wortley LRC	November	1905
Heavy Woollen LRC (Batley and Dewsbury)	March	1903
Wakefield LRC	June to September	1903
Huddersfield LRC	January	1904
Keighley LRC		1904

Source: Labour Party Archive, Labour Representation
Committee Correspondence, boxes 1-31.

Moreover this support for the West Yorkshire
Labour movement was quickly transmitted into both
parliamentary and local election results. For the
first time, as Table 5.3 indicates, the Labour movement made tremendous gains in the parliamentary general elections. This was complimented by the steady
progress which was made in local elections throughout this period, as indicated in tables 5.4 and 5.5.
Although Labour's big breakthrough in local politics
did not occur until after 1906, the period 1900 to

Table 5.3: The Number of Votes and the Proportion of
Votes received by the leading political parties of
West Yorkshire at general elections, 1885 - 1910

Year		Liberals		Conservative and Liberal Unionist		Labour	
		Votes	%	Votes	%	Votes	%
1885		113,712	59.1	78,640	40.9		
1886		66,903	56.4	51,759	43.6		
1892		107,777	54.0	88,844	44.6	2,749	1.4
1895		106,861	49.0	100,899	46.1	10,623	4.9
1900		105,960	48.3	104,034	47.4	9,491	4.3
1906		113,194	50.3	72,913	32.4	38,595	17.3
1910	(J)	140,586	49.2	100,257	35.7	42,871	15.1
1910	(D)	94,681	47.5	76,601	38.5	27,962	14.0

Source: F.W.S. Craig, British Parliamentary Election
Results 1885 - 1918 (Macmillan, London, 1974).

1906 did see tangible gains.
　　The first success by a legitimate Labour candidate at Leeds did not occur until 1903, but by
November 1906 there were nine Labour representatives
on the City Council. The euphoria which resulted
from such growth led the Leeds LRC to push for the
contesting of three Leeds parliamentary seats in the
1906 general election. J. O'Grady was the LRC candidate for Leeds East, after a bitter and protracted
contest with Owen Connellan, Secretary of the Trades
Council, for the nomination.[14] But there were
feelings expressed that O'Grady should contest Leeds
South instead, and John Macrae wrote to Ramsay Mac-
Donald expressing his view that 'Our most tried and
fullest strength is in South & West divisions and
it is galling to them to be without a candidate'.[15]
In the final analysis, only Leeds East and Leeds
South were contested, though, as we shall see, a
determined effort was made to put a candidate forward for Leeds West. The determined resistance of
MacDonald, and his control over central funds, made
a contest in Leeds West impossible.[16]
　　Municipal successes in Bradford were more grad-
ual and, on the whole, led to less ambitious parliamentary aspirations in 1906[17] Elsewhere in West
Yorkshire there was a steady accretion of municipal,
urban district and local successes for Labour.

Table 5.4: The Number of Municipal Representatives returned for Labour in Four West Yorkshire Towns and Cities, 1900-6

Year	Bradford	Halifax	Huddersfield	Leeds	Total
1900	6	2	1	0	9
1901	8	5	1	0	14
1902	8	6	1	0	15
1903	7	6	1	1	15
1904	10	6	4	4	24
1905	10	5	6	8	29
1906	11	4	8	9	32

Sources: November issues of Bradford Observer, Halifax Guardian, Huddersfield Examiner; T. Woodhouse, 'The working class', in Derek Fraser (ed.), A History of Modern Leeds (Manchester University Press, Manchester, 1980), p. 363.

Table 5.5: The Number of Labour Representatives on Local Political Bodies in West Yorkshire, 1900-6

Year	Municipal	CC,UDC RDC[a],PC	Board of Guardians	School[b] Board	Total
1900	19	10	3	21	53
1901	26	20	8	24	68
1902	26	13	8	22	69
1903	27	15	8	22	72
1904	37	21	6	22	86
1905	41	34	6		81
1906	47	36	6		89

Note: a. County Council, urban-district councils, rural-district councils and parish councils.
    b. School boards were abolished in April 1904 and their functions assumed by the West Riding County Council and the municipal authorities.
Sources: Labour Leader, ILP News, Bradford Observer, Halifax Guardian, Huddersfield Examiner and the records of a number of trades councils and Labour Party branches.

What is evident, from both local contests and

parliamentary activity, is that the West Yorkshire
Labour movement was gathering pace from 1900 onwards. It is clear that it was not particularly hampered by the Boer War nor was it overly encouraged
by the Taff Vale decision of June 1901. The organisational changes which went on in the Labour movement paved the way for steady and real improvements
in Labour's position before 1906.

In recent years the political impact of the Boer War
has been subjected to close scrutiny. In the early
1970s, Richard Price took to task those historians
who have suggested that the Conservative government's conduct of the war attracted significant
support from the working classes who were largely in
support of aggressive imperial policies. Price
suggests that most working-class organisations were
divided over the war, that despite the relief of
Mafeking, and 'Mafeking Night', the war did not
spark widespread interest and that this is reflected
in the fact that the 'Khaki' election of October
1900 provoked much less interest, and a smaller
turnout, than did the 1895 General Election.[18]
    It is clear that the implications of the Boer
War for the ILP and LRC, who opposed the war, would
either be politically disastrous as the tide of
working-class support for imperialism swept Labour's
parliamentary, and local, challenge aside, or ir-
relevant owing to the relatively unimportant nature
of the issue amongst working-class supporters. The
evidence of West Yorkshire tends to support the latter assumption. On the whole the Boer War made
little difference to the prospects of the independent Labour movement in West Yorkshire, and there is
no evidence to suggest that the movement found its
political hopes blighted by the war.
    Part of the reason for the drop in Labour's
proportion of the parliamentary vote in the 1900
General Election, as indicated in Table 5.3, is that
the West Yorkshire Labour movement fielded fewer
candidates than in 1895. In the 1895 General Election there were five Labour candidates whilst in the
1900 General Election there were only three, and
only two of those, Jowett, in West Bradford, and
Parker, in Halifax, could be accurately described as
Labour candidates.[19] Byles, who stood for East
Leeds, was, as previously suggested, imposed upon
Labour with the support of the 'Irish party'.
    All three ILP/Labour candidates were opposed to
the Boer War, supporting the official ILP line,
presented forthrightly at the Seventh Annual

110

Conference of the ILP, at Leeds in 1899, that it
was 'a capitalist clique, who are seeking, through
Mr. Chamberlain, his colleagues or the Government,
and an unscrupulous Press, to further their own ends
against what we believe to be the true interests of
England' and calling the Government to cease the war
and 'submit all subjects of difference to arbitration'.[20] Jowett promoted the joint ILP and Trades
Council anti-war public meeting which was held in
the Bradford Mechanics' Institute in September 1899
and was prominent in organising and speaking at a
peace demonstration at Peckover Walks, Bradford, in
March 1900.[21] Byles was the leading force in the
Bradford South African Conciliation Committee, and
James Parker actively opposed the war.[22]
   Fenner Brockway, in his biography of Jowett,
suggested that despite the unpopularity of the pro-
Boer stance adopted by Jowett he continued to press
the 'peace' campaign during the election.[23] More
recently this view has been challenged by two historians, one of whom has argued that Jowett and the
ILP 'deliberately avoided the issue during the
election'.[24] Indeed, Jowett does appear to have
played down the significance of the Boer War and concentrated upon the issue of social reform. Yet his
pro-Boer position was well known and his Tory opponent did concentrate upon the war. Moreover, Jowett,
admittedly in a two-cornered election, did come
within 41 votes of victory. The war was clearly the
key issue being fought out in the 1900 General Election, and the key issue in the Bradford campaign,
and yet the ILP candidate was almost successful.
Similarly, the Boer War was important in the contests fought by two other Labour candidates, and
whilst both lost the contests they polled quite well;
Byles obtaining 20.1 per cent of the vote in Leeds
East and James Parker obtaining 16.3 per cent of
the vote in the four-way Halifax contest. As with
the national trend, the turnout in all three contests was lower than in the 1895 General Election
contest.[25] Political apathy rather than political
bellicosity appears to have been the major feature
of the 1900 General Election. The independent labour position does not appear to have been worsened
by the Boer War, and Jowett's impressive performance in West Bradford gave the ILP/LRC hope for the
future.
   Part of the explanation for Labour's relative
success in riding the patriotic tide which could
have overwhelmed it may be that there was still a
strong sense of Liberal Nonconformist opposition to

the war which still espoused the old Liberal shibboliths of 'peace, retrenchment, and reform'.
H.J. Wilson, the Liberal MP for Holmfirth, was ve-
hemently opposed to the war, as were most of the
leading Bradford Liberals, such as Alfred Illingworth.[26] Indeed, there was no Liberal Imperialist
group active within Bradford Liberalism, though one
suspects that there were many individuals within
the Liberal Party who kept silent and either did not
vote in the 1900 General Election or voted Conservative.[27] J.H. Whitley, one of the two Halifax MPs,
was also staunchly opposed to war, as was Sir J.T.
Woodhouse in Huddersfield.[28] There were, of course,
exceptions, Sir James Kitson, the Leeds engineering
employer and one-time organiser of Leeds Liberalism,
was a fervent imperialist and projected his views on
the Colne Valley electorate in 1900.[29] On balance
then, there was a substantial proportion of West
Riding Liberalism which was just as much opposed to
the war as was the ILP and LRC. Although 'peace' or
'pro-Boer' meetings were broken up by a few activists, there is sufficient evidence to suggest that
a large proportion of the voting public, were equivocal about the war, admiring the British victories
but leaning back to their Liberal upbringing on the
matter of seeking peace. The political climate was
by no means hostile to the pro-Boer opinions held
by ILPers and Liberal alike and the Conservative
Party, which pressed the war issue, did not improve
its parliamentary position in West Yorkshire, still
holding nine of the 23 seats as it had done in the
1895 General Election.[30]

The identification of Liberal and Labour candidates on the war issue could, of course, have
blurred the distinctions between the organisations
and tended towards the submergence of Labour within
Liberalism. This was a possibility which could have
been further galvanised by the common stance which
the Labour and Liberal parties assumed in opposing
the 1902 Education Act, which transferred elementary
education from school board to local authority. But
in reality this did not occur for at least two reasons. The first is that most sections of West Yorkshire Liberalism were opposed to compromising with
Labour. In Halifax and Leeds East both the ILP and
Labour candidates were opposed by Liberals, whilst
in West Bradford, a good portion of the Liberal
Party, led by Alfred Illingworth objected to Fred
Jowett being given a straight run with the Conservatives after the Liberal progressives had secured
the withdrawal of Jarratt, the Liberal candidate.[31]

Liberals, such as Illingworth, were prepared to
share the 'peace' platform with Labour but were un-
prepared to endorse a Labour candidate in the place
of a Liberal. As previously suggested, this arrangement in West Bradford led to Illingworth's temporary departure from the Bradford Liberal Association.
The second reason why Labour's submergence within
Liberalism did not occur is that neither the ILP nor
the LRC in West Yorkshire were prepared to entertain
such an alliance, as is witnessed by both the vol-
umnious correspondence which flowed by Keir Hardie
and Ramsay MacDonald in the eventful years of the
early twentieth century.[32] On the whole, West Yorkshire Labour leaders favoured more parliamentary
contests whilst the ILP and the LRC national leader-
ships were intent upon keeping the number of contests to a minimum.[33]

Thus the Labour movement was growing rapidly
and independently of the Liberal Party from 1900,
barely touched by any unpopularity which might have
resulted from the Boer War because of the strong
Nonconformist tradition of West Yorkshire which
tempered the patriotic fervour of war. The Bradford
Trades Council and the Leeds Trades Council, the
General Union of Textile Workers, and many other
trade union organisations had been won to the LRC
by the end of 1900. The Taff Vale decision of 1901
merely galvanised an existing trend in West Yorkshire. The events are well known enough not to need
recounting in detail. The Taff Vale Railway Company
successfully sued the Amalgamated Society of Railway
Servants for damages incurred by picketing and won
its case in the High Court. The Court of Appeal reversed the decision; but the company won damages
against the ASRS in the House of Lords in 1901.[34]
The immediate significance from the Bradford point
of view is that the chairman of the ASRS at this
time was J.H. Palin, a prominent member of the
Laisterdyke branch of the ASRS and a leading figure
on the Trades Council and in the ILP. He broadcast
his views to the Trades Council and the Bradford
ILP and gained further support for the LRC.

In Huddersfield the situation was similar to
that of Bradford. The ILP-dominated executive of
the Trades Council had established an LRC as early
as November 1900,[35] and the Taff Vale decision, and
other similar legal positions at this time, merely
served to strengthen the trade union link with
Labour. Although the Huddersfield LRC floundered,
William Pickles, President of the Huddersfield
Trades Council, wrote a letter to MacDonald in

January 1902 asserting that

> with the organisation of capital for defensive
> and aggressive purposes ... we see that in
> industry as well as politics, the next step
> must be in the direction of socialisation of
> the means of production ... This step the
> Liberals are not prepared to take.[36]

Many trade union organisations within the Hudders-
field Trades Council still showed reluctance to drop
Liberalism, but the Taff Vale decision did help the
ILP and LRC to win over the waverers.

Faced with a growing Labour movement the Liberals in
West Yorkshire attempted to use political tactics to
thwart Labour rather than to offer the new Liberal
ideology as an alternative to the collectivist tend-
encies of the ILP and the LRC. In Leeds, the Liberals had attempted to control the Trades Council by
offering some of the officials opportunities to
stand as Liberal municipal candidates.[37] In Bradford, Liberals had resorted to a similar tactic in
1891, after the Bradford Labour Union had begun to
challenge Liberal hegemony on the Trades Council.[38]
In Huddersfield, the Liberals constantly claimed
Allan Gee to be a Liberal councillor, despite the
fact that he was a member of the ILP, the only Labour councillor for Huddersfield in the 1890s, and a
leading national figure in the LRC from 1900 onwards.[39] Where Labour was making some inroads, and
where there was still Liberal support amongst trade
unions and within the trades councils, the West
Yorkshire Liberal parties appear to have made some
minor concessions to working-class representation.
    But these palliatives did not halt the growth
of the ILP and local Liberal parties were forced to
campaign more solidly for working-class support in
1902 and 1903. Attempts at a Liberal rapprochement
with Labour were inaugurated, and in May 1903, one
prominent Bradford ILPer noted that 'every effort
is being made by the Liberals to draw the Trade
Unionists into an alliance'.[40] But such efforts evaporated quickly in the face of ILP and LRC campaigning amongst trade unionists and as the euphoria of
rising municipal success drove the Labour movement
forward in Halifax, Huddersfield, Bradford, Leeds
and other Labour centres.
    The definite turning-point for Labour appears
to have been 1903. In that year the Leeds ILP/LRC
won its first seat on the municipal council.[41]

This was also the time when, according to David
Clark, there was the beginnings of a massive swell-
ing of support and activity within the Labour movement of Colne Valley.[42] In many respects the final
dashing of Liberal hopes of compromise was symbolised by Keir Hardie's clear hostility to the established parties at a May Day Demonstration in Bradford when he stated that 'Liberalism and Toryism
had divided the workers, Independents had come to
unite them'.[43] This statement was taken to be an
irrevocable declaration of war against both Bradford and West Yorkshire Liberalism. It was an attack born of confidence rather than hope for Labour.
Indeed, the local election result began to reveal
that Labour was undermining Liberal domination in
several municipalities between 1900 and 1906, and in
areas such as Bradford the Liberal Party was beginning to face financial strains as well as a loss of
support.

Table 5.6   The Municipal Balance of Power in Bradford, Leeds and Huddersfield, 1900-6

Year	Bradford				Huddersfield				Leeds		
	L.	C.	Lab	O.[a]	L.	C.	Lab	O.	L.	C.	Lab
1900	28	42	6	8	37	19	1	3	27	37	0
1901	42	31	8	3	33	24	1	2	28	36	0
1902	45	29	8	2	33	24	1	2	30	34	0
1903	49	26	7	2	30	27	1	2	29	34	1
1904	45	28	10	1	32	22	4	2	40	20	4
1905	42	31	10	1	32	19	6	3	37	19	8
1906	38	34	11	1	32	17	8	3	34	21	9

Note: a. The abbreviations are L for Liberal, C for
Conservative, Lab for Labour and O. for Others.
Sources: Bradford Observer, Huddersfield Examiner,
Nov. issues; T. Woodhouse, 'The working class' in
Derek Fraser (ed.), A History of Modern Leeds
(Manchester University Press, Manchester, 1980), p.
363.

Clearly then, the formation of the LRC had achieved
the object of strengthening the independent Labour
movement. Yet there were other factors at play
which also furnished support for that movement. One
was the emergence of workers' election committees
outside the LRC. A second was the extension of the

cultural activities of the ILP and wider Labour
movement.
     From the outset many trades councils joined the
LRC and, in some areas, additional LRC branches were
formed. In Bradford and Halifax, however, no LRC
branch organisation was formed. Instead workers'
electoral or municipal committees were formed to act
as go-betweens for trades unionists and ILPers, very
much the same role as LRC branches without actually
joining the National LRC.
     In Bradford the Workers' Municipal Federation
was formed - as a more formal organisation than the
Municipal Election Committee which had been formed
in 1900 - in order to 'secure the return of Labour
representatives on the City Council, Board of Guardians and the now defunct School Board'.[44] Thus it
sought to avoid the truculunt political conflict
within the Bradford Labour movement which had emerged in the late 1890s when the Trades Council had
insisted that its candidates for local office should
be Socialists.[45]
     Notwithstanding an early setback, when the ILP
eventually decided not to join the WMF, the formation of the new organisation anticipated a movement towards political unity within the ranks of
the Bradford Labour movement. Even without formal
membership the ILP found its views well represented
on the WMF through the many trade union and Trades
Council representatives, such as W.H. Drew, George
Licence, A.T. Sutton, Tom Brown and James Bartley,
all of whom were leading figures in the ILP.[46] Of
the first 16 members of the Executive at least five
were pominent ILP members.[47] It was this informal
presence which helped to pave the way for more
formal consultations between the two bodies. In
1904, the WMF resolved to endorse the ILP nominees
contesting municipal elections and, in 1905, the
Executive Committee of the WMF decided to 'receive
a deputation from the I.L.P. with a view to avoid
clashing in contest of seats'.[48] In 1907 relations
were so good that it helped form a committee to run
ILP and WMF candidates jointly in municipal elections. Although formed to get the best arrangements
from any political party, the WMF in reality worked
with the ILP and in opposition to Liberals and Tories. In effect, they fought as a united group on
the City Council. The WMF was partly encouraged in
this policy by the continued intolerance of the
Bradford Liberal Association, which had been unwilling to withdraw its candidate and allow A.N. Harris,
president of the WMF, a straight run with the

Conservatives in the 1902 municipal election in
Listerhills ward.[49] This experience imbued the WMF
with a sense of its own independence which meant
that subsequent Liberal overtures were rejected.[50]
After the events of 1902 Liberal vicissitudes had no
place in the discussions and debates of the WMF and
the organisation looked to its own strength and the
ILP for political gains. By 1905 it could claim
five representatives on the City Council, half the
Labour group at that time.

The Halifax Workers' Election Committee fulfil-
led a similar role to the WMF. It was formed in
1900 and by 1905 had 22 trade societies plus the ILP
affiliated to it, representing between 4,000 and
5,000 workers. The Committee was responsible for
all the local election work of the local Labour
movement, had six borough council representatives
and four board of guardian representatives by 1905.
It was reported that although the Halifax Trades
Council was affiliated to the LRC 'they do no election work'.[51] Labour's unifying force in Halifax
was the Workers' Committee.

Underpinning much of this political work, and
that undertaken by the ILP and the LRC, was the
growth of Labour's cultural and social institutions.
We have already suggested that there was such growth
in the 1890s and the early twentieth century, with
the rapid emergence of clubs, Labour churches and
Socialist sunday schools. It is true, as previously
suggested, that the number of ILP clubs diminished
in the late 1890s and that the Labour churches began
to lose their appeal. By 1900 the Keighley and
Leeds Labour churches were clearly experiencing difficulties, and the Leeds organisation was toying
with the idea of joining with the Bradford Labour
Church.[52] The Spen Valley Labour Church had apparently ceased to exist by the turn of the century and
the three Labour churches in Huddersfield, at Lock-
woold ILP club, Longwood and Milnsbridge, had practically expired by 1895, following the defeat of
H.R. Smart, a leading Labour Church activist, in the
1895 General Election.[53] There is certainly evidence that the cultural side of the movement was declining, but Yeo has clearly written the obituary
of the 'religion of socialism' for too early a
date.[54] The Labour churches in Bradford and Halifax
were still active, the Clarion movement and the
Socialist sunday schools were just emerging, and the
general cultural side of the movement was still prevalent until the First World War.[55]

There is strong evidence that the Clarion

movement, formed by Robert Blatchford in the early
1890s, had begun to expand its activities in the
years between 1900 and the First World War. The
Clarion movement had always been well-established in
Keighley, Bradford and Halifax, where there were
numerous cycling, field, scout, glee and vocal unions in existence. In Keighley, the movement had
its own brass band.56 From 1900 the membership of
some sections of the movement, particularly the
Clarion cyclists, began to increase. From about
1903 the Clarion movement also became better organised in areas where its impact had, hitherto, been
limited. The movement began to make an impact in
Huddersfield after 1902 and by 1906 the Huddersfield
movement had a glee club, a vocal union, a brass
band, a swimming club and a cycling club.57
     It was not until the formation of the Yorkshire
Socialist Sunday School Union in 1900 that Socialist
sunday schools began to emerge with vigour, though
there had been some earlier attempts to form such
schools, most notably at Bradford in 1895 and in
Huddersfield in 1896.58 The Yorkshire Socialist
Sunday School Union was committed to the Hardie,
rather than Blatchford, strand of the movement, de-
siring to capture youngsters for Socialism whilst
'their minds and suspectibilities are plastic and
impressionable'.59 Its emergence quickly strengthened and spawned other similar organisations throughout West Yorkshire.60 The Bradford Central
Socialist Sunday School was formed in June 1899.
This organisation, which was started by Sam Wood,
initially attracted about 90 children and their parents to the one-hour long Sunday meetings which it
held in the Labour Institute.61 It was the only
organisation of its type in Bradford until 1905 when
the Great Horton, Manningham and Little Horton Socialist sunday schools were formed.62 Similar schools were established in West Bowling and East Bowling
in 1906, to be followed by another three schools in
later years.63
     Always limited to a minority of Socialists, the
Socialist sunday schools nevertheless provided an
important strut to the Labour movement, underpinning
the wider movement with a solidity of support and
commitment. In 1900 the Bradford school had 112
scholars, the Halifax school 159 and the Huddersfield school 40.64 By 1906 the movement had widened
considerably and in Bradford alone there were between about 250 and 300 regular scholars attending
these schools, plus their parents. In total there
were probably 150 or more families involved in

Bradford Socialist Sunday schools, probably representing 700 or more people, and the movement was
still growing. They included such prominent figures
as Nora Fineburgh, the daughter of Joseph Burgess,
the famous editor of Labour newspapers, and her son
Willie Fineburgh who was later to become a Labour
MP.[65] The Fineburghs attended the Great Horton
Socialist Sunday School. Victor Feather, as a young
lad, attended East Bradford Socialist Sunday School.
    Although these Sunday schools helped to swell
the support for the Labour movement in West Yorkshire, their primary aim was to produce the next
generation of Socialists. This objective was the
crux of their activities. The normal Sunday meeting
took place between 2 pm and 3 pm and consisted of
children singing some Socialist hymn, group discussion, further singing and a rendering of the 'Socialist Ten Commandments', which would have been attached to the wall throughout the proceedings. The
group discussion consisted mainly of moral instruc-
tions drawn from a variety of texts. At East Bowling, Bradford, in 1906, J.J. Gould's book The Child's
Book of Moral Lessons was used.[66] The adult classes, usually held at the same time, were based mainly
on a variety of lectures, such as George H. Frogg-
ett's 'Labour Attitude towards Religion', which was
delivered at East Bowling in 1906. On occasions
specific lectures led to the formation of other
classes which might meet in the houses of members
during the week. One lecture on Esperanto led to
the formation of an Esperanto class in connection
with the East Bowling Socialist Sunday School.[67]
These activities, with the formation of drama societies and other organisations, formed the basis of
what was a thriving Socialist culture in West Yorkshire until the end of the First World War. Like
the chapels and churches of Victorian England, the
ILP was providing what, in fact, was a total way of
life in which whole families could participate.
Indeed, one of the most notable features of such cultural activity was that it encouraged, and attracted,
family participation.

It was the conflation of a variety of factors - the
formation of an LRC, the rapid extension of trade-
union support, for a variety of reasons, the emergence of workers' election committees, and the development of the cultural side of the movement -
which explain the dramatic improvement in the political fortunes of independent Labour in the period
between 1900 and 1906. Yet what made this growth

insuperable was the emergence of class conflict and class division over many of the vital issues which separated the Labour and Liberal parties. The most dramatic divisions in policy occurred over the problems of unemployment and the attitudes of Liberals towards municipalisation.

Unemployment was the most important economic issue in West Yorkshire in the early years of the twentieth century. The woollen and worsted textile economy had suffered badly in the 1890s, due largely to foreign competition and foreign tariffs which reduced the demand for West Yorkshire woollen and worsted pieces. The manufacturers' response to these pressures had been to speed up machinery, rather than to introduce new machinery, and to reduce wages. In addition unemployment, or 'broken time', the gap between a weaver's completing one piece and taking an order to produce another piece of cloth, increased. Unemployment was usually high but, intensified by tariff restrictions, was appreciably higher during the period between the autumn of 1891 and the early months of 1895 and between the winter months of 1902/3 and 1905/6. We have already noted that the high unemployment of the early 1890s nurtured support for independent Labour from a number of quarters, and it is clear that similar support was forthcoming between 1902 and 1906.[68]

The return of high unemployment provoked the town and city councils of West Yorkshire to take action. Most set up a Lord Mayor's Fund in order to finance relief for the unemployed and their families, and some set up their own unemployment committees, which occasionally led to the formation of joint unemployment committees between the municipal authorities, boards of guardians and voluntary organisations.[69] Labour registers for the unemployed were also opened by town, or city, councils. Bradford City Council set up such a register in the winter of 1902/3, and repeated the operation in the winter months of 1903/4 and 1904/5.[70] Leeds City Council did much the same from the autumn of 1902 onwards, continuing the operation for a number of winters.[71] Leeds City Council also provided £10,000 from the City funds to relieve unemployment, and there was discussion about employing the unemployed on the town hall extension being built in Bradford.[72] Bradford Corporation sent a deputation to the Nidd Valley to see whether the land there was was suitable for farm colonies, and Forward, the journal of the Bradford ILP, eagerly supported the

intention behind the visit, arguing that 'if you
could experimentally place 100 unemployed Bradford
men on the land and give them a chance of living
upon it, you would not displace more than the farm-
er and his family.[73] There was a scheme to send
some of those on the Bradford Labour Bureau register
to Canada.[74] There was certainly no lack of schemes
to deal with the unemployed in West Yorkshire.

Most of these schemes were cosmetic. There
were many schemes blending both charity and public
relief into the relief of the unemployed but they
were trifling when compared with the scale of unemployment. In the autumn of 1903, before the onset
of winter which would add many outdoor workers to
those unemployed, it was 'computed by workmen that
in the industrial centres of the West Riding there
are 20,000 unemployed, and what is nearly as bad,
an equal number of operatives only partially employed'.[75] In Bradford alone it was suggested that at
least 6,000 men were unemployed, plus a large number of women who were employed in the woollen and
worsted industries, by December 1903.[76] The dis-
tress was equally severe in Leeds and Owen Connellan, Secretary of the Leeds Trades and Labour
Council, stated in December 1903 that 'As a matter
of fact he believed that in Leeds several industries
were suffering from very great depression indeed,
notably in the engineering and clothing trades'.[77]

Trades councils were to the fore in pressing
the municipal and local authorities to offer relief
to the unemployed, and in passing motions that the
Government ought to take action to deal with the
problem.[78] Numerous unemployment demonstrations and
conferences were organised by trade unions and trades councils. The Yorkshire Factory Times, the
journal of textile trades unionists in the West
Riding, ran regular columns on the problems of the
unemployed, as did the local Labour press. What
became obvious is that unemployed registers barely
reflected the true extent of unemployment. The unemployed register set up in Bradford in the autumn
of 1902 attracted only 335 men - most of them woolcombers - though there were 61,355 textile workers
in the city. But as a correspondent to the
Yorkshire Factory Times noted:

> It is convenient to forget that those employed
> were male workers and that the lower-paid lab-
> our of women had displaced men in the textile
> industry. Further, hundreds of dyers and other
> operatives refused to register their names

because they were unable to bear the strain of
outdoor labour, and a little army of out of
work, who were in receipt of out of work
pay from the trade union, because of their antipathy to a free labour agency avoided the
Corporation Bureau as a pesthouse.79

Even when a large number of unemployed registered
with a labour bureau it was highly likely that the
bureau would, for a number of reasons, only deal
with a small section of those registered. In the
winter of 1904/5 there were almost 4,500 unemployed
registered with the Bradford Labour Bureau. Of
these, 1,303 found regular work before they were
dealt with, 534 were put on relief work, and the
other 2,660 were either out of work, had been lost
sight of, transferred to a new register, or had been
struck off the register because they were not sufficiently destitute.80 The Labour bureau registers
thus proved to be an inefficient tool for dealing
with the unemployed. The Labour bureaus failed to
offer relief work to the vast majority of those unemployed workers who even bothered to register.
    The inadequacy of public relief and charity did
much to bring the Liberal and Labour parties into
conflict in West Yorkshire. The local Liberal organisations, and their spokesmen, did much to extoll
the virtues of charity and essential, if limited,
public provision. Their view tended to be that if
charity was failing then it had to be re-organised,
not abandoned. The independent Labour organisations,
on the other hand, stressed the need for an extension of municipal provision. The difference of approach adopted by the two political parties produced bitter conflict over the scale of relief for
the unemployed, the issue of municipal contracts,
school feeding and other related issues.
    It is beautifully demonstrated in the struggle
to provide free municipal school meals in Bradford81
Despite the fact that the Bradford Cinderalla Club
admitted that it was unable to provide a sufficient
number of free meals for the children of the unemployed, though it had provided 110,000 free meals in
the winter months of 1903/4, and that is was practically without funds, the Liberal Association in
Bradford refused to consider the necessity of municipal provision. It was only political expediency,
forced upon it by the impending municipal elections
of November 1904, which eventually led the Liberal-
dominated Bradford City Council to accept the possibility of municipal school feeding in October 1904,

an action which it reversed immediately after the
municipal elections. For almost three years, until
the early months of 1907, the Bradford Liberals re-
sisted the demand for municipal provision of free
school meals, largely on the grounds that such an
action would lead to the widespread municipalisation
of poverty. Instead they supplemented the work of
charity by setting up a Lord Mayor's Fund, which was
to be administered by the representatives of the
City Council and of the Cinderella Club. When the
Fund was exhausted the task of feeding the children
of the poor was passed on to the Board of Guardians,
who quickly demonstrated their inability to deal
with the full extent of the problem. It was only
when the actions of Charity and the Poor Law had
foundered, when the Bradford Liberals began to experience political reverses in local elections, when the
Liberal government passed a permissive act providing
for municipal school feeding in December 1906, and
when Alfred Illingworth - a leading opponent of municipal school feeding - died in February 1907 that
the Bradford Liberal Association capitulated and accepted the need for municipal school feeding.[82]
    It is clear that faced with the obvious failings
of charity Liberals were, on the whole, inclined to
favour its re-organisation rather than to engineer
moves towards municipal responsibility. Charity
began to alter its form to deal with the new scale of
economic problems in West Yorkshire. For many years
the Charity Organisation Society had been offering
relief to the poor by providing the worthy with money
for self-help activities. In Bradford, when the
Charity Organisation Society appeared to be faltering, many of its leading figures, such as H.B.
Priestman, the leader of Bradford Liberalism, decided
to set up an entirely new body, the Guild of Help,
in 1904.[83] The main purpose of this body was to
tackle poverty at its source, rather than to examine
it before a committee, which had been the style of
the Charity Organisation Society. The Guild of Help
established a network of helpers throughout Bradford
who would enter the houses of the poor and provide
help and relief for these people. Social casework
was to be the focus of its work, and poverty was to
be grappled at first hand. Guilds of Help were formed in other parts of the country and in West Yorkshire, one of the most notable organisations being
formed at Huddersfield in 1908.[84]
    On the whole, however, Labour politicians were
sceptical of these cosmetic exercises. To them,
rising unemployment, and its consequential poverty,

123

had exposed the failures of charity and the Poor
Law. Harry Smith, Secretary of the Bradford Cinderella Club, and a leading member of the ILP, considered that 'at best in Yorkshire there exists a state
of things that no system of private almsgiving can
alleviate'.85 To him, and many other members of the
ILP and trade union organisations, what was required
was the two-fold intervention of local and central
government to provide relief, investment and jobs.
The focus of ILP and trade union activity was, therefore, to pressure for municipalisation at all levels
- whether it be of hospitals, industry, coal supply
or school feeding. On the issue of school feeding,
the Bradford ILP vigorously demanded 'the provision
of at least one free meal a day at each school' for
each child.86 Whilst strongly advocating municipalisation, however, there were some ILPers who were
willing to entertain Liberal attempts to re-organise
charity. Harry Smith, for instance, was quite prepared to join in the activities of the Bradford
Guild of Help, though many ILP members, such as
James Bartley, were bullish in their opposition to
the Guild.87

In the end, however, charity and the Poor Law
were left to provide relief. Charity was incapable
of dealing with the problem and the Guardians, who
assumed more responsibility for school feeding in
1905, following an instruction from the Local Government Board, were clearly seen to be incapable of
dealing effectively with the issue.88 The established means of dealing with unemployment and poverty were effete.

There is no doubt that the failure of the local
Liberal-dominated town and city councils to consider
and tackle the problems of unemployment, and the
recourse which was made to charity and the Poor Law,
forced many trade unionists and workers over to the
ILP and LRC. The surge in Labour's local representation partly reflects the concern for unemployment
and also partly reflects the rising concern for a
municipal solution. In addition, however, there was
the issue of fair contracts, the payment of trade
union wage rates, which it became clear could only
be firmly established on public bodies if there was
adequate Labour representation.89 ILP and LRC
members, most of whom were also trade unionists,
were quick to seize the problem of enforcing fair
contracts resolutions to strengthen their support.90
They were also adept at using the attempts of employers to increase work burdens to enlist support.
This was particularly obvious in the Huddersfield

Labour movement, where there was strong Labour and trade union opposition to the moves by employers in the woollen industry to introduce the two-loom system, whereby weavers minded two looms instead of one.[91]

Yet the course of Labour growth did not run smoothly in the early years of the twentieth century. In West Yorkshire there appear to have been two main problems which created difficulties. The first is that, despite its weakness in West Yorkshire, the Social Democratic Federation created tensions within the Labour movement in both Dewsbury and Bradford. The second is that the exuberance of many local Labour leaders led them to demand that Labour candidates should be put forward in their constituency at the next general election, despite the entreaties of Ramsay MacDonald that only a few prime constituencies ought to be fought.

The SDF had never been well-established in the West Yorkshire textile district in the 1890s, nor had it ever made the efforts to win support as it had done in London and Lancashire.[92] Although there were a number of prominent individuals who were members of the SDF there were few SDF branches in West Yorkshire. There had been an SDF branch in Leeds during the 1880s and a small Bradford branch was in existence between 1895 and 1898, but by the end of 1901 there was probably only one branch in West Yorkshire, at Dewsbury, though a Bradford branch was re-established soon afterwards.[93] It was the Dewsbury branch which caused most difficulty for the ILP and LRC, and which created related problems in Bradford.

The conflict between the ILP and the Trades Council, on the one hand, and the SDF, on the other, was most protracted between October 1901 and January 1902. As we have already suggested, Dewsbury was a promising centre for ILP activity in the mid 1890s. The constituency contained ILP branches in Dewsbury itself, Batley and Thornhill Lees and a membership of 800 to 900 by the mid 1890s. During the late 1890s, however, this support had been partly dissipated by the fact that the local ILP had appointed an SDF man from Lancashire as its local agent, and he had converted the Dewsbury ILP into a Socialist Society and, finally, into an SDF branch.[94] Much of the old ILP support had drifted away quickly, and by 1901 the SDF branch in Dewsbury had only about 40 or 50 members.[95] The ILP, weakened as it was, still retained a substantial membership in

Batley, where Ben Turner the ILP was active, and in
Thornhill Lees, where Tom Myers was prominent.96
Turner and Myers, were both active members of the
Dewsbury Trades Council and kept support for the ILP
strong in that organisation.

Relations between the local ILP and the SDF
organisations were never very easy, but they deteriorated markedly when the SDF pushed for a local
conference with other Labour organisations in November 1901, and then pre-empted the issue by announcing their intention to contest Dewsbury with Harry
Quelch, a leading figure in the SDF and the editor
of Justice, before the local conference was held.
Although the SDF argued that it took such action
because it felt that the Trades Council and the ILP
would accept Sam Woods, the Liberal nominee, as the
effective Labour candidate it was well known that
the Trades Council and the ILP would support E.R.
Hartley who had unsuccessfully contested Dewsbury
in 1895. The spurious claims of the SDF did much
to fuel the fusillade of abuse hurled at it by the
leading figures in the ILP. The Labour Leader
registered the official ILP view, as presented by
its sub-committee set up to examine the affair, that
Quelch and the SDF were the first in the field 'only
by breaking away from the starting line'.97

Although the focus of much of the ILP criticism
was that the SDF had cheated whilst the ILP and the
Trades Council had played by the rules of selection,
many ILP leaders felt that the affair had demonstrated what was to be expected of the much lauded Socialist unity campaign which was being waged by the SDF.
One writer reflected that 'The S.D.F. has taken up
the attitude of having its own isolated impossibil-
ist way, and setting at defiance the I.L.P. and the
Trades Council. It is unity, no doubt - the unity
of itself'.98 The same writer later added that

> We are disputing the pretence under which he
> has been placed in the field as "the Socialist
> and Trades Union candidate", and we are disput-
> ing the suggestion that his candidature can
> result in anything but an unnecessary and hum-
> iliating reproach upon the reputation of Social-
> ism.

The ILP News felt that the imposition of Quelch
would be disastrous for Socialism:

> An isolated S.D.F. candidate would prove a very
> lamentable and futile political escapade, and

would provide a very bad advertisement for
Socialism in the West Riding of Yorkshire.
Without the cardinal co-operation of the Trade
Unions, no third, not to speak of a fourth
candidate, would receive an effective vote in
the division.[99]

Despite the criticism of Keir Hardie, Bruce
Glasier, Philip Snowden, and local figures, such as
Ben Turner and Tom Myers, the tactical advantage was
with the SDF who were supplied with the additional
bonus of the decision of Hartley, mooted as the ILP
and Trades Council candidate, to stand down in favour of Quelch. The defeat of Quelch in the January
1902 by-election - where he obtained 1,597 votes or
13.6 per cent of the vote - was not the end of the
affair for its ramifications extended into Hartley's
position with the ILP in Bradford. Hartley was a
highly respected figure in the ILP and when the NAC
of the ILP censured his action the Bradford movement
came to his defence.[100] But he was soon to develop
his relations with the SDF alongside his ILP and
Clarion Van activities. He joined the SDF in 1902
and helped the re-formation of the Bradford SDF
branch in the same year. He also pressed to be
adopted by the ILP as the Socialist candidate for
Bradford East, in tandem with Fred Jowett who had
been endorsed by the ILP and the LRC for Bradford
West. In this action, many Bradford ILPers saw him
acting as the representative of the SDF and feared
that the SDF was attempting to obtain ILP support to
secure the return of a parliamentary candidate.
Neither the Bradford ILP nor Fred Jowett were prepared to divide the resources of the Bradford ILP between Bradford West and Bradford East[101]and Keir
Hardie reflected the official ILP line on Hartley's
candidature when he wrote to Cunninghame Graham, who
had been to Bradford East to help Hartley's campaign,
in vitriolic style - arguing that Hartley's candidature was the outcome of 'vanity', that the SDF had
refused to find 'money for the candidature' and that
Jowett's prospects of winning Bradford West would
be impaired.[102] Hardie also noted that MacDonald,
and the LRC, agreed with this advice not to divide
the ILP forces.
The Quelch affair and the Hartley action continued to fuel hostility between the ILP and the SDF in
West Yorkshire up to the First World War. In a
broader sense, however, the whole issue of the selection of candidates was encapsulated within the
events which took place at Dewsbury. Both the ILP

127

and the LRC were very much feeling their way in the
selection of candidates. Whilst the National ILP
appears to have been less pedantic; it is clear that
both the ILP and LRC were concerned that proper and
extensive consultations with all local labour organisations should take place and that only seats capable of returning a Labour candidate should be contested. This approach was evident in Hardie's attitude towards Hartley's contesting Bradford East
and putting Bradford West at risk. But it was even
more evident in the relations between the LRC and
local LRC constituency organisations. MacDonald,
Secretary of the LRC, was strongly opposed to the
assumption by many constituency organisations that
they should run a Labour candidate in the parliamentary elections just because a local LRC had been
formed or because the local trades council had affiliated to the National LRC. The resulting correspondence was often heated.

In West Yorkshire the LRC gradually adopted
seven candidates for the forthcoming election
- James O'Grady (Leeds East), Fred Jowett (Bradford
West), James Parker (Halifax), Ben Turner (Dewsbury),
T.R. Williams (Huddersfield), A. Fox (South Leeds)
and Dr. Stanton Coit (Wakefield). Most of these
candidates were selected without acrimonious debate.
Some discussion was raised about Fox standing for
Leeds when, at one time, it appeared to be the view
that only Leeds East, of the five Leeds constituencies, would be contested by Labour.[103] But Mac-
Donald fought a determined rearguard action against
the promotion of Labour candidates for other seats.

Joe Walker of the Pudsey ILP tried to pressure
MacDonald to find a 'Trade Union candidate (a
Socialist preferable) who is yet without a constituency' to fight Pudsey.[104] The difficulty with the
enormous Pudsey division, which surrounded Bradford,
was that the ILP was weak; the trade union movement
insignificant, that there was only one small trades
council, at Stanningley, and, above all, that about
5,000 Leeds freeholders were to be found amongst
its electorate of between 15,000 and 16,000.[105]
Despite some minor political successes which were
achieved in the Pudsey constituency, MacDonald was
forced to conclude that the area was not worth
fighting.[106] Similarly in Todmorden, though the
Trades Council advocated the selection of a Labour
candidate for the Sowerby Division, James Parker,
the Halifax ILP man who, with Keir Hardie, was one
of the two ILP representatives on the LRC Executive,
advised that 'The Sowerby Division is a hopeless

place for a Labour candidate, it is a county division, very little trade unionism in the division
& Todmorden itself has very few voters in the division'.[107]
     Whilst the situations in the Pudsey and Sowerby
divisions were not promising, and MacDonald was
probably wise not to get the LRC to give its support, this was not the situation in all constituencies. Bradford East was a promising area for a
Labour parliamentary candidate, but animosity towards Hartley ruled out LRC support there. In Leeds
West it was the secret pact of 1903, between Herbert
Gladstone and Ramsay MacDonald which intruded into
relations between the Leeds LRC and the National
LRC. Relations between MacDonald and the Leeds LRC
had never been particularly easy but they worsened
considerably when J.D. Macrae, Secretary of the
Leeds LRC, wrote to MacDonald indicating the intention of his organisation to contest Leeds West as
well as Leeds East and Leeds South. The argument
which Macrae put forward was that the November 1905
municipal elections suggested that there was more
support for Labour in Leeds West than there was for
the Liberal Party.[108] Indeed, Macrae had been returned for Armley/Wortley ward and A. Shaw had been
returned for New Wortley. Two of the four wards in
West Leeds had been won by Labour in the 1905 municipal elections. MacDonald's reaction to Macrae's
letter was to suggest that the LRC would probably
pass a strong resolution against the contest, that
O'Grady' society, which permitted him to stand for
Leeds East on the understanding that he would be
the only Labour candidate in the Leeds constituencies, would probably have to be contacted, and that
'my Executive will even go to the length of publishing a condemnatory resolution in the newspaper
if you insist upon a third candidate'.[109] The
riposte to MacDonald and J.S. Middleton was impressive, and clearly touched a nerve. Macrae replied
in mocking style:

> What is the matter with West Leeds? Dear me,
> national responsibility, only one candidate,
> condemnatory resolution in the newspaper,
> national movement has suffered, dissociating
> ourselves from such a policy. What a flutter
> in the dovecotes. What did you say?
> Chief Liberal Whip, how very rude, it really
> is too bad for you. Now do be good boys,
> remember the honour and dignity of the move-
> ment depend upon your conduct.[110]

MacDonald's furious reply complained of Macrae's
'reckless charges' regarding the 'Chief Liberal
Whip'.[111] But Macrae had hit bullseye, for MacDonald did not wish to endanger the secret agreement
he had made with Gladstone, to avoid needless Liberal and Labour clashes in certain constituencies,
by allowing a Labour candidate to be put forward
against Herbert Gladstone in Leeds West. In the
end, MacDonald successfully blocked the efforts of
the Leeds LRC.

The West Yorkshire Labour movement progressed enor-
mously between 1900 and 1906. Traditional areas of
Labour strength - such as Bradford and Halifax -
continued their inexorable growth. More unstable
areas of Labour support - such as Huddersfield,
Leeds and Dewsbury - showed real signs of Labour's
improving position. On the other hand, the once
promising Keighley constituency saw a regression in
Labour support after 1900. There had been a marked
improvement in Labour's position in 13 of the 14
constituencies covered by these six towns in the
period 1906 to 1914. The other ten constituencies
in West Yorkshire experienced more mixed fortunes.
Labour strength was only marginally improved in
Otley, Sowerby, Elland, Holmfirth, Morley, Pudsey,
Spen Valley and Shipley. Yet, as David Clark has
ably revealed, there were major improvements in
Labour's propaganda work, lecturing activities and
club activities in Colne Valley, although the constituency was not contested by Labour in the 1906
General Election.[112] Yet the most dramatic improvement for Labour in West Yorkshire occurred at
Wakefield.
      Wakefield was a traditional stronghold of
Conservatism. A Conservative or Unionist candidate
had been returned for the constituency in all the
general election contests since the mid 1880s,though
the margin of victory was often comparatively small.
This Conservative dominance had been confirmed in
the 1900 General Election when the Unionist candidate, Viscount Milton, had been returned unopposed.
Up to that time the Liberal Party was effete and the
Labour movement had barely begun to stir. The
Wakefield Federated Trades Council had been formed
in 1891, but is remained a weak and ineffective
organisation throughout the 1890s. There does not
appear to have been an ILP organisation in the constituency, though there were clearly some ILP members in Wakefield. The meaningful starting date of
the Wakefield Labour movement was March 1902 when,

due to Viscount Milton's becoming Earl Fitzwilliam, there was a by-election at Wakefield. Since the Liberals did not intend to contest the by-election Philip Snowden stepped in and, with both Liberal and Labour support, recorded just under 2,000 votes, or just over 40 per cent of the vote, in a two-sided contest. It is true that Snowden acted as the radical candidate, and that there was some criticism from the SDF which claimed to have given him some support at Blackburn in the 1900 General Election, but it is also clear that his entry transformed Labour's position in Wakefield. In the wake of his campaign, the Wakefield Trades Council affiliated to the LRC about September 1902 and a Wakefield LRC was formed in the late spring or summer of 1903.[113] By June 1903, the Wakefield LRC was requesting a list of Trade Union/Labour candidates from the National LRC and showing distinct signs of wishing to make Wakefield one of the official LRC seats to be contested at the next general election.

Initially, it was Robert Morley, one of the stalwarts of the Halifax ILP, who acted as the organising secretary of the Wakefield LRC,[114] and it may have been his influence which provoked the formation of the Wakefield ILP. This became very active throughout 1903.[115] By the end of 1903, the ILP, the LRC and the Trades Council had gone through the business of selecting Dr. Stanton Coit, from London, as the Labour candidate for Wakefield.[116] Once selected, Stanton Coit set about strengthening Labour's position within Wakefield, and did so dramatically by purchasing the Wakefield Echo at the end of April 1905. Coit informed Arthur Henderson, of the LRC, that

> I have just taken over, in the interests of the Labour Party, the "Wakefield Echo", a half-penny eight-page paper which has been in existence 27 years. The first issue under the new regime will appear on Friday morning of this week. As you are well known to all the people of Wakefield, I write to ask whether you will not send us a short letter ... expressing your good will and congratulating the Labour Party here upon having an organ which will set forth its principles.[117]

The Wakefield movement had indeed surged forward and, despite some concern at the appearance of a Liberal candidate, Dr. Coit came within an ace of winning Wakefield for Labour in the 1906 General

Election.[118]

The 1906 General Election marked the breakthrough
of Labour into national politics, with the return of
29 Labour/ILP MPs. The events in West Yorkshire
were a mirror image of the euphoria which overtook
the national independent Labour movement at the
beginning of 1906. Nine Labour or Socialist candidates contested seats in West Yorkshire, seven for
the ILP/LRC, one for the ILP, and one for the SDF.[119]
Of these, three were returned to Parliament - Fred
Jowett (Bradford West), James Parker (Halifax) and
James O'Grady (Leeds East) - all of them for the
ILP/LRC. Admittedly, O'Grady won a straight fight
with the Conservatives and Parker had only one Liberal opponent in the two-seat Halifax constituency,
but elsewhere there were victories and narrow de-
feats for Labour in the face of stiff Liberal opposition. Jowett was an impressive victor in Bradford
West, forcing the Liberal candidate into third place,
T. Russell Williams was only narrowly defeated by
Sir J.T. Woodhouse in Huddersfield, and Stanton Coit
pushed the Conservative candidate close in Wakefield,
and was well ahead of the Liberal candidate. As
Table 5.3 indicates, the Labour Party did remarkably
well in West Yorkshire in an election which saw the
Liberals recover some of their vote and the Conservative vote collapse. Labour did remarkably well on
the progressive tide.
     There were, however, deep divisions between
Labour and Liberalism which made the contests in
Yorkshire more overtly based upon the conflict of
class issues than any previous General Election.
In Bradford, the Liberal and Conservative parties
were united over the issues of

> Free Trade, Welsh Disestablishment and Tariff
> Reforms, with reference to Home Rule for Ire-
> land, religious teaching in schools, licencing
> reforms and 'Chinese slavery" in South Africa.
> Jowett gave most attention to the poverty
> question, and particularly to unemployment and
> school feeding, and showed that on these issues
> there was little difference between the
> Conservatives and Liberals.[12]

Even though the O'Grady victory in Leeds East was
due to the Gladstone-MacDonald pact arrangement, Tom
Woodhouse concludes:

> If allowing James O'Grady a free run in

> East Leeds is seen as an example of progressive
> Liberalism it must be observed that the con-
> cession was opposed as damaging by local Lib-
> eral activities. The reason was that the
> Labour Party in Leeds simply did not respect
> the policy of <u>rapprochement</u>. Given its head
> in East Leeds it was all the more ready to
> attack the other Liberal seats. Joseph Henry
> watchdog of Liberal interests in their strong-
> hold of West Leeds, pointed out the effects
> of the policy: 'I hope the party is not going
> to go as it did at the last election - leave
> the Labour man at liberty to fight a Tory and
> then allow him to fight a Liberal whenever he
> likes ...[121]

In Halifax, James Parker, despite effectively running in tandem with a Liberal in the two-seat constituency, pressed home the issues of unemployment and
poverty at the general election. E.R. Hartley,
though officially an SDF candidate, held joint
meeting with Fred Jowett, at St. George's Hall,
where poverty and school feeding were on the menu of
topics for discussion.[122]
   It was the exigencies of working-class life
which both coloured the Labour campaigns throughout
West Yorkshire in the 1906 General Election and
distinguished them from the Liberal and Conservative
campaigns. This distinction of approach persisted
even where Liberal candidate had given way to Labour candidates, and it is wise to remember that,
whatever MacDonald might have arranged with the Liberal leadership at the national level, the local
Labour leaders in West Yorkshire were resolute in
their opposition to the ideas of an alliance with
Liberalism. Contrary to the views recently expressed by David Howell, a Progressive unity between the
Liberal and Labour parties did not dominate the political events surrounding the growth of Labour in
Bradford, and evidence of such a Progressive alliance is thin for the West Yorkshire area as a
whole.[123] The political and social divisions between the Labour and Liberal parties were, by now,
too deep to permit such an accommodation. The intransigence of Liberal industrialists and the aloof-
ness of Liberal politicians to the need for municipal provision, and their penchant for charity provision, cast them adrift from an increasing proportion of the working class whose economic and
social conditions required more than the limited financial resources of charitable institutions. The

infrequent parliamentary contests cannot accurately
and precisely chart this loss of Liberal support
over a short period of time and their unrepresent-
ative nature can often obscure the political meta-
morphosis which was occurring. In contrast, the
more representative local elections and muncipal
contests provide a more accurate year by year bench-
mark of Labour's growth.[124] Between 1900 and 1906,
as Table 5.5 reveals, that growth was steady. As
we shall argue in the next chapter, Labour's growth
became more rapid therafter.

On the face of it, the Liberal Party had done well
in West Yorkshire at the 1906 General Election. It
had increased its parliamentary representation from
14 to 19, the Conservatives were reduced to one
representative instead of nine, and Labour was still
only a modest parliamentary opponent with three
representatives, though they were the first parliamentary victories for Labour in West Yorkshire. But
any complacency that such a Liberal victory engendered was short-lived in the face of the furious
assault of Labour in local contests which was eating
into the grass-roots support for Liberalism. All
was not well with West Yorkshire Liberalism.
    P.F. Clarke has argued that Progressive Liber-
alism changed in order to accommodate the newly-
emerging working-class aspirations within the Liberal fold, that this was successfully accomplished
in Lancashire and probably achieved in other areas.
But there is little evidence that this occurred in
West Yorkshire. There are, perhaps, two main
reasons for this absence of Liberal approbation of
working-class interests. In the first case, West
Yorkshire Liberalism was still overwhelmingly dominated by the Nonconformist textile magnets such as
Alfred Illingworth, James Hill and John Brigg.
These men, and their like, continued to dominate
West Yorkshire Liberalism, dominated local politics,
and stifled opposition to the old Liberalism. Under
their rule there was no synthesis between Liberalism and Socialism. Secondly, it is quite clear
that the unrestricted Labour challenge in local
politics, and the rising grass roots demand for
political independence, prevented the Liberal Party
from re-absorbing Labour supporters into the Progressive fold.
    The years between 1900 and 1906 had seen the
revival of the West Yorkshire Labour movement from
its nadir of the late 1890s. Many factors account
for this revival. The steady expansion of the

cultural side of the movement and the continued and
growing support of religious leaders helped broaden
the appeal of the ILP and LRC. But, in the end, the
revival of Labour fortunes was largely achieved by
the mere formation of the national LRC, which broad-
ened the possibility of obtaining trade-union support which was not Socialist. Typical of the new
trade unionist who was active within the LRC was
Ernest Wimpenny, a leading figure in the General
Union of Textile Workers and prominent in the Huddersfield LRC. It was written of Wimpenny that he
'sailed his political craft under the LRC flag. He
is not a Socialist, but a sound trade unionist'.[125]
By winning this type of support the West Yorkshire
Labour movement was able to quickly expand its activities. The events of Taff Vale were of marginal
importance to this growth of Labour support for
major inroads had been achieved before the decision
of the House of Lords in the summer of 1901. The
1906 General Election was the icing on the cake for
the West Yorkshire Labour movement. One local Labour leader, Robert Morley, of Halifax and Wakefield
fame, noted that some Labour MPs were 'flushed with
victory and talking foolishly' and that, in some
areas, the ILP was buzzing with activity: 'Huddersfield & the District is simply alive with ILPism'.[126]
However, from the 1906 General Election onwards, the
West Yorkshire Labour movement had to settle down to
the responsibility of consolidating its position.
It became highly attuned to its new role, expanding
its activities as the vehicle of working-class aspirations at a rate which the West Yorkshire Liberal
parties were unable to withstand.

NOTES

1.   Labour Party Archive, LRC Correspondence
5/233,10/453.
2.   Ibid., 20/112; Workers' Municipal Federation Minutes, Bradford Trades and Labour Council
Collection, Archives Department, Bradford Central
Library.
3.   Labour Party Archive, LRC Correspondence
3/191.
4.   Roberts, 'The Liberal Party in West Yorkshire', epilogue.
5.   J. Foster, Class Struggle and the Industrial Revolution (Weidenfield and Nicolson, London,
1974).
6.   P. Joyce, Work, Society and Politics: The
Culture of the Factory in Later Victorian England

(Harvester Press, Brighton, 1980).

7. H. Pelling, The Origins of the Labour Party (Macmillan, London, 1954), chapter x.

8. J. Saville, 'Trade Unions and Free Labour: The Background to the Taff Vale Decision' in A. Briggs and J. Saville, (eds.) Essays in Labour History (Macmillan, London, 1960, 1967), pp. 348-50.

9. Labour Party Archive, LRC 1/58.

10. Ibid., 1/53.

11. Ibid., 1/219-24, 2/192.

12. Huddersfield Trades Council, Minutes, 24 Feb. and 23 Mar. 1904; Yorkshire Factory Times, 1 Apr. 1904.

13. The General Union of Textile Workers appears to have joined the National Labour Representation Committee at its formation in Feb. 1900.

14. Labour Party Archive, LRC 13/267, 13/269, 14/212, 15/52, 15/54, 20/145.

15. Ibid., 20/149.

16. J. O'Grady fought Leeds East and A. Fox fought Leeds South in the 1906 General Election.

17. The Bradford ILP concentrated upon the return of Fred Jowett for Bradford West and though it gave its general support for E.R. Hartley, a member of both the ILP and the SDF, it put no resources into Hartley's Bradford East contest.

18. R. Price, An Imperial War and the British Working Class (Routledge and Kegan Paul, London, 1972), introduction and chapter three.

19. Jowett and Parker were both active in the ILP and the LRC; Byles does not appear to have been directly connected with either organisation.

20. Seventh Annual Report of the I.L.P. at Leeds, April 1899; Bradford Observer, 11 Jan. 1900.

21. Bradford Observer, 15 Sep. 1899, 26 Mar. 1900.

22. S.J. King, 'Bradford Politics and the Boer War', unpublished M.A. dissertation, Huddersfield Polytechnic, 1982.

23. Brockway, Socialism over Sixty Years, pp. 64-7.

24. King, 'Bradford Politics and the Boer War', p. 26.

25. Price, An Imperial War and the British Working Class, chapter three.

26. A. Illingworth, Fifty Years of Politics: Mr Alfred Illingworth: Retrospect (Bradford & District Newspaper Co. Ltd., Bradford, 1905).

27. The poll was low and the progressive vote ought to have been larger, which implies that there was a significant proportion of abstentions.

28. One of the significant exceptions was C.P. Trevelyan, the Liberal, and later Labour, MP for Elland. Refer to Morris, C.P. Trevelyan 1870-1958: Portrait of a Radical, p. 35.

29. E.D. Steele, 'Imperialism and Leeds Politics, c. 1850-1914' in D. Fraser (ed.) A History of Modern Leeds (Manchester University Press, Manchester, 1980), pp. 335-7, 343-6.

30. Table 5.3 suggests that the 1900 General Election saw the Liberals reach a new low in parliamentary popularity in West Yorkshire, though there was comparatively little deterioration from the 1895 General Election position.

31. W.E.B. Priestley had led a secret delegation to meet Herbert Gladstone in order to secure Jarratt's withdrawal.

32. ILP Archive, Francis Johnson Collection and the Labour Party Archive, LRC Correspondence 1900-7 contains numerous examples of advice tendered against Labour being involved in alliances with the Liberals. Labour Party Archive, LRC 8/24 illustrates the hostility of the Bradford ILP to an alliance with the Liberals.

33. ILP Archive, Francis Johnson Collection, 1907/70, 1908/156, 1908/159, 1908/199, 1908/202.

34. Pelling, Origins of the Labour Party, pp. 225-7.

35. Yorkshire Factory Times, 30 Nov. 1900; Huddersfield Chronicle, 24 Nov. 1900.

36. Labour Party Archive, LRC 1/466.

37. Woodhouse, 'The Working Class', p. 361.

38. Samuel Shaftoe, Secretary of the Trades Council from the 1870s to 1893, was returned as a Liberal councillor for West Bowling in 1891.

39. Gee was on the Executive Committee of the LRC in 1900.

40. Labour Party Archive, LRC 8/34.

41. Woodhouse, 'The Working Class', p. 363.

42. Clark, Colne Valley: Radicalism to Socialism.

43. Bradford Daily Telegraph, 4 May 1903.

44. Workers' Municipal Federation, Minute Book, 1902-19, Archives Department, Bradford Central Library. The Constitution appears at the beginning of the book.

45. Bradford Trades and Labour Council, Minutes, 1895, passim.

46. Drew was the first Secretary of the WMF and Secretary of the Bradford Trades Council at the same time, as well as being a prominent member of the ILP. G. Licence was Secretary of the WMF between 1905 and 1909. A.T. Sutton became a member of the Executive

Committee of the WMF in 1905, at a time when he was
also Secretary of the Bradford ILP, and became
President of the WMF in 1913. Tom Brown was on the
Executive Committee of the WMF in 1902 and, again,
between 1902 and 1908. He acted as Fred Jowett's
election agent during the 1906 General Election contest for Bradford West. James Bartley was on the
first Executive Committee of the WMF in July 1902.

47. W.H. Drew, Tom Brown, James Bartley, J.H.
Palin and G. East.
48. WMF, Minutes, 17 Jul. 1905.
49. Ibid., 3 Oct. 1902.
50. Ibid., for 1904.
51. Labour Party Archive, LRC 20/112.
52. James, 'The Emergence of the Keighley Independent Labour Party', charts the rise and fall of
the Labour Church in Keighley.
53. K.S. Inglis, Churches and the Working Classes in Victorian England (Routledge and Kegan Paul,
London, 1963), chapter six; Labour Prophet, May
1893, Jan., Mar., Apr., 1894; Yorkshire Factory
Times, 3 Mar. 1893, 11 Jan., 1 Feb., 15 Feb. 1895.
54. S. Yeo, 'A New Life: The Religion of Socialism in Britain 1883-1896', History Workshop, issue 4,
autumn 1977, pp. 5-56.
55. K. Laybourn, 'The Trade Unions and the ILP:
The Manningham Experience' in J.A. Jowitt and R.K.S.
Taylor, Bradford 1890-1914: The Cradle of the Independent Labour Party (Bradford City Occasional Papers No. 2, University of Leeds Centre of Adult
Education, Bradford, 1980), pp. 34-40.
56. Keighley Labour Journal, 24 Mar., 30 Dec.
1894, 24 Apr., 2 Jun. 1897, 26 Jan. 1898.
57. Huddersfield Examiner, 14 Apr. 1906, 16 Feb.
1907.
58. Labour Leader, 15 Sep. 1900; Young Socialist, Mar. 1901.
59. Labour Leader, 25 Mar. 1895; F. Reid,
'Socialist Sunday Schools in Britain, 1892-1939',
International Review of Social History, X1(1966), pp.
18-47.
60. ILP Archive, Francis Johnson Collection,
1917/61.
61. Bradford Labour Echo, 24 Jun. 1899.
62. Forward, 14, 21 Jul. 1906.
63. Taped interview with Ada Dalby, August 1979.
In the possession of Dr. K. Laybourn.
64. Labour Leader, 15 Sep. 1900.
65. Burgess was the editor of the Yorkshire
Factory Times and the Workman's Times in the early
1890s, fell on hard times in 1894, and went to live

in Scotland for a number of years before coming to live in Bradford. Mrs. A. Dalby remembered Burgess and his daughter attending the Great Horton Sunday School and provided Dr. Laybourn with photographs of the Fineburghs.

66. Forward, 27 Oct. 1906.

67. Ibid., 24 Nov. 1906.

68. Laybourn, '"The Defence of Bottom Dog": The Independent Labour Party in Local Politics', pp. 229-33.

69. Such a body was set up to deal with unemployment and the provision of school meals in Bradford at the beginning of 1905.

70. Yorkshire Factory Times, 4 Dec. 1903.

71. Ibid.

72. Ibid., 28 Oct. 1904.

73. Forward, 11 Feb. 1905.

74. Ibid., 9, 16, 23 Sep. 1905.

75. Yorkshire Factory Times, 30 Oct. 1903.

76. Ibid., 18 Dec. 1903.

77. Ibid., 4 Dec. 1903.

78. Ibid.

79. Ibid., 13 Nov. 1903.

80. Forward, 18 Mar. 1905.

81. Laybourn, '"The Defence of Bottom Dog": The Independent Labour Party in Local Politics', pp. 237-9; K. Laybourn, 'The Issue of School Feeding in Bradford, 1904-1907', Journal of Educational Administration and History, Vol. XIV, No. 2, Jul. 1982, pp. 30-8.

82. This change in direction occurred dramatically, and swiftly, between December 1906 and March 1907, and was partly implemented by the fact that the medical evidence supplied by Dr. Crowley, son-in-law of H.B. Priestman, the Bradford Liberal leader, revealed the acute problem of starvation and undernourishment which faced many children in the winter months.

83. M. Cahill and T. Jowitt, 'The New Philanthropy: The Emergence of the Bradford City Guild of Help', Journal of Social Policy, Vol. 9, Pt. 3. Jul. 1980, pp. 359-82.

84. C. Parton, 'Liberal Individualism and Infant Mortality: The Infant Welfare Movement in Huddersfield 1900-1918', unpublished dissertation, Huddersfield Polytechnic, 1982.

85. Yorkshire Factory Times, 30 Oct. 1903.

86. Forward, 29 Oct. 1904.

87. Cahill and Jowitt, 'The New Philanthropy', p. 377.

88. Forward, 10 Feb, 17 Feb., 30 Jun. 1906.

89. Bradford Trades and Labour Council Year Book, 1903 (Bradford Trades and Labour Council, Bradford, 1903), p. 11; Year Book, 1904 (Bradford, 1904), pp. 39-41; Year Book, 1905 (Bradford 1905), pp. 93-101.

90. ILP Manifestoes. Deed Box 13, Case 64, Archive Department, Bradford Central Library.

91. Yorkshire Factory Times, 27 Nov. 1903, 2 Feb. 1894, 27 Nov. 1895.

92. P.A. Watmough, 'The Membership of the Social Democratic Federation, 1885-1902', Bulletin of the Society for the Study of Labour History, no. 34, Spring 1977, pp. 35-40; ILP News, April 1902.

93. Hartley was responsible for re-starting the SDF branch in Bradford during 1902.

94. ILP News, Nov. 1901.

95. Ibid., Dec. 1901.

96. Yorkshire Factory Times, 19 Feb. 1904.

97. ILP Archive, Francis Johnson Collection, 1901/49, 1901/53-4, 1901/68; Justice, 2 Nov. 1901.

98. ILP News, Oct. 1901.

99. Ibid., Oct. 1901.

100. Ibid., May 1902.

101. Forward contains numerous references to this throughout 1905.

102. ILP Archive, Francis Johnson Collection, 1906/6.

103. Labour Party Archive, LRC Correspondence 24/263, 28/211.

104. Ibid., 17/534.

105. Ibid.

106. Ibid., 17/536.

107. Ibid., 8/298.

108. Ibid., 28/215.

109. Ibid., 28/216.

110. Ibid., 28/217.

111. Ibid., 28/218-19.

112. Clark, Colne Valley: Radicalism to Socialism, pp. 112-16.

113. Labour Party Archive, LRC 9/443.

114. Ibid., 10/454.

115. Ibid., 11/487.

116. Ibid.

117. Ibid., 23/54.

118. Coit obtained 2,068 votes, only 217 less than his Conservative opponent and more than 800 ahead of the Liberal candidate. The Snowden by-election candidature of 1902, when there was no Liberal candidate, appears to have established the credability of Labour.

119. The ILP/LRC candidates were O'Grady (Leeds

East), Fox (Leeds South), Coit (Wakefield), Turner
(Dewsbury), Parker (Halifax), Jowett (Bradford West)
and Williams (Huddersfield).Newlove was endorsed
by the ILP for Keighley and Hartley had SDF support,
and some ILP sympathy, in Bradford East.

120.   Brockway, Socialism over Sixty Years, p. 68.
121.   Woodhouse, 'The working class', p. 361.
122.   Forward, 13 Jan. 1906.
123.   Howell, British Workers and the Independent
Labour Party 1888-1906, p. 197.
124.   M.G. Sheppard, 'The Effects of the Franchise Provisions on the Social and Sex Compositionof
the Municipal Electorate 1882-1914', Bulletin of the
Society for the Study of Labour History, no. 45
(Autumn, 1982), 19-25.
125.   Yorkshire Factory Times, 4 Mar. 1904.
126.   ILP Archive, Francis Johnson Collection,
1906/55.

Chapter Six

LIBERAL DECLINE AND LABOUR GROWTH 1906-14

The ever-increasing pace of working-class defections
from Liberalism to Labour prior to the 1906 General
Election turned into a torrent in the years immediately prior to the First World War. Although the
Liberal Party did increase its parliamentary representation from 19 to 20 in 1910, and despite the
fact that it recovered some municipal ground in
1908, it is evident that Labour was enhancing its
political claims to West Yorkshire after 1906.
Grayson's Colne Valley by-election success of 1907
temporarily increased Labour's parliamentary representation in West Yorkshire to four, reducing the
number of Liberal MPs to 18, and it is evident that
much of the Liberal parliamentary success of 1910
was based upon a dip in Conservative rather than
Labour support. Liberalism was no longer garnering
the working-class support which it once commanded
and the real drift of that support to Labour appears
in the enormous surge of Labour's municipal and local victories, especially after 1910. The inexorable
political growth of Labour was borne upon the development of class politics, which had seen trade unionism, and through it the working class, attach itself to the Labour Party. Had the parliamentary
franchise been more democratic, and had the financial position of the Labour Party been stronger,
there is little doubt that Labour's parliamentary
position in West Yorkshire would have risen as dramatically as did its local and municipal successes.
Despite this, it is clear that by the First World
War, the Labour Party was much stronger than the
Conservative party in the whole spectrum of politics
and if not as comprehensively powerful as the Liberal Party it was challenging it for political predominance in some areas of West Yorkshire. Indeed
there is little to suggest that the Labour and

Liberal parties could be 'subsumed in Progressivism'[1] or that Labour 'fared abysmally' in all contests with the Liberals from December 1910 to the outbreak of war.[2] In West Yorkshire, Labour was pressing Liberalism on all political fronts between 1906 and 1914 and there are few signs of Liberalism arresting the development of the ILP/Labour Party.

West Yorkshire Liberal leaders were well pleased with the result of the 1906 General Election. The party had regained the five seats it had lost in the 1895 General Election. But they soon realised that there was no ground for complacency. The Liberal candidate had been pushed into third place in Bradford West and the Labour candidate had come within 400 votes of victory in Huddersfield. Whilst Liberals could quickly come to terms with the influence which Fred Jowett exerted over Bradford West they were less enamoured of the Labour challenge in the southern parts of the region, where Liberalism had shown few signs of weakness. Two parliamentary by-elections, at Huddersfield in 1906 and Colne Valley in 1907, did much to puncture Liberal confidence.

The resignation of Sir J.T. Woodhouse as Liberal MP for Huddersfield led to a parliamentary by-election in November 1906. The Liberal candidate, A.J. Sherwell, was returned despite the stiff opposition of Williams, the Labour candidate, and in the face of the revival of a serious Conservative challenge: Sherwell receiving 5,762 votes, Williams 5,422 and Fraser, the Conservative, 4,844. The closeness of the contest, which was said to have swung to Sherwell 'in the closing hours of the campaign' was reflected in the statement of Bruce Glasier, one of the leading ILP figures, when he wrote of the by-election that it was the 'most distinctively socialist contest fought in this country'.[3]

The Liberal Party had been shocked by the narrowness of their victory particularly since it had begun to re-organise itself in Huddersfield following the closeness of the Labour challenge in the 1906 General Election. Throughout 1906 the Liberals had been improving their organisation. The Huddersfield Liberal Association had increased its organising body from 300 to 500, divided the constituency into six districts, and re-organised the Liberal Club. It has been argued that the Huddersfield Liberal Association did respond to the Labour challenge and thus stifled its growth before the First World War.[4] Even so, and assuming that this view is

143

correct, what is evident is that there was no attempt to offer a new progressive Liberalism to the constituency. What was offered was the old Liberalism based upon an improved organisation.

As for the Labour Party, it is clear that Williams was not an ideal candidate for Huddersfield. His ethical brand of Socialism, emphasising that 'all things socially needed should be socially owned', was not specific enough for many trade unionists looking for trade union policies in his manifesto and his speeches.[5] His employment as a mill manager in the Keighley area also presented him with difficulties from trade unionists in Huddersfield. It is clear that relations between Williams and the local Huddersfield Labour Party were by no means harmonious. The local trade-union dominated ILP and LRC organisations appear to have considered him to be a Socialist of the quasi-Marxist SDF type, whilst more extreme Socialists of the SDF type were inclined to dismiss his credentials as a serious Socialist candidate.[6] Ben Riley summed up the prevailing Labour opinion in Huddersfield, however, when he wrote to Keir Hardie after the by-election discouraging haste in the selection of a Labour candidate for Huddersfield and suggesting that 'we require a man for Huddersfield' of 'good Trade Union standing' and a 'thoroughly competent Labour politician'.[7]

Notwithstanding such criticism of Williams, it is evident that the internal conflict within Labour was confined to Williams and the trade unions. If it did anything to harm Labour support then the performance of Williams at the 1906 General Election and the by-election were even more impressive. The Liberals were badly shaken on both occasions by the narrowness of their victory.

If growing Labour support found expression in the Huddersfield parliamentary contests then there was even more evidence of Labour breakthrough in Victor Grayson's dramatic and 'splendid victory' in the Colne Valley by-election of July 1907. This victory provoked one national newspaper to write, exaggeratedly, that 'The Red Flag Waves over the Colne Valley ... the fever of Socialism has infected thousands of workers who ... seem to think that Mr. Grayson's return means the millennium for them'.[8]

Colne Valley had been an early centre of ILP activity in the 1890s. The Colne Valley Labour Union had supported Tom Mann's parliamentary contest there in the 1895 General Election and, despite a decline in the movement in the late 1890s there had been an enormous resurgence of Labour support in the

valley from about 1903 onwards. David Clark has
suggested that much of this growth occurred outside
the trade-union movement, which was weak in Colne
Valley, and was to be found emerging from the ethical side of the movement, Labour club organisation,
religious support for Labour, and in the frustrations of Liberals at the lack of democratic decision-making within their party.9 But Colne Valley was
one of the seats which MacDonald had given to the
Liberals in the secret Gladstone-MacDonald pact of
1903, and it was not contested by Labour at the 1906
General Election. Acutely annoyed at this failure
to contest, the local ILP organisation, the Colne
Valley Labour League as it was by 1907, decided to
contest the seat at the earliest opportunity.

That moment arrived with the raising of Sir
James Kitson to the House of Lords in the summer of
1907. For some time there had been rumours of this
possibility. There was speculation about an impending by-election in April 1906 and in December 1906
Ben Riley wrote to Keir Hardie on the matter asking
to be informed when Sir James Kitson was raised to
the House of Lords and informing him that the Colne
Valley branches were 'sure to insist upon a fight
if possible'.10

Both Reg Groves and David Clark have examined
the Grayson candidature and the campaign in detail.11
Their accounts of the events differ slightly but
what is evident is that the local Labour movement
was determined to contest the by-election. Indeed,
the Colne Valley Labour League had already begun
the process of selecting a candidate in April 1906,
when the Executive Committee put forward four names,
including Victor Grayson, as possible candidates.12
Behind the scenes, there had been a good deal of
discussion and confusion as letters flew from Sam
Eastwood, the Secretary of the CVLL, to the ILP and
Labour Party, though it was not always clear which
of the two, about the selection of a candidate and
the possibility of the CVLL forming the basis of a
Colne Valley LRC.13 As David Clark has explained,
the confusion partly arose from the fact that whilst
the CVLL should have only communicated with the
National Administrative Council of the ILP, it was
the practice of ILP branches to seek endorsement of
all organisations within an area who were attached
to the Labour Party. In addition, confusion often
occurred over the fact that Ramsay MacDonald was
Secretary of the LRC and Chairman of the ILP.14
Despite feverish activities and tactical moves by
both national and local Labour figures it was

decided not to select a Labour candidate until the
end of January 1907.[15] After a protracted process
of discussion, two ballots, and the withdrawal of
W.C. Anderson as one of the two names put forward
by the Executive of the CVLL to the whole membership, it was eventually agreed to nominate Grayson
in February 1907.[16]

The eventual election of Grayson for Colne
Valley created difficulties for both the Liberal and
Labour parties. In the first instance, it is quite
clear that local Labour groups, and especially the
ILP organisations, considered themselves to be autonomous, or semi-autonomous, bodies, to which the
national ILP and LRC organisations should pay due
respects. If the national leadership intervened in
local difficulties, as it did in Halifax in 1894 and
1895, then it was swiftly given its marching orders
in no uncertain terms. But in the late 1890s and
early twentieth century the balance of power had
swung more to the national leadership which, through
its increasing control of party organisation and
funds was able to impose some semblance of discip-
line upon local Labour organisations, although its
efforts to do so often provoked conflict and bitter-
ness.[17] But even the national Labour leadership of
the ILP/LRC had limits to its power. Since the normal practice was for the local bodies to pay for the
election expenses of candidates and for the national
organisations, and particularly the LRC, to help
support Labour MPs who were returned and to pay
about a quarter of the registration officer's fee,
the real problem was that if local bodies could
comply with the procedures imposed by national Labour organisations then they could do practically
what they wanted and impose a financial burden upon
the national organisations. The only way in which
the national organisations could control local events was thus to find fault with the selection procedure and thus threaten to withhold funds. This
is precisely what the ILP and the LRC tried to do
with the Grayson candidature.

Both the ILP and the LRC examined the selection
procedure in Colne Valley. The ILP, which agreed
to pay for the services of a full-time organiser
for three months, sent a deputation consisting of
Philip Snowden and J. Howard to meet the Executive
of the CVLL in April 1907.[18] They found the CVLL
in healthy condition and resolute in its determin-
ation to contest the seat with Victor Grayson.[19]
They recommended that 'in the circumstances the NAC
try to meet the branches' desire'. In the event the

NAC procrastinated and the Annual Conference of the
ILP at Derby in 1907 resolved to invoke a rule that
all ILP candidates, except in exceptional circumstances, should be chosen in accordance with the
Constitution of the Labour Party. This necessitated
that all organisations affiliated to the Labour
Party in any locality should be drawn together in a
properly convened conference.[20] MacDonald used
this resolution to suggest that the CVLL should
first of all approach the NAC before calling a conference, whilst the CVLL rightly pointed out that
the resolution was passed after it had selected
Grayson as its candidate.[21] The animus created by
these tactical ploys of the ILP and LRC national
organisations lapped over into the acrimonious correspondence between Eastwood and Grayson, on the one
hand, and MacDonald on the other. In the confusion
of debate, and the occurrence of the by-election,
Grayson and the CVLL fought without the endorsement
of the Labour Party and with only partial support
from the ILP.[22] At one point, the Labour Party
Executive advised that no Labour Party member should
go to Colne Valley to aid Grayson but the ILP eventually approved of the contest and appealed for
funds in the columns of the Labour Leader.[23] For
the independent political Labour movement the Colne
Valley by-election proved to be an embarrassing
episode revealing difficulties within the Labour
movement which will be examined later. The core of
this was MacDonald's attitude towards the relationship between the Labour and Liberal parties and the
relationship between trade unionists and individual
Socialists within the Labour movement. Although
the Labour movement went through the whole gamut of
public internecine conflict for which it has become
famed, the fact is Grayson was victorious.

A second consequence of the Grayson by-election
victory was clearly the traumatic impact which it
exerted upon Colne Valley Liberalism. Sir James
Kitson, the Liberal candidate, had been unopposed in
the 1906 General Election and it was expected that
his successor, P. Bright, would have little difficulty holding the seat, especially given that it was
the Liberals who held the ultimate control over the
timing of the by-election and held the advantage of
prior knowledge: One local writer recalls how 'the
result dumfounded everybody, more especially the
Liberals, who imagined that their candidate, Philip
Bright, would be safely returned.[24] The editor
of the Colne Valley Guardian, a staunch opponent of
Socialism, reflected that

> Last week's election result suggests the his-
> toric question, 'Stands Colne Valley where it
> did?' The answer to which is emphatically
> 'no'. In the estimation of the country, Colne
> Valley has greviously fallen and it will take
> a decade, perhaps a generation, to restore it
> to its former position.[25]

In the event, the Liberal Party recovered the seat
in the January 1910 General Election. Yet one must
reflect that, given that Colne Valley was considered to be a staunch Liberal seat and that the trade
union movement was weak in the area, the seat should
never have been lost in the first place.

The Huddersfield parliamentary by-election of 1906
and the Colne Valley by-election of 1907 disabused
West Yorkshire Liberals of the idea that their
traditional centres of support were sacrosanct. The
Labour Party and the ILP had delivered a political
jolt to which they were forced to respond. That
Huddersfield Liberalism did respond to make the parliamentary seat safer and that Grayson was beaten
into third place in the 1910 General Election is not
proof positive that the West Yorkshire Liberal
parties were absorbing the Labour challenge on the
eve of the First World War. The fact is that the
Labour vote was increasing in local elections and
that the Labour Party was doing well in parliamentary by-elections, despite the apparent tensions
which were occurring within Labour ranks.
    M.G. Sheppard and John L. Halstead have sugg-
ested that there was a strong upward trend in the
Labour vote and the number of Labour candidates
returned at municipal elections in provincial England and Wales from 1900 onwards, and that despite
fluctuations from year to year the Labour Party's
position was strengthened, not diminished, after
1910.[26] The municipal and local returns for West
Yorkshire support this viewpoint. Table 6.1 indicates the extent to which progress was made in some
of the more successful Labour areas. Table 6.2, on
the other hand, indicates the full extent of Labour
representation on local bodies in West Yorkshire.
Taking them both, it is clear that despite some
political setbacks in 1908 and 1909, Labour was
rapidly cutting into the Liberal political stronghold of West Yorkshire on the eve of the First
World War.
    Faced with the municipal and local challenge
of Labour the Liberal organisations in West

Table 6.1 Municipal Representation in Four West Yorkshire Municipalities, 1906-14

Year	Bradford	Halifax	Huddersfield	Leeds	Total
1906	11	4	8	9	32
1907	13	6	6	10	35
1908	10	7	5	4	26
1909	8	8	3	6	25
1910	8	7	2	6	23
1911	13	7	4	10	34
1912	17	8	5	11	41
1913	20	8	5	16	49
1914	20[a]	8	5	16	49

Note: a. A political truce operated in Bradford, Halifax and Leeds in November 1914.
Sources: November issues of Bradford Observer, Halifax Guardian, Halifax Courier, Labour Leader; T. Woodhouse 'The working class', A History of Modern Leeds (Manchester University Press, Manchester, 1980), p. 363.

Table 6.2 The Number of Labour Representatives on Local Political Bodies in West Yorkshire, 1906-14

Year	Municipal	CC, UDC, RDC, PC	Board of Guardians	Total
1906	47	36	6	89
1907	51	39	18	108
1908	44	45	18	107
1909	47	53	21	121
1910	44	60	24	128
1911	61	69	24	154
1912	70	68	24	162
1913	85	70	33	188
1914	85[a]	77[b]	40	202

Note: a. The municipal returns are the same as in 1913 as a result of the political truce which operated at the beginning of the First World War. Only Huddersfield appears not to have operated such a truce in November 1914.

b. The numbers of local labour representatives indicated are, if anything, likely to be under-estimates. Whilst it is possible to obtain reason-ably accurate information on municipal authorities and boards of guardians there is the possibility that the Labour press have not provided full details on the urban-district, rural district and parish council results where by-election and election suc-cesses may have gone unnoticed. Also since rural-district councils often acted as local board of guardians as well no attempt has been made to dis-tinguish such bodies as guardians.
Sources: <u>Bradford Observer, Halifax Courier, Halifax Guardian, Huddersfield Examiner, ILP News, Labour Leader</u> and the records of a varied assortment of trades councils and Labour Party branches.

Yorkshire preferred, where necessary, to join with the Tories in a local alliance against Labour rather than to offer a more progressive form of Liberalism. Liberal-Tory alliances were not uncommon, especially where the Labour challenge was considered to be serious. Tom Woodhouse notes that 'A Tory-Liberal alliance had actually come to pass in Armley and Wortley in 1907', though there appears to have been some Liberal reluctance to enter such an agreement therafter.[27] A Liberal-Tory alliance sprang up at Halifax in 1906 when the ILP and the Trades Council put forward 13 candidates for the municipal elections. 'This challenge, says the Yorkshire Ob-server, was accepted, and as a result of an arrange-ment between the·Liberal and Tories, three-cornered contests were avoided in wards where there was a Labour candidate'.[28] In the 1908 urban-district council elections for Farsley and Pudsey, where Labour was beginning to make a minor mark, a simi-lar agreement was forged. 'A dead set was made by a Liberal and Tory combination at Farsley, resulting in the loss of Allerton and Walker. At Horsforth a ratepayers' association composed of the old par-ties combined, managed to throw Hazelip out'.[29]
    What is clear, however, is that such alliances were of only marginal value in stemming the tide of Labour successes. The position of the ILP/Trades Council strength on Halifax Town Council was only marginally reduced, from five in 1905 to four in 1906.They appear to have worked best between about 1907 and 1910. Even then the advantage was often gained by the Tories rather than the Liberals. In Bradford, for instance, the Tories did much better out of the arrangement. Between 1906 and 1913,

16 of the 21 Bradford wards were involved in the local Tory-Liberal alliance and, as Table 6.3 indicates, the Tories had a higher ratio of success than the Liberals. In addition, it is clear that the Liberal control of the council was weakened not

Table 6.3: The Liberal-Conservative Municipal Pact in Bradford, 1906-13

Year	Liberal straight fights with Labour		Conservative straight fights with Labour		Total	
	Contested	Won	Contested	Won	Contested	Won
1906	3	2	4	4	7	6
1907	4	2	1	1	5	3
1908	4	4	4	3	8	7
1909	5	5	4	4	9	9
1910	3	1	2	2	5	3
1911	3	1	4	4	7	5
1912	1	0	1	1	2	1
1913	3	2	5	4	8	6
Totals	26	17	25	23	51	40

Source: Bradford Observer, Nov. issues between 1906 and 1913.

strengthened during the period in which the alliance operated. In November 1905 the Bradford Liberal Association had 42 representatives on the City Council, compared to the 31 of the Conservatives, the ten of Labour and the one Independent. By November 1913 the Liberals were down to 29 representatives, the Conservatives had 34, Labour had 20 and there was one Independent. Labour also gained 43.1 per cent of the municipal vote in the 1913 municipal elections, compared with the 27.2 per cent gained by the Liberals and the 29.7 per cent of the Conservatives.

The evidence suggests that West Yorkshire Liberalism preferred to enter an alliance with Conservatism where its municipal position was particularly vulnerable to the Labour challenge, rather

Table 6.4: The Municipal Balance of Power in
Bradford, Leeds and Huddersfield, 1906-13

Year	Bradford				Huddersfield				Leeds		
	L.	C.	Lab.	O	L.	C.	Lab.	O	L.	C.	Lab.
1906	38	34	11	1	32	17	8	3	34	21	9
1907	30	40	13	1	37	15	6	2	26	28	10
1908	32	42	10	2	37	16	5	2	23	36	4
1909	33	41	8	2	40	14	3	2	23	34	6
1910	35	39	8	2	42	15	2	1	26	31	6
1911	36	34	13	1	34	20	4	2	28	26	10
1912	35	31	17	1	27	25	5	1	33	34	11
1913	29	34	20	1	28	26	5	1	18	34	16

Note: a. The abbreviations are L. for Liberal, C.
for Conservative, Lab. for Labour and O for Others.
Sources: Bradford Observer, Huddersfield Examiner,
Nov. issues; T. Woodhouse, 'The working class' in
Derek Fraser (ed.), A History of Modern Leeds
(Manchester University Press, Manchester, 1980),
p. 363.

than offer a new more progressive type of Liberalsim
which might attract the working-class vote. Its
emphasis was to harness the anti-Labour or anti-
Socialist vote rather than to unite progressives
under the 'new' Liberal label.
     It is true that the parliamentary position of
Labour did not improve in West Yorkshire, and that
this could be construed to suggest that Labour was
being held in check by the Liberals. But even this
evidence is not as clear as it seems. The Labour
Party continued to poll well in general elections,
and its by-election record was quite impressive in
West Yorkshire. Table 5.3 has already suggested
that the Labour proportion of the general election
votes decreased from the 17.3 per cent peak in 1906
to 15.1 per cent in January 1910 and 14.0 per cent
in December 1910. Yet at the same time, the Liberal proportions fell from 50.3 per cent in 1906 to
47.5 per cent in December 1910. It was not the Liberal Party which was reducing the parliamentary
vote of Labour so much as the Conservative Party
staging something of a political revival at the expense of both Labour and Liberalism, though it held
no parliamentary seat in West Yorkshire from December 1910 to the war. Also, whilst the number of

Labour candidates, of all types, increased from
the 1906 election to the January 1910 election,
the 14 per cent of the vote obtained in the December
1910 General Election derived from only four
contests; three in the Labour seats of Bradford
West, Halifax and Leeds East, the fourth in Huddersfield where Harry Snell came bottom of the poll.
What this indicated, as we shall stress, was
the weak financial state of the West Yorkshire
Labour movement rather than its lack of electoral
support. Despite the class-representative nature
of the unequal parliamentary franchise, it is
evident that the Labour Party was doing particularly
well in West Yorkshire constituencies. In the
four seats it contested in the December 1910
General Election - admittedly including three Labour strongholds where there was no Liberal opposition - it obtained just over 41 per cent of the
vote.[30]

Labour's performance in parliamentary elections was also very encouraging, particularly so
after 1910. The Labour Party contested eight by-
elections between 1906 and 1914, winning only the
Colne Valley seat in 1907. All these contests were
three-sided affairs and, as Table 6.5 suggests, the
tendency was for Labour to improve its percentage
of the poll.

Table 6.5: Parliamentary By-Elections in West
Yorkshire at which Labour candidates were involved

Constituency	Date		Labour % of poll		Previous Labour % of poll	
Colne Valley	July	1907	35.2	(Victory)	1895	13.4
Dewsbury	April	1908	20.2		1906	21.3
Holmfirth	June	1912	28.2	(J)	1910	14.9
Huddersfield	November	1906	33.8		1906	35.2
Keighley	October	1911	28.9		1906	26.6
Keighley	November	1913	29.8		1911	28.9
Leeds South	February	1908	19.4		1906	32.6
Pudsey	June	1908	10.7[a]			

Note: a. J. Benson stood as an Independent Labour
candidate in the June 1908 parliamentary by-election
for Pudsey, though he was not officially sanctioned
by the ILP or the Labour Party.

Source: F.W.S. Craig, British Parliamentary Election Results 1885-1918 (Macmillan, London, 1974).

As we have already suggested, Labour did well in Huddersfield and Colne Valley in 1906 and 1907. In 1908, a bad year for Labour in local contests, Labour lost three by-elections with substantial reductions in its support, but from 1910 onwards, the period in which P.F. Clarke suggests that the Liberals were winning by-elections and Labour was doing badly, it is evident that Labour was making progress. In Keighley there was a steady improvement of the Labour position. In Holmfirth, Labour almost doubled its percentage vote in two and a half years. The switch of allegiance amongst miners, from the Liberal Party to the Labour Party, might help explain the improvement in Holmfirth, but the fact is that Labour's position in by-elections does not suggest the enervating impact of Liberal progressivism existed in West Yorkshire. The dwindling trade-union support for Liberalism was, incidentally, further proof of the inroads which Labour had made into trade union, and working-class, support.

By any yardstick, Labour had made substantial political gains in West Yorkshire between 1906 and 1914. Whilst Liberalism remained the preponderant force at the parliamentary level, the roots of its parliamentary success were being rapidly eroded by Labour at the local level. When Labour chose to contest parliamentary elections, or found the financial wherewithal to do so, it tapped a welling of support for Labour candidates. To many Labour observers, at least, the three or four MPs it returned between 1906 and 1914 were simply the tip of the iceberg of Labour support, the vast majority of which remained unrevealed, due to the fact that the party could not afford to contest all parliamentary seats and, perhaps, due to the inequities of the parliamentary franchise. Yet, for a time, it appeared that the Labour movement nationally and locally might be faltering. There were political setbacks in 1908 and 1909, especially in parts of West Yorkshire where political truces were forged between Liberals and Tories. The national movement appeared to be convulsed with conflicts between the members of the ILP and Labour Party, and over the direction which the political movement was taking. For two or three years there even seemed to be the distinct possibility that internecine conflict or apathy might consume the movement and force Labour

supporters back to Liberalism, pushed by Labour
failures rather than won by the new Liberal ideology. This in-fighting within the Labour movement
was more apparant in West Yorkshire than was new
Liberalism.

The source of much of the temporarily rising
frustration with the ILP and the Labour Party arose
from the sense of irritation at the slow place of
parliamentary reform. It is true that Fred Jowett,
and other Labour members, had pushed the House of
Commons into introducing municipal school feeding in
December 1906, and that this was followed by other
concessions to Labour. Yet progress appeared slow
to some, and partly based upon Labour support for
Liberalism. Indeed, by 1909 and 1910 some branches
of the ILP, such as Farsley, were passing resolutions condemning any move towards establishing a
Lib-Lab pact.[31]

It was Victor Grayson who most effectively am-
plified the suspicions of many Labour supporters
that Labour might be becoming a mere adjunct to Liberalism. When he entered Parliament in 1907, Grayson remained aloof from his ILP and Labour colleagues. He harboured resentment over the ILP and
the Labour Party's reluctance to endorse him for the
Colne Valley by-election. As Groves suggests, he
gained some revenge in his politely discourteous
treatment of Keir Hardie at the great bazaar day in
Huddersfield shortly before the ILP Annual Conference was held there in 1908. The ensuing conference
saw some compromise arrangement by which the ILP
agreed to pay his parliamentary salary, he was allowed to attend Labour Party meetings and have the
Party Whips but was not forced to sign the constitution of the Labour Party. As he reiterated at the
ILP Conference: 'I cannot sign the constitution of
the Labour Party under any circumstances. I esteem
it a pearl of great price that we should have independent socialism represented in the House of
Commons, instructed by the conference. I cannot
accept any other conditions'.[32]

In Parliament, Grayson refused to abide by the
ILP and Labour Party decisions, and Fred Jowett
later recalled that Grayson had always placed himself above party politics.[33] As is well known,
Grayson protested when the debate concerning the
King's visit to the Czar spluttered to a halt. The
Labour group, and particularly Hardie, had protested
against the Russian treatment of political prisoners
and were concerned that secret treaty arrangements
might have been forged between Britain and Russia.

But when Grayson was called Arthur Henderson moved the closure of the debate on the behalf of the Labour Party. The subsequent discussion in the pages of the Labour Leader presented Grayson's view that the whole affair had been contrived although the statements of Henderson and Hardie indicated that a decision to close the debate at that partic- ular point had been made by prior agreement before the debate occurred.[34] More obviously, there was the unemployment debate, in which, on two consec- utive days, Grayson was suspended from the House of Commons for cutting across the business of the House and demanding the discussion of unemployment, on one occasion shouting to the Labour members that 'You are traitors! Traitors to your class'.[35]

Throughout 1908 and 1909 the actions of Gray- son in Parliament attracted the derision of the Liberal and Conservative press and the acclaim of some sections of the Socialist movement, particu- larly in Colne Valley and in other parts of West Yorkshire. As Reg Groves stresses, it is clear that he did garner considerable support for his views in some areas, though this must be qualified by the fact that Keir Hardie was extremely popular in West Yorkshire and that Fred Jowett, James Parker and Philip Snowden carried substantial local support throughout West Yorkshire.

Grayson's conflict with his Labour colleagues became even more pronounced when he joined the staff of the New Age towards the end of 1908. For three months he worked a joint editorship of the paper with Orage but left to join the staff of the Clarion in February 1909. From these news- paper platforms he mounted his campaign against the ILP and Labour Party leadership. He was involved in the famous Holborn Hall rally, or non-rally, where the refusal of Hyndman and himself to stand on the same platform as Hardie to address the Clarion Scouts led to Hardie's withdrawal from the meeting. Groves gives a graphic, if totally unbal- anced account of these events, where the strident Grayson set himself against the 'hurt' and 'reproa- chful' Hardie.[36] However, if one examines the whole range of evidence presented in the Labour Leader then it quickly becomes clear that, whilst Grayson had touched a nerve amongst some of the younger members of the ILP, it was the established leadership which carried the weight of ILP support in the country and in West Yorkshire.

Grayson was just one of a number of ILP members who were at odds with the ILP leaders, parliamentary

procedures, and the trade-union domination of the
movement. Amongst his group of supporters was
H. Russell Smart, who had been the ILP candidate for
Huddersfield in the 1895 General Election. Smart
had become increasingly critical of the leadership
of Hardie, Snowden, MacDonald and Glasier - refer-
ring to them as the 'Junta'. He had written a
number of articles in The Worker, the organ of the
Huddersfield Labour movement, in 1907 and 1908, and
repeated his accusations against the 'Junta' in the
Labour Leader. The gist of his argument was that
'The I.L.P. is in Danger' of ceasing to be a democratic organisation:

> and is becoming, if it has not become, a mere
> machine for registering the desires of three
> or four men who for so many years have formed
> the inner circle of the N.A.C. I pointed out
> that this body had obtained control of the
> Party, all the wires are in their hands, one
> of them always occupies the chair at the
> annual Conference, one of them in on the
> Agenda Committee, and the powers that they have
> acquired enables them to impose their will
> upon the Conference and the Party even when the
> general sentiment of the Party is in opposition
> to them.[37]

Leonard Hall, once of Manchester but by now of
Birmingham, was equally critical of what he saw as
a challenge to the democracy of the party by its
four main leaders. But whilst Smart and Hall hov-
ered in the wings it was Grayson who took the
centre stage.

The final showdown came at the ILP Annual Conference at Edinburgh in April 1909. The National
Administrative Council of the ILP had sought to censure Grayson for his actions in Parliament, his refusal to sign the constitution of the Labour Party
and his public insult of Hardie at Holborn Hall.
The conference decided to refer the offending pas-
sage back to the NAC and Hardie, Snowden, MacDonald
and Glasier resigned from the NAC. It was Hardie
who explained the position of the 'Old Gang'. He
objected to the notion that he, and the others,
should be regarded as 'limpets clinging to the rock
of office', and accused Grayson of being used 'by
others who were even more unscrupulous than he was'.
He made it clear that the resignations should be
seen by the ILP as the opportunity to demonstrate
whether it was to stand for consolidation of the

working-class movement, or whether departing from
the lines of sanity, they should follow some
chimera called Socialism and unity, spoken of by men
who did not understand Socialism and were alien to
its very spirit'.[38]

Made a matter of confidence in the old leadership, the offending paragraph was reinstated by a
vote of 249 to 110. But Hardie, and his three
colleagues decided to adhere to their resignations
and, although there was a move throughout the
country to force them to stay in office, they were
steadfast in their decision and only Glasier returned to the NAC at the 1910 Annual Conference.[39]

The reactions to the events at Edinburgh were
fought out in the pages of the Labour Leader during
subsequent weeks. Smart attacked the 'Old Gang'
or 'Junta' for their mistakes and failure to push
for Socialism and yet suggested to branches throughout the country that they should not let the four
resign, as inconstitency of argument which was
eagerly seized upon by W.C. Anderson, a supporter of
Hardie, who became party chairman in 1910.[40]

A letter, signed by the 'Old Gang', demonstrated the depths to which this fissure extended
into the ILP. It was clear to them that Grayson
wished to form a new Socialist party which excluded
trade unions and did not seek 'the advancement of
Labour'. They particularly criticised the pamphlet
The Problem of Parliament which had advocated the
formation of Socialist Representation committees in
the place of the Labour Party, and which stated
that

> The basis of a Socialist Party must be the
> I.L.P., the S.D.P., the Clarion, and, if it
> can possibly be brought to the point of making
> up its political mind, the Fabian Society.
> There are also various local societies which
> are small but powerful in their neighbourhood.[41]

Despite Groves's view that there was massive
support for Grayson throughout the country, and
particularly in Yorkshire, this is not borne out by
the evidence of the conference nor by the evidence
of branch opinion which appeared in the Labour
Leader. Grayson did find support for his views
and position in Colne Valley, but the Halifax ILP,
the Batley ILP and the Manningham branch of the
Bradford ILP signalled their support for the 'Old
Gang'. Jowett was active in getting the Bradford
movement behind Hardie; Robert Morley, James Parker

and Henry Brockhouse did the same in Halifax, and Alderman Ben Turner was similarly active in Batley. Even the Huddersfield ILP, despite its close proximity to Colne Valley, was divided on the issue of who to support.42 In the event the four members of the 'New Gang' who replaced the 'Old Gang' on the NAC, including Smart and Hall, resigned from the NAC after a year and eventually left the Party, having issued the 'Green Manifesto' Let us Reform the Labour Party, in 1910. Grayson's parliamentary defeat in the January 1910 General Election led to his further estrangement from the party.

By the early months of 1910 the main threat to the ILP, and the Labour Party, had passed and what is clear is that in West Yorkshire, as well as in the country as a whole, the dissident group's attempt to form a rival Socialist party was abortive, despite the publicity which Grayson, through the Clarion, and Hyndman, through Justice, gave to it. The attempt to form the British Socialist Party as an effective alternative to the ILP flickered briefly and failed miserably between 1911 and 1914.

It was Grayson who first announced the formation of the British Socialist Party in the Clarion during August 1911 with his opening sentence that 'The time for the formation of the BRITISH SOCIAL-IST PARTY has definitely come'.43 He then called for others to follow his example and withdraw from the ILP, vowing never to join another Socialist organisation until the BSP, 'the one socialist party', had been formed. Grayson's example worked briefly. There was a period of ecstatic enthusiasm leading to the Socialist Unity Conference at Manchester in September 1911 where the clamour of support was evident. Within nine months the BSP had been formed and had held its first annual conference, but it was soon in difficulties. The vast majority of ILP members were not attracted to the BSP and it quickly became obvious that it was simply the Social Democratic Party (the old Social Democratic Federation) in a new form with H.M. Hyndman, Dan Irving and Harry Quelch pressing established policies on the new organisation.

As we have already noted, the idea of Socialist unity, based upon the ILP and the SDF, never attracted significant support in West Yorkshire during the 1890s. The preponderant Bradford and Halifax ILP branches saw no value to be gained in uniting with an organisation which could not muster a thirtieth of their combined strength. Also,

whilst Grayson was a popular figure in Yorkshire and
Lancashire, no Socialist Representation committee
was formed in West Yorkshire. Despite the fact that
Grayson was able to get the Colne Valley Socialist
(ex-Labour) League to join the BSP, with its 600
members, it is clear, according to a letter from
Albert Inkpin, Secretary of the BSP, that it paid
infrequently after the first four months.[44] Indeed
the CVSL returned to the ILP in 1916.

Nevertheless, Grayson made determined efforts
to win support for the BSP in West Yorkshire. Within a week of his pronouncement in favour of the BSP,
he wrote that

> On Saturday I addressed a magnificent meeting
> in the Colne Valley, and at the close a reso-
> lution to the following effect was put to the
> meeting "That in the opinion of this meeting
> immediate steps should be taken towards the
> formation of a united British Socialist Party".
> The forest of hands that shot up in favour of
> the resolution was a beautiful sight to see,
> and there was not a single hand raised in
> opposition.[45]

On 24 September 1911, Grayson and H. Dawson Large
opened their campaign on behalf of the BSP at St.
George's Hall, Bradford. They filled the hall and
Grayson made a determined appeal for the formation
of a strong Bradford branch of the BSP. The following week some of the Yorkshire ILP branches were
represented at the Socialist Unity Conference, held
at Manchester, most notably the thirteen branches of
the Colne Valley Socialist League.[46] The first
branch of the BSP in Bradford was opened in October
and the first meeting of the Halifax BSP was held
the same month in the SDP rooms at Mount Street,
Cow Green.

There is no denying that Grayson did win support in West Yorkshire. Apart from the CVSL, the
Wakefield ILP branch withdrew from the ILP, and a
BSP branch of 70 members was formed.[47] A large
number of individual members of the ILP also appear
to have joined the BSP. But Grayson's estimate that
30 per cent of ILP members had joined the BSP is
excessive.[48] If correct, that would have meant that
at least 2,000 of the ILP's West Yorkshire members
who had paid their fees to the ILP would have joined
the BSP and that something in the region of 3,000
to 4,000 of the estimated membership would have left
the ILP. The West Yorkshire district of the BSP,

whilst not including every branch of the BSP, claimed to represent 1,000 members in March 1912, when
the local and national BSP movements were at their
zenith.[49] Add to this the estimate of up to 800
members for the CVSL, and allow for some members
who may have been overlooked, and a figure of 2,000
BSP members for West Yorkshire would not have been
an unreasonable estimate. Yet perhaps 300 of these were members of the SDF/SDP, whose membership
had increased in West Yorkshire since 1902, a large
number of previously 'unattached' members were also
admitted to, and much of the membership was short-
lived and nominal.[50] Including Colne Valley's 800
members, soon to be reduced to 600, there were
perhaps 1,000 to 1,300 ILP members who went over to
the BSP. Most had drifted back to the ILP by the
beginning of the First World War. Exclude Colne
Valley from the totals and Grayson's influence
was, of course, greatest there and the West Yorkshire ILP defections become relatively insignificant. Within four years, the ex-ILP members who
remained within the West Yorkshire branches of the
BSP did not number 200. J.B. Glasier's comment of
October 1911 ultimately proved correct: 'The new
party is merely the S.D.P. under a new name'.[51]
Early incursions into ILP support only flattered to
deceive.

This was obvious in Bradford, which saw
Grayson begin his BSP campaign in the West Riding.
Four Bradford branches of the BSP had emerged within a few months of Grayson's appeal. The first
to be formed was the Bradford Central branch which
quickly claimed 200 to 300 members, 'mostly unattached', and was eventually to claim 500 members.[52]
Other branches were formed at Clayton, at Dudley
Hill and Tong, and in the Bradford East parliamentary constituency. They all appear to have been
energetic in 1911 and early 1912, but therafter
faded badly. In the absence of E.R. Hartley, the
Socialist candidate for East Bradford in 1906 and
January 1910, who was touring New Zealand in 1911
and 1912, the only local BSP figure of any note was
Dr. Dessin. No prominent Bradford ILP member,
other than Hartley, joined the BSP and many, such
as J.H. Palin, Fred Jowett and W. Leach were extremely critical of its presence in Bradford.[53] The
Bradford BSP branches soon slimmed down to their
SDP core and were prone to frequent bouts of inactivity. Indeed, only the East Bradford branch and
the Central branch appear to have made any showing
throughout 1912 and 1913. Even these two branches

were prone to difficulties, particularly when
national BSP imposed John Stokes, Secretary of the
London Glass Blowers' Society and Secretary of the
London Trades Council, upon East Bradford as the
parliamentary candidate in place of E.R. Hartley.54
Local members were dissatisfied with the decisio-
and a conference in February 1913 failed to heal
the rift.55

Nevertheless, Harry Quelch, writing in
Justice, gave the impression that matters were going
well in Bradford and that in November 1913 there
were three ILP and BSP candidates returned to
Bradford City Council, after originally announcing
that they were BSP candidates.56 In fact the three
men they named - Thomas Grundy, Charlie Glyde and
F. Lockwood Liles - were all long-established
members of the ILP. Grundy was most certainly not
a member of the BSP, though Glyde, who had joined
the SDF in 1887, and Liles were. Glyde was most
certainly returned for Tong because of his long-
association with Labour politics in the town, and
only Liles could be really described as a success
for the BSP as such, being described as 'One of
Mr. E.R. Hartley's band of Socialists. Member of
the British Socialist Party, a trade unionist, and
a member of the I.L.P.'57

Few other BSP centres in West Yorkshire reached
even the minimal success of the Bradford branches.
The 1912 BSP Conference report suggests that there
were about 20 BSP branches in West Yorkshire, 13 of
them connected with the CVSL.58 There was also a
West Yorkshire District Council. Branches emerged
and collapsed quickly and few BSP branches had claim
to any successes. The Wakefield BSP soon became
ineffective, despite its early success at winning
the support of the local ILP branch. In Halifax,
the BSP was largely based upon the old SDF/SDP, and
won a little support in the Trades Council.59

The only other centre of BSP activity to rival
Bradford in the West Yorkshire area was Leeds.
Though there were no municipal successes, as in
Bradford, there were five active branches of the
BSP in Leeds - Leeds Central, the Clarion Scouts,
Leeds North, Leeds West and Leeds West Ward. These
branches produced a myriad of minor figures but the
only one to emerge to national importance was Bert
Killip, Secretary of the Leeds West branch. He
became a member of the Executive of the BSP in 1913,
and was a faithful supporter of H.M. Hyndman.60
He was largely responsible for organising many of
the BSP propaganda meetings on Woodhouse Moor and

appears to have been responsible for getting the
local BSP organisation to affiliate with the Leeds
Labour Party, well beforeof the national BSP adopted the same policy.61

The results of Grayson's campaign were not
impressive. The BSP, even at its apogee, was unable to attract more than about 20 per cent of the
membership of West Yorkshire ILP organisations, and
many of those came from the Colne Valley Socialist
League. Within a few months there was strong evidence of decay within the BSP branches in West
Yorkshire, and they were never able to secure more
than one or two municipal seats, and then only in
conjunction with the ILP. Ranged against the membership and successes of the ILP, the BSP's impact
was embarrassingly poor and failure generated failure. Most ILP members attracted to the BSP quickly
drifted back to the ILP. Indeed, the impetus to
the movement disappeared when Grayson quickly lost
interest in the BSP, partly due to his l -health
in 1911 and 1912 and partly due to the conflicts
which occurred between himself and the Hyndman
section of the BSP.62 As the Hyndmanites became
predominant so Grayson withdrew from active work
for the BSP. His short story 'The Lost Vision: A
Spring Fantasy' which appeared in Justice during
May 1912 reflected, in a vague and veiled way, his
loss of hope and faith in the BSP.63 A grave ill-
ness in 1913 removed Grayson from the political
scene and a biographical sketch of Grayson's life,
which appeared in Justice, perhaps summarised the
whole Graysonian episode when it said that his was
'A story of buried talents and wasted opportunities'.64

The Grayson challenge was, in West Yorkshire,
merely an irritant to the ILP and the Labour Party.
Nevertheless, it did tap some of the local frustrations which had developed as a result of the
tendency of MacDonald and Hardie to thwart local
ambitions of sponsoring parliamentary candidates.
In West Yorkshire these tensions had become most
apparent in two relatively unpromising constituencies for Labour - Pudsey and Keighley.

Before the First World War the Pudsey constituency
surrounded the three Bradford constituencies.
There were indeed some overlaps between Bradford
and Pudsey for whilst the Tong and Dudley Hill
areas returned councillors to Bradford City Council
they were in the Pudsey parliamentary division.
Prominent Bradfordians, such as E.R. Hartley and

Charlie Glyde, were also active in the Pudsey division because of this overlap with the City of Bradford. Yet whilst Bradford was the centre of the
West Yorkshire Labour movement, and helped to establish a nucleus of Socialist support within the
overlapping Pudsey division, the ILP and the Labour
Party never became powerful in Pudsey. Glyde did
much fine missionary work in Tong, Joe Walker did
the same in Farsley, helping to produce the Labour
Herald and Joseph Hazelip mounted a Socialist
challenge in Horsforth. Yet these efforts were
merely straws in the wind. There were a number of
urban-district council and school board successes
achieved by the ILP in the constituency but these
were always fitful.[65] There were three major
reasons for the weakness of Labour in Pudsey. The
first was that the trade union movement was weak,
although the Stanningley Trades Council was formed.
The second was that there were a large number of
outvoters, possibly about 5,000 out of an electorate
of more than 15,000. This fact had dissuaded the
ILP from contesting the seat in the 1906 Election. The third problem was that in the Horsforth
area, in particular, there was a Ratepayers'
Association, consisting of the Liberals and Conservatives, which had led to the defeat of Hazelip in
the District Council elections of April 1908. In
the same year, a Tory and Liberal combination at
Farsley had resulted in the defeat of two ILP councillors, Walker and Allerton, in the Farsley District Council elections.[66]

Despite the difficulties which Pudsey posed for
Labour candidates, Joe Walker, Secretary of the
Pudsey ILP, kept up a barrage of letters to Hardie
and MacDonald, insisting that there was a need to
find a suitable candidate for Pudsey.[67] The
National ILP's response was predictable. They
rejected the demands on the grounds that the size of
the ownership vote, the lack of funds and the weak
commitment of trade unions meant that there was
little prospect of success.[68]

Walker adopted a petulant tone in subsequent
letters and the Pudsey ILP did warn the ILP not to
make an alliance with the Liberal Party towards the
end of 1909. But such irritant action failed to
budge the NAC of the ILP. Pudsey was not officially
contested by the ILP or the Labour Party before the
First World War, though Hartley only withdrew from
the 1900 General Election contest on the eve of the
poll and though there was an Independent Labour
candidate, J. Benson, in the June 1908 parliamentary

by-election.
    The situation in Keighley was even more pro-
tracted. W.T. Newlove had unsuccessfully contested
the seat in the 1906 General Election. But the
real problem was that despite the good Labour showing J. Brigg, a local wool manufacturer, was easily
at the head of the poll and local as well as national, opinion appeared to be that whilst Brigg was
contesting the seat for the Liberals there would be
little prospect of success but that a Labour candidate ought to be selected in order that the seat
could be contested if Brigg retired because of his
advanced years. The NAC appears to have accepted
the view of Tom Mackley, a leading local Labour
leader, that the 'National I.L.P. cannot afford to
throw away such a good constituency as Keighley',
but were unsure whether or not Herbert Horner should
be the candidate.69 Horner was a founder member of
the Keighley ILP, a teacher and Secretary of the
West Riding Teachers' Association, a member of the
National Union of Teachers, and had been returned
as a County Councillor in April 1907.70 A much
respected local figure, he was nevertheless considered to be a rather weak character by many of the
leaders of the National ILP. After some lengthy
correspondence and selection arrangements he was
selected to be the Labour candidate for Keighley
and was to be supported in his election expenses to
the tune of £100 by his union.71 But it was clear
that he felt that he had little chance of beating
J. Brigg, the sitting Liberal MP, and he withdrew
his candidature, in the hope that Brigg would
retire and cause a parliamentary by-election, at the
January 1910 General Election.72 The death of
J. Brigg, towards the end of 1911, forced a by-
election but it was W.C. Anderson, chairman of the
ILP, who was put forward, not Horner. In the 1913
parliamentary by-election W. Bland won the nomination instead of Horner.
    Apart from the fact that the NAC was evidently
opposed to Horner's candidature it is clear that the
period between 1909 and 1913 also saw a change in
the political structure of the Keighley Labour movement. The Keighley LRC had joined the Trades Council by 1911 and the ILP, which had not advanced in
membership from its position in the early 1890s, was
divided between Horner, and some of the older established members, and W. Bland, and younger members.
Indeed, by 1913 there were real fears that the local
ILP would split. Horner threatened to form a second
ILP branch in opposition to the Keighley ILP,

annoyed at the fact that Bland, and the 'Blandite'
section of the Keighley ILP were excluding him
from an active part in Keighley Labour politics.
He obviously held grounds for resentment against
Bland and the national leadership, particularly in
the light of a Labour agent's report which was produced on Keighley, and correctly indicated that he
had stood down in the January 1910 General Election
on the advice of Philip Snowden. He had also stood
down in favour of W.C. Anderson, the chairman of
the party, in the Keighley by-election of 1911,
'although I had £100 guaranteed by the Executive of
the National Union of Teachers'. He claimed that
Anderson had assured him 'that I should lose nothing
through my magnanimity'.73
     The blunt tone of Hardie's reply, and the
suggestion that Horner had no just cause for being
aggrieved, hardly fitted the facts and was an indel-
icate response to a party faithful whose parliamentary ambitions had been thwarted by the misleading
advice and promises of the leaders of the National
ILP.74
     Compared to the threat which Grayson posed,
these local turbulences were mere pinpricks to the
growth of the Labour movement in West Yorkshire and,
as we have made abundantly clear, Labour's growth
continued unabated from 1909 and 1910 onwards.

The West Yorkshire Liberal organisations were quite
clearly losing control of municipal centres, such
as Bradford and Leeds, in the face of the erosion
of their working-class support by the Labour movement. In many areas, Labour was making inroads
into the number of Liberal municipal representatives, even if the Liberals retained their predominance. But why did this occur? Why was it
that Liberalism was unable to staunch the flow of
support to Labour?
     Part of the reason may well have been that
the changes which P.F. Clarke detects for Lancashire did not occur in West Yorkshire. Clarke
suggests that Lancashire Liberalism, particularly
after 1910, was dominated by a new career-minded
type of politician who replaced the local industrial, often textile, magnates as Liberal candidates and MPs. They were less steeped in Nonconformity, more interested in national rather than
local issues, and in tune with the more progressive demands of some sections of the Liberal
Party.75 Even the most sanguine of historians of
the Clarke school of thought could not suggest that

the Lancashire features pertained in West Yorkshire.
The fact is that Liberalism in West Yorkshire con-
tinued to be dominated by the textile millocracy,
Nonconformity still shaped the thinking of local
Liberals, Liberal MPs rarely exhibited progressive
policies and local politics remained important.
What is blatently obvious is that the 1910 General
Elections in no way represented a watershed for the
West Yorkshire Liberal parties. West Yorkshire Liberalism continued along established lines and failed
to respond to the rising identification of the working classes with the Labour Party. The development
of class politics, insofar as there was a move by
the working classes to attach themselves to the
Labour Party, cut deeply into Liberal support well
before the First World War and particularly, as we
have noted, after 1910.

The evidence for these assertions in plentiful.
In the first place, many of the Liberal MPs were
still drawn from textile families and not from a
career-minded type of politician.   At the parliamentary level, which is the main location of
Clarke's argument, many MPs were still drawn from
the manufacturing classes. W.E.B. Priestley, Liberal MP for Bradford East between 1906 and 1918,
was the son of Briggs Priestley - one of Bradford's
leading industrialists, a Baptist, and Liberal MP
for Pudsey between 1885 and 1900. Rowland Barran,
MP for Leeds North between 1902 and 1918, owned a
clothing firm in Leeds. Robert Armitage, MP for
Leeds Central between 1906 and 1922, was a substantial ironmaster.[76] Percy Illingworth, who represented Shipley between 1906 and 1915, was the nep-
hew of Alfred Illingworth and connected with the
Illingworth firm, Whetley Mills, Bradford.[77] Many
other MPs had business and textile connections.
But even those who were not drawn directly from the
local business community rarely exhibited what
might be considered to be progressive Liberal ideas.
A.J. Sherwell, returned as the Liberal MP for Huddersfield in the November 1906 parliamentary by-
election, and represented Huddersfield until 1918,
was a fairly traditional Liberal. He had been
trained to enter the Wesleyan ministry and became
involved in Wesleyan mission work. He worked with
the Charity Organisation Society in the 1890s, produced a sociological study of the slums of Soho
entitled Life in West London, and had become an
international expert on drink and temperance.
Although his views on temperance were less pedantic
than those held by many Liberal Nonconformists, he

tended to view poverty in terms of personal failing, and proposed self-help, not state intervention, as a solution. Sherwell's views, therefore, stopped short of the state intervention or collectivisation of the new Liberalism.

Those Liberal MPs who were not drawn from local business families or Nonconformity rarely showed evidence of new Liberal ideas. Sir George Scott Robertson, who was MP for Bradford Central between 1906 and 1916, and who might be regarded as a career politician, showed no inclination to offer progressive policies in his election campaigns.[79] In addition, there were comparatively few new Liberal MPs, contesting seats for the first time, appearing in the January and December general elections of 1910.[80]

Only two of the Liberal MPs could claim strong new-Liberal credentials. One was Walter Runciman who was returned as Liberal MP for Dewsbury in 1902. Although Martin Pugh's study of 'Yorkshire and the New Liberalism', largely about Dewsbury, stresses that he was a new Liberal it also points out that it was old Liberal Nonconformity, rather than new Liberal ideas, which ensured that Runciman was returned for Dewsbury. The other new Liberal was C.P. Trevelyan, Liberal MP for Elland from 1899 to 1918. Although Trevelyan's collectivist views eventually led him to join the Labour Party in 1918, it is clear that he barely pushed his new-Liberal views in the more traditional Liberal seat of Elland.[81] Whilst some new-Liberal MPs, and their supporters, were present in West Yorkshire before the First World War there is little to suggest that they exerted any marked influence upon the local Liberal parties, much less the working-class electorate.

The lack of support for Liberal progressivism in West Yorkshire is perhaps part of the explanation for the failures of Liberalism to prevent the haemorrhage of working-class support to Labour. Another factor must be that despite the Liberal reforms at the national level, local Liberalism, because it was unbending in its support for self-help and charity was reluctant to sanction local collectivist action by the town or city councils which it controlled.

In Bradford remarkably little was done to encourage collective responsibility for the ill and needy. We have already suggested that Bradford became a centre of the municipal school-feeding movement, largely in the face of Liberal opposition which fought a determined rearguard action against

what it saw as the 'municipalisation of poverty'.[82]
The provision of municipal housing in Bradford was
also only accomplished against a background of Liberal and Conservative opposition. Only after a
vigorous ILP campaign from the late 1890s, led by
Fred Jowett, was the trenchant opposition of Liberals and Conservatives overcome when the Council
agreed to press forward with the Longland scheme in
August 1901. A slum area was to be cleared, tene-
ments were to be constructed to accommodate 432
people, and 'through' houses were to be built in
Faxfleet Street for the 925 displaced persons.[83]
Limited as this scheme was, compared to the total
slum problem of Bradford, it was strongly disap-
proved of by Tories, and some Liberals, who fought
to prevent any further extension of municipal housing. ILP leaders later argued that:

> The leaders of the Liberal party in Bradford,
> Alderman H.B. Priestman, has recently been
> claiming that his party is just as anxious to
> remove slums and remedy poverty as the Social-
> ists. Whilst we do not doubt that in the main
> both Liberals and Tories have the kindliest
> feelings towards their poorer fellow citizens,
> yet we feel compelled to point out that when
> it comes to an actual conflict between the
> sacredness of human life and the sacredness
> of property, they are generally to be found on
> the side of property.[84]

A similar reluctance to consider progressive
measures occurred in Huddersfield. Ben Riley, a
Labour councillor and later Labour MP for Dewsbury,
reflected:

> How completely out of touch modern local
> official Liberalism ... is with the real pro-
> gressive spirit of the time ... the leading
> dominant Liberals on the Council are either
> entirely opposed to enlarging the purpose of
> their politics or they are far too timid, too
> nervous, achieving no great aims.[85]

Riley's comment is in fact borne out by the
facts. The Huddersfield Liberal Association, and
its membership, placed its faith in the efficacy of
charity to deal with the social problems of the day.
The Charity Organisation Society was the main focus
of a charitable self-help approach which, in the
face of rapidly rising unemployment in the first

decade of the twentieth century, gave way to the
more community-based and social casework approach
of the Huddersfield Guild of Help. As with the
Bradford Guild of Help, formed in 1904, many of the
leading C.O.S. figures were to be found within the
Guild and in essence the new organisation was merely
a revamped version of the C.O.S. The Huddersfield
Guild was also considered by Labour leaders to be
a Liberal 'surrogate for municipal action'.[86] It
was clearly the hope of the Guild that poverty could
be dealt with without the need for additional
legislation. It is true that the development of
the Guild softened the traditional attitude of Liberal Nonconformists that much poverty was self-
induced as a result of recourse to drink, but
Samuel Bull, a Liberal manufacturer, still reflected
the view of many Liberals that 'if the unemployed
drank less it would raise their efficiency and give
them employment'.[87] In the face of this lingering
opposition to poverty being dealt with by the
direct action of the state or the municipal authorities, it is not surprising that the Huddersfield
Liberals dragged their heels in connection with
social welfare. The Liberal-dominated town council
did not commit itself to a housebuilding programme
for the working classes until 1907 and did nothing
on the matter until 1912.[88] Its only significant
concession to district municipal action before 1914
was its decision to set up a Canteen Committee,
financed from the rates, to provide school meals to
necessitious children under the 1906 Eduction
(Provision of Meals) Act.[89]
     The exigent needs of working-class life were
producing a demand for collectivisation which the
Liberal parties of West Yorkshire were unwilling to
meet. It was only the West Yorkshire Labour movement which was prepared to meet these needs with
an advanced social programme, a programme which was
attracting trade-union, and thus working-class,
support.

Yet the rapid drift of working-class support to
Labour, whilst it was encouraged by the rising
level of industrial unrest which occurred in Britain and West Yorkshire in the years between
1909 and 1914, does not appear to have been influenced by the rise of syndicalist activity before
the First World War. It is clear that there were
a large number of industrial disputes in West Yorkshire between 1909 and 1914. It is equally
evident that these disputes added to the support

for the Labour Party. But is must be remembered
that the Manningham Mills strike of the early 1890s
had encouraged the working-class drift towards
Labour and that the trickle of disputes from the
1890s to 1909 re-enforced the message of Manningham
- the need for the working classes to support an
independent working-class political party. The
militancy of the immediate pre-war years served to
galvanise the Labour position, since so many of
the leading West Yorkshire figures were in fact
trade unionists. What is equally clear, however, is
that syndicalism played a very limited role in the
industrial unrest which occurred in West Yorkshire
and that had it been more significant it might well
have dampened the support for the Labour Party
rather than have exposed the social and industrial
failures of Liberal Britain.

The syndicalists were a group of activists, by
and large led by Tom Mann, who hoped to capture the
existing trade-union structure for the rank and
file, to bring unity and militancy to trade unionism through the formation of industrial unions,
which united all the unions of one industry into
one union and to bring about the collapse of capitalist society by a General Strike which would pave
the way for some type of workers' control. In
essence, the syndicalist was an advocate of industrial as opposed to political action. Their
policies were at odds with the Labour Party where,
despite its close connection with trade unions,
primacy lay with political rather than industrial,
means of bringing about change. Labour leaders,
such as Ramsay MacDonald and Philip Snowden, wrote
pamphlets and books attacking syndicalism as an
imported French movement which was alien to the
British way of life. Indeed, it would appear that
the vast majority of Labour leaders in West Yorkshire agreed with this view, though there was some
sentimental support for Tom Mann and for the support
which syndicalism gave to the emerging strategies
of trade unions. But there is little evidence that
syndicalism was ever prevalent in West Yorkshire.
Several years ago, J.E. Williams, in an article on
the Leeds Gas Strike of 1913, dismissed notions that
syndicalists or syndicalism played a part in the
dispute. When Bob Holton wrote his polemic on
British Syndicalism, attempting to prove that it
both achieved some degree of international success
and that its influence did not expire after 1912 but
continued up to the First World War, it is notice-
able that he provided no hard evidence of the

movement thriving in West Yorkshire.[90]
     Indeed, the only real evidence of syndicalist
activity in West Yorkshire emerges in the conflicts
of the British Socialist Party. At the national
level it was torn between the essentially political
approach of Hyndman, who was opposed to strike
activity, and Leonard Hall and H.R. Smart, both of
whom believed in the need for industrial unionism.
Hall wrote:

> The great defensive and destructive duties
> of Industrial Unionism must not be allowed to
> overshadow its essentially constructive func-
> tion in the transition to Socialism ... Under
> Socialism itself the co-ordinating centres
> would be Parliaments of Industry not Parlia-
> ments of Politicians. No free and self-
> respecting community would have any need or
> room for partisan "Punch and Judy" politics.[91]

He was naturally opposed by Hyndman, and other SDF
and BSP leaders, who had 'never known ... a successful strike'.[92]
     The only serious support for Hall and Smart
came from the Huddersfield branch of the BSP. A
number of factors conflated to make the Huddersfield
branch pro-syndicalist. In the first instance,
Smart carried a little weight in the constituency,
having been the ILP parliamentary candidate at the
general election of 1895 and having retained his
contacts in the area. In addition, E.J.B. Allen,
one of the leading members of Tom Mann's Industrial
Syndicalist Education League, had lived, worked and
agitated for his views, in the Huddersfield area.[93]
Also, leading members of the Huddersfield BSP, such
as Arthur Gardiner, were trade unionists and
committed to industrial action. It is hardly surprising then that the Huddersfield BSP resolved
that its meeting

> realising the necessity of the return of
> Socialist members of Parliament, and on the
> local governing bodies, as well as the organ-
> isation of the workers industrially in their
> unions, both movements aiming at the abolition
> of the wages system of slavery, and the
> entire emancipation of the working class,
> pledges itself to secure Socialist
> representation where possible, and to assist
> in the building up of a powerful union
> movement.[94]

Yet even in Huddersfield there appears to have been
little evidence of syndicalist presence in strike
activity, no matter what the Huddersfield Examiner
and the Liberal press might say.
     The militant strike activity before 1914 did
help to galvanise the links between the Labour
Party and the trade union movement. Some of the
Liberal legislation, such as the Unemployment section of the National Insurance Act of 1911 did en-
gender some criticism from trade union ranks. But
on the whole the militant period of industrial
activity merely served to buttress the class alliances which had already been forged between trade
unions and the Labour Party.

The West Yorkshire Liberal parties failed to meet
the challenge of Labour between 1906 and 1914.
Without needing to enter the involved and protracted
debate about the inequalities of the parliamentary
and local franchises which might, or might not,
have helped the Liberals at the expense of Labour,
it is evident that the Liberal voters were moving
to Labour. Labour did well in both general elections and parliamentary by-elections and made deep
inroads into the local position of the Liberal
Party from 1910 onwards, after the setbacks of 1908
and 1909. There is no evidence that Labour's
political growth was being checked in West Yorkshire between 1910 and 1914, and little evidence
to suggest that local Liberalism was making the
attempt to capture the working-class vote with its
progressive social policies. On the whole West
Yorkshire Liberalism was still dominated by the
factory master and Nonconformity. The shibboliths
of self-help and charity were offered by Liberals
as an alternative to greater intervention and
collectivisation. When these failed the Liberals
often united with Tories as anti-Socialist combines.
It was a ploy which both demonstrated the lack of
Liberal progressivism and the seriousness of the
Labour challenge. Labour was much stronger in West
Yorkshire by 1914 than it had been in 1906 or 1910,
and much of its growth was at Liberal expense.
The First World War served to speed up the decline
of the Liberal Party, of that there is no doubt.
But it is clear that the signs of Liberal decay
were already apparent before the war. Moreover,
the identification of the working classes with the
progressive policies of the Labour Party foreshad-
owed Liberal decline. There is also no reason to
suppose that the Liberal Party should be more

seriously affected by the war than was the Labour
Party. The political turbulence created by the
First World War was just as pronounced in the West
Yorkshire Labour movement as it was within the
Liberal Party. The fact that Labour survived and
that Liberalism collapsed owes much to the class
nature of political support which had accreted to
the Labour cause before 1914.

NOTES

1. Clarke, Lancashire and the New Liberalism,
p. 406.
2. Wilson, The Downfall of the Liberal Party
1914-35, p. 19.
3. Labour Leader, 30 Nov. 1906; Independent
Review, Feb. 1907.
4. R. Perks argues this in his CNAA PhD study,
at Huddersfield Polytechnic, on Huddersfield politics in the late nineteenth and early twentieth
centuries.
5. Independent Review, Jan., Feb. 1907.
6. ILP Archive, Francis Johnson Collection,
1908/263, letter from Williams to Keir Hardie, 30
Jun. 1908.
7. Ibid., 1906/43.
8. Daily Express, 20 Jul. 1907.
9. Clark, Colne Valley: Radicalism to Socialism, pp. 5-6.
10. ILP Archive, Francis Johnson Collection,
1906/403.
11. Clark, Colne Valley: Radicalism to Socialism, pp. 129-61; R. Groves, The Strange Case of
Victor Grayson (Pluto Press, London, 1975), pp. 20-
42.
12. Colne Valley Labour League, Minutes, 13
Oct. 1906.
13. Yorkshire Factory Times, 22 Jun. 1906;
Labour Party Archive, LP/CAN/06/2/65, circular
issued by the Colne Valley Labour League in response
to an ILP statement.
14. Clark, Colne Valley: Radicalism to Socialism, p. 131.
15. CVLL, Minutes, 13 Oct. 1906.
16. Ibid., 25 Feb. 1907.
17. Howell, British Workers and the Independent
Labour Party 1888-1906, pp. 301-26.
18. Labour Party Archive, LP/CAN/06/2/40.
19. Ibid.
20. ILP Report, 1907.
21. Labour Party Archive, PL/CAN/06/2/42.

22. Yorkshire Factory Times, 12 Jul. 1907.
23. Labour Leader, throughout Jun. 1907.
24. E. Lockwood, Colne Valley Folk (Heath Cranton, London, 1936), p. 73.
25. Colne Valley Guardian, 26 Jul. 1907.
26. Sheppard and Halstead, 'Labour's Municipal Election Performance in Provincial England and Wales 1901-13', p. 42.
27. Woodhouse, 'The working class', p. 361.
28. Labour Leader, 9 Nov. 1908.
29. Ibid., 17 Apr. 1908.
30. Bradford West, Halifax, Leeds East and Huddersfield.
31. ILP Archive, Francis Johnson Collection, 1910/530.
32. Groves, The Strange Case of Victor Grayson, p. 59.
33. Ibid., p. 62.
34. Labour Leader, 20 Nov. 1908.
35. Groves, The Strange Case of Victor Grayson, p. 67.
36. Ibid., pp. 92-6.
37. Labour Leader, 15 May 1908.
38. Ibid., 16 Apr. 1909.
39. Ibid., 23, 30 Apr. 1909, 1 Apr. 1910.
40. Ibid., 30 Apr. 1909, 1 Apr. 1910.
41. Ibid., 16 Apr. 1909.
42. Ibid., 30 Apr, 1909 and subsequent issues.
43. Clarion, 4 Aug. 1911.
44. Letter from SBP to CVSL, 6 Jun. 1916 in the Colne Valley Labour Party records, The Polytechnic Library, Huddersfield.
45. Clarion, 11 Aug. 1911.
46. Ibid., 22 Sep., 6, 13 Oct. 1911.
47. Ibid., 8 Dec. 1911.
48. Ibid., 13 Oct. 1911.
49. Ibid., 2 Mar. 1912.
50. Ibid., 10 Nov. 1911.
51. L. Thompson, The Enthusiasts: A Biography of John and Katherine Bruce Glasier (Victor Gollancz, London, 1971), p. 169.
52. Clarion, 10 Nov., 7 Dec. 1911.
53. Bradford Pioneer, 7 Feb. 1913.
54. Justice, 30 Nov. 1912.
55. Clarion, 4 Nov. 1912, 14 Feb. 1913.
56. Justice, 18 Oct., 8 Nov. 1913.
57. Bradford Daily Telegraph, 4 Nov. 1913.
58. First Annual Conference of the British Socialist Party, 1912 (Communist Party of Great Britain, London, 1970 reprint), pp. 50-2.
59. Justice, 13 Oct. 1913, 26 Mar. 1914.

60. Ibid., 10 Sep. 1914.
61. Bradford Pioneer, 11 Apr. 1913.
62. W. Kendall, The Revolutionary Movement in Britain 1900-1921 (Weidenfeld & Nicolson, London, 1969); Clarion, 5 Jan. 1912; First Annual Conference of the British Socialist Party, 1912, pp. 9-10.
63. Justice, 4 May 1912.
64. Ibid., 21 Dec. 1912.
65. Labour Party Archive, LRC 17/534-6.
66. Footnote 29.
67. Labour Party Archive, LRC 17/534; ILP Archive, Francis Johnson Collection, 1907/70, 1908/156, 1908/159, 1908/199.
68. ILP Archive, Francis Johnson Collection, 1908/22.
69. Ibid., 1907/144.
70. Ibid., 1907/51, 1907/189. There was also a Labour Party agents' report which was critical of Herbert Horner 1909/500.
71. Ibid., 1909/549.
72. Ibid., 1909/549-50, 1909/568-9.
73. Ibid., 1913/306.
74. Ibid., 1913/307.
75. Clarke, Lancashire and the New Liberalism.
76. E.D. Steele, 'Imperialism and Leeds politics, c. 1850-1914', in D. Fraser (ed.), A History of Modern Leeds (Manchester University Press, Manchester, 1980), p. 328.
77. He replaced W.P. Byles as Liberal candidate for Shipley in 1897.
78. Huddersfield Examiner, 24 Nov. 1906.
79. W.D. Ross, 'Bradford Politics 1880-1906', unpublished PhD thesis, University of Bradford, 1977, particularly the biographical section.
80. Four in January 1910 and three in December 1910.
81. Morris, C.P. Trevelyan 1870-1958: Portrait of a Radical, p. 81.
82. Laybourn, 'The Issue of School Feeding in Bradford, 1904-1907', pp. 30-8.
83. Brockway, Socialism over Sixty Years, p. 52.
84. Forward, 18 Oct. 1907.
85. Huddersfield Examiner, 22 Oct. 1910.
86. M. Cahill and Tony Jowitt, 'The Bradford Guild of Help Papers', History Workshop, Issue 15, Spring 1983, p. 151; M. Cahill and Tony Jowitt, 'The New Philanthropy: the emergence of the Bradford City Guild of Help', Journal of Social Policy 9: 3 (July, 1980), pp. 359-82; Huddersfield Examiner, 22 Nov. 1913.

87. Huddersfield Examiner, 16 Dec. 1893.
88. Ibid., 19 Oct. 1907; Huddersfield Trades
Council, Minutes, 28 May 1913.
89. Huddersfield Borough Council, Minutes,
24 Apr. 1907.
90. J.E. Williams, 'The Leeds Gas Strike, 1913',
in A. Briggs and J. Saville, Essays in Labour
History (Macmillan, London, 1971).
Bob Holton, British Syndicalism, 1900-1914 (Pluto
Press, London, 1976).
91. Clarion, 3 May 1912.
92. Kendall, The Revolutionary Movement in
Britain 1900-1921, pp. 28-9.
93. The Industrial Syndicalist, passim.
94. Alfred Gardiner scrap book, p. 3, though
the source of the newspaper cutting is not indicated. Photocopies of parts of the scrapbook are in
the hands of Dr. K. Laybourn. Gardiner was a
member of the Dyers' Union and a delegate to Huddersfield Trades Council.

Chapter Seven

THE FIRST WORLD WAR

Recent research on the First World War and domestic
politics has divided historical opinion into two
major schools of thought. The first, in which we
include ourselves, maintains that the Labour Party
had made deep inroads into Liberalism well before
1914. It has been our contention that the Labour
Party was eroding the political support of the Liberal Party in West Yorkshire before 1914, and that
the First World War merely speeded up the erosion of
that support. The second school of thought, dominated by P.F. Clarke, Trevor Wilson and Roy Douglas,
has emphasised the crucial impact of the War in
dividing Liberalism and allowing a political vacuum
to emerge which the Labour Party was able to fill.
Wilson set the parameters of this particular school
of thought when he wrote that

> The war not only inflicted such a disaster on
> the Liberals but provided Labour with the
> impetus to seize the opportunity. The impact
> of the war on the nation's economy so increas-
> ed the importance of trade unions and so stim-
> ulated their political consciousness, that it
> correspondingly enhanced the position of the
> Labour Party, which had all along derived much
> of its limited importance from its association
> with organised labour.[1]

The problem with this second viewpoint is that it
first of all ignores the substantial improvements
made by Labour before the First World War and,
secondly, it assumes that the war was more condu-
cive to the growth of Labour opinion than it was to
Liberal opinion. In West Yorkshire, Labour had
made rapid inroads into the local political power
of Liberalism, and it was also evident that the war

posed just as many problems for the Labour movement
as it did for Liberalism. There is no particular
reason why the Liberal Party should have been any
more inconvenienced by the war than was the Labour
Party, which faced its own leadership crisis.
Labour's political resilience, on the other hand,
appears to have resulted from the inexorable growth
of its working-class support. Conversely, Liberalism's loss of working-class support, rather than
conflict amongst the leading Liberals, was the fundamental difficulty which it faced.

The 1914 ILP Conference, the 'Coming of Age Conference' as it was known, was the apogee of the ILP
before the War. Apart from the fact that the
meeting was held at the time of ILP growth and
success, it was held in Bradford, the birthplace of
the National ILP. Despite an excess of local pride,
which coloured the speeches of many Bradford delegates, the conference did accurately reflect the
local confidence of the movement. In his welcoming
address to the 1914 Conference, J.H. Palin, reflecting upon the fact that the Bradford ILP had
1,600 members, 20 members on the City Council,
three members on the Board of Guardians and one MP,
asserted:

> they would see that the ILP was not only the
> political party of the future, but that, so
> far as Bradford was concerned, it was the
> political party of the present. ... and there
> was no danger of the Bradford branch going
> wrong and if they would follow its lead the
> party would go on, and would eventually become
> the dominant party in British politics.[2]

This confidence and sense of unity within the Bradford and West Yorkshire ILP organisations was to be
quickly undermined by the First World War.
    In the years immediately prior to the war, the
Bradford and West Yorkshire Labour movements had
committed themselves to oppose militarism. Both
the Bradford ILP and the Bradford Trades Council
responded to the increasingly threatening international situation by supporting international
Socialist resolutions opposed to war. In 1912 the
Bradford Trades Council resolved to express its
approval 'of the proposal for a general stoppage of
work in all countries about to engage in war, and
further we urge upon all workers the necessity for
making preparations for a simultaneous stoppage of

work in those countries where war is threatened'.[3]
Arthur Gardiner and the Huddersfield Socialist
Party, which was briefly attached to the British
Socialist Party, were also staunchly opposed to the
war, despite the patriotic pressure applied by
H.M. Hyndman.[4] On the eve of war numerous articles
appeared in the Bradford Pioneer and the Huddersfield Worker, the local ILP newspapers, exposing
the workings of secret diplomacy and the Armaments
Trust, and advocating the fostering of unity across
international boundaries.

The driving force behind such concern was the
moral indignation of many ILPers who felt that the
taking of human life was never justifiable. Underpinning this heartfelt rejection of violence was a
traditional Nonconformist opposition to war which
was galvanised within the ILP by the presence of a
number of prominent Nonconformist ministers. One
of the most frequent writers in the Bradford Observer was the Reverend R. Roberts, a Congregational
minister who had had a somewhat stormy relationship
with the ILP in the previous twenty years.[5] In
early 1914, Roberts wrote:

> Alone amongst the parties of Britain the
> Labour Party is pledged against militarism...
> We must take up the Fiery Cross and carry it
> to the remotest hamlet in the country, call
> every man and woman to the colours. "Down
> with militarism". That is our cry - as it is
> also the cry of our comrades all over Europe.
> Blazon it on the banners. Write it on the
> pavements. Sing in the streets.[6]

The outbreak of the First World War came with
startling suddeness. As late as 1 August 1914
Continental Socialist leaders were still not convinced that war was even a likely possibility. As
Haupt suggests, they were captive of their own
myths about their ability to prevent war and unaware
of the depths of national chauvinism.[7] They were
caught out by the events, pushed on to the defensive
and literally became disoriented spectators,
waiting to be submerged by the gathering wave of
nationalism.

In Bradford, in the midst of the period of
national ultimatums, the ILP called a mass meeting
on 2 August which deplored the threatened war but
did not advocate immediate working-class action to
prevent it. Fred Jowett, the ILP MP for Bradford
West, hoped that Britain would not be involved in

the coming conflagration but, bowing to events, concluded: 'Let us who are Socialists keep our minds calm, our hearts free from hate, and one purpose always before us - to bring peace as soon as possible on a basis that will endure'.[8]

Such a unanimity of purpose evaporated with the declaration of war. Throughout West Yorkshire the ILP branch membership divided into pro-war and anti-war factions, divisions which rapidly became evident within cognate Labour organisations. In essence, there emerged three main strands of opinion. At one extreme there were pacifists who were opposed to war *per se*. At the other there were those who felt that the war had to be pursued to its successful conclusion for Prussianism to be defeated. Between these two groups were those, probably representing a majority of the movement, who were equivocal about the war. Whilst they supported the national and international peace movements they felt the need to protect Britain and to defend Belgium, some even going so far as to suggest that Socialist objectives had to be suspended for the duration of the war.

The National ILP had its fair share of pacifists whose ideas became more or less fully accepted by the ILP's National Conference in 1917. Bruce Glasier, Clifford Allen, Arthur Salter and Fenner Brockway, with Philip Snowden on the edge of this group though he was never a fully committed pacifist, set the pacifist tone of the national party which initially maintained the front that Socialists of all countries were solid against the war.[9] There was a professional, middle-class temper about this group, which was almost entirely composed of writers, journalists, academics and doctors. Though it included many prominent members of the ILP, it was never very numerous either at the national or the local level. In West Yorkshire there were few prominent individuals in its ranks. The pacifist strand in Huddersfield was led largely by Arthur Gardiner, although he was temporarily a member of the British Socialist Party rather than the ILP at this time. The leading ILP pacifists in Bradford were William Leach and Arthur Priestman, both of whom were employers who had joined the Bradford ILP in the mid 1890s. Arthur Priestman was a Quaker and a member of one of the largest business families in Bradford.[10] Leach, who was to become one of Bradford's MPs during the inter-war years, had originally been drawn into the ILP by Fred Jowett, whom he had once employed as an overlooker, and had

become a prolific writer within the Labour movement.
He was a frequent contributor to the <u>Bradford
Labour Echo</u>, the Bradford ILP paper of the late
1890s, became editor of <u>Forward</u>, the ILP's paper
between 1904 and 1909 and, from October 1915, in the
stead of the increasingly pro-war Joseph Burgess,
became editor of the <u>Bradford Pioneer</u>. He articulated the paper's policy in the following manner:

> We hate all war, especially the present one.
> This is a pacifist or peace journal conducted
> among other purposes, with the object of
> stating as well as we can, the ILP position on
> the hideous tragedy now being enacted in
> Europe... Human life is the most sacred thing
> we know, and its preservation, its development,
> its best welfare, must therefore be our reli-
> gion on this earth.[11]

Under Leach's editorship the <u>Bradford Pioneer</u>
reported extensively on the activities of pacifists
and opponents of war controls, such as the No-
Conscription Fellowship and the Union of Democratic
Control. When Bertrand Russell lectured at the
ILP's New Picture House in Morley Street, Bradford
in 1917, the <u>Bradford Pioneer</u> referred to him as
'a recent and very valuable acquisition to the
I.L.P.'.[12] When E.D. Morel, of the Union of Democratic Control, lectured at the Picture House he was
affectionately described as 'that distinguished
jail bird... now a member of the I.L.P. and of the
Bradford Branch'.[13]
    Though Leach was badly defeated when he stood
as the ILP/Labour Party candidate for Bradford
Central in the 1918 General Election he still stuck
firmly to his pacifist views, stating that 'I have
never felt so pugnaciously right in my life. I
still disbelieve in war. As long as I am in public
life I will not support bloodshed for any cause,
whether that cause appears right or does not. It
looks as if this victory fervour has swept us out.
But it will pass. Liberalism is defunct, Socialism
is deferred, and the Coalition will be deflated'.[14]
    Such passion of conviction was equally evident
amongst those members of the ILP who did support
the war effort. Jessie Cockerline, the regular
trade union correspondent of the <u>Bradford Pioneer</u>,
and a leading contributor to the <u>Yorkshire Factory
Times</u>, the weekly paper of the Yorkshire textile
workers, constantly argued that the cry must be 'My
Country Right or Wrong', occasionally tempered with

The First World War

the thought that the War was not so much concerned
with patriotism as the issues of right and wrong,
might and right. [15] Cockerline wrote frequently on
need to fight against Caesarism, one one occasion
maintaining that 'The sword is drawn and it is
drawn in the cause of democracy, in the cause of
liberty and honour and we must, each one of us,
realise that it can never again be sheathed whilst
the terror of the Kaiser's dreams of universal
domination have the most remote possibility of
being realised'. [16]
    There were certainly many other ILPers, often
springing from a trade union background, who
supported Cockerline's views. J.H. Palin, Hector
Munro and Councillor A.W. Brown of Bradford, and
James Parker of Halifax, were strongly pro-war.
    Palin was a prominent trade unionist, had been
chairman of the Amalgamated Society of Railway
Servants at the time of Taff Vale, and a prominent
public figure in Bradford, acting as an ILP councillor, and later alderman, up to and during the
war. Until early 1917 he was the trade union
correspondent of the Bradford Pioneer, having taken
over from Cockerline, and prominently displayed his
support for the War. At first his views were tol-
erated in the confusion of opinion over the War
within the ILP ranks, but he became an increasing
embarrassment to Leach and the anti-war Bradford
Pioneer and was obviously out of step with resolutions passed by the Bradford ILP. This difference
of opinion was sharply indicated at the 1916 ILP
Conference when, despite being mandated to support
a resolution advocating all Socialist parties of
all nations to refuse to support every war entered
into by any government, Palin cut across the comparative equanimity of the meeting and bluntly
stated that

    We do not want the Germans here. Assume that
    the workers of this country had carried out
    this resolution at the beginning of the war,
    and the Socialists of other countries had not,
    and had rallied or been forced to join the
    Army, where at the moment would Great Britain
    have been? At any rate, it seems to me that
    more time is required to get a considered
    opinion to start afresh after the war. [17]

Although Palin was reprimanded by T.W. Stamford,
President of the Bradford ILP, he remained unrepen-
tant and subsequently went to France to help with

war transportation.

Others campaigned strongly for the war effort and took themselves to France. Dr. Hector Munro, a prominent Bradford ILPer and sometime member of the Board of Guardians, went to France with an ambulance wagon at the beginning of the conflict.[18] Censuses of the Bradford ILP membership confirm that many young men volunteered to go to the front. A census in February 1916 indicated that of 461 young men in the local party membership of 1,473, 113 were in the trenches, four had been killed, one was missing, nine had been wounded, three were prisoners of war, 118 were in training in England, six were in the navy and 207 attested under the Derby Scheme were necessary home workers.[19] A similar survey in 1918 found that of the 492 members liable for service, 351 were serving in the forces whilst 48 were conscientious objectors or were on national war work.[20]

Such patriotism was to be found more broadly throughout the West Yorkshire Labour movement. Indeed, perhaps the most prominent of the ILP's pro-war contingent was James Parker, ILP/Labour MP for Halifax. From the outset, Parker identified himself with the war effort and the recruiting campaign. One critic, attacking the Keighley Labour Party for not supporting the war effort in early October 1914, noted that this neglect was being more than made up for by James Parker:

> Mr. James Parker, M.P., in pleading for more recruits in the Halifax district, declared that if Britain were defeated in the war, the working class would have everything to lose and nothing to gain. They would not be asked to serve in the army but would be bludgeoned into it not only in times of war but in times of peace. ... Parker is not a man to talk like this unless thoroughly convinced that the war is a joint one on our part.[21]

Parker's commitment to the war effort was amply demonstrated when he wrote to Francis Johnson, Secretary of the National ILP, in April 1915 responding to an ILP Conference resolution criticising his action: 'In reference to the Resolution re my recruiting campaign in Eccles Division and Bishop Auckland. I have nothing to add to my former letter beyond that I have been doing my duty'.[22] Parker's influence appears to have told on the Halifax Trades Council, most of whose leading

members were ILPers. When they discussed the recruiting campaign in September 1914 they supported
it by 24 votes to 16. Alderman Arthur Taylor, a
leading figure in the Amalgamated Society of Engineers and the doyen of the Halifax ILP, reflected
that 'while he hated wars, there were times when it
was absolutely necessary that people should recognise war was inevitable. England did not belong
to the people, but neither did any other country.
At any rate, England was the best country among
"a blooming bad lot"'.[23]

Although not as forthright in his views as
Parker and Palin, Ben Turner, the leader of the
weavers and textile workers, who was re-elected as
Mayor of Batley in November 1914, quickly accepted
the need to fight and identified himself with the
relief of the Belgian refugees.[24] Elsewhere in
West Yorkshire, ILPers were to be found putting
forward similar arguments for the putative involvement of Socialists in the war effort.

The majority of ILP/Labour supporters in West
Yorkshire do not appear to have accepted either the
pacifist or patriotic line as such, but to have
stood somewhere between the two positions, fluctu-
ating in their emphasis as the mood of the nation
altered. Generally they opposed the war but recognised the need for National Defence. Fred Jowett,
Bradford West's Labour MP, reflected the opinion
of this section. Throughout the war he articulated
a viewpoint of what caused the war and how wars
could be eradicated in the future. As he argued in
his Chairman's speech to the 1915 ILP Conference at
Norwich 'Now is the time to speak and ensure that
never again shall the witches' cauldron of secret
diplomacy brew the war broth of Hell for mankind'.[25]
He later wrote that 'I believe that the war would
never have arisen if the government had carried
out an open and honest foreign policy and disclosed
to the people who had most to lose the relations
between themselves and foreign governments with
whom they were acting in collusion'.[26] Jowett
was a belligerent critic of the British Government
which had arranged, though frequently denied the
existence of, secret treaties. As the Standard
said 'His fad is the democratic control of foreign
affairs'. Given that there was a war, however,
he demanded an end to the conflict as soon as possible and that the Government should specify its war
aims to be forced to the negotiating table.

Although Jowett was clearly a stern critic of
the Government he was equally adamant that a

British victory over 'Prussianism' had to be won
and that he could not agree to a peace settlement
which did not include the 'restoration of Belgium
to complete sovereignty'.[28] He maintained that a
nation had a right to defend itself and frequently
paid homage to those who had given their lives in
the war.[29] In many respects Jowett's policy closely
resembled the views expressed by Keir Hardie in his
famous article 'We must see the War Through, but
denounce Secret Diplomacy'.[30] Although Jowett's
position on the war, as with the stance adopted by
Hardie, often appeared ambiguous and at odds with
the ILP's declared opposition to the war, he was
categorical in his wish to see it speedily concluded
in favour of the allies. This point is illuminated
by his comment on the anti-war resolution passed at
the 1916 ILP Conference, of which he was chairman,
'The I.L.P. resolution to which you refer only
expressed the view that Socialist Parties
as organised bodies should support no war. It did
not attempt to lay down such a policy for individuals. If it did I should be opposed to it in
principle'.[31] Such semantics confused Jowett's
critics and permitted him to both support and oppose
the war by turns.
   Such equivocation found widespread support
throughout the West Yorkshire textile district.
Many leading ILP figures who were formally committed to peace found the First World War to be the
exception which proved the rule. The Rev. R.
Roberts who, as already indicated, was taking up
the 'Fiery Cross' against militarism in early 1914
was a converted man by the middle of August 1914,
and argued that the legend of 'blood and iron' had
to be shattered unless Socialism wished to be set
back for generations.[32] He later elaborated:

> Through 40 years of public life, I have
> preached peace ... I have never believed hum-
> anity would so far break down as to make it
> necessary to pay the extreme price of waging
> a war to preserve the peace. Yet, for my
> sins, I have lived to see that ... We are
> threatened with the ruin of civilized society.
> The success of Prussia in the awful tussle for
> life means that humanity will sink in smoking
> ruin.
>   In the first what is our duty as a
> British people? We must fight the battle to
> a truimphant finish. At whatever cost of life
> and treasure we must fight (I cannot tell the

> pain it cost me to write that sentence. I
> never thought I should live to do it) ...
> Better to die than be Prussianised. Better to
> be wiped off the face of the earth than to
> exist squealing and squirming under the
> Prussian jack boots.[33]

Roberts's conversion reflects the difficulties
which the 'Anglo-German War' or 'European War'
imposed upon ILP and Labour Party organisations in
West Yorkshire. For instance, the Sowerby Division
Labour Representation Committee, which had been
formed in April 1908 as the Labour Party organisation for the division, does not appear to have
expressed a clear viewpoint on the war until May
1915 when it urged the Labour Party to oppose conscription 'unless it is accompanied by the conscription of all the material wealth of the country'.[34] For the rest of the war it protested against conscription and increasingly veered towards the
peace initiative of 1917. It declared its intention
to send representatives to the August 1917 Workers
and Soldiers' Council Conference in Leeds, organised in the wake of the earlier June conference,
although that conference was subsequently abandoned.[35]
It is hardly surprising that there was political fragmentation within the Labour movement and
some obfuscation about the ILP's precise position
on the war, given that Labour organisations were
not always unequivocal about the war and that many
ILPers did fight at the front. The claim to individual rights of opinion, as opposed to the collective will of the ILP, does appear to have led to
further confusion but this confusion does not
appear to have unduly damaged the ILP position in
West Yorkshire or to have weakened the bond with
the trade unions, and thus the working classes.

The trade union movement in West Yorkshire appears
to have been similarly divided over the war. We
have already stressed that the Halifax Trades Council co-operated in the war effort, goaded on by
James Parker and Arthur Taylor. The General Union
of Textile Workers, later to become the National
Union of Textile Workers, was led by Ben Turner,
Mayor of Batley and supporter of Belgium independence. There was also some ambivalance over the
fact that whilst the Socialist leaders of the Textile Workers' Union might deprecate the events
which led to war there were clear advantages in

terms of employment and wage rises for their
members.[36] The <u>Yorkshire Factory Times</u> also remained neutral projecting both the pro-war views of
Jessie Cockerline and the anti-war sentiments of
'Sweeper Up'. The importation of national trade
union leaders to help in local recruiting campaigns,
as occurred when Jimmy Thomas, of the National
Union of Railwaymen, helped out in the Wakefield
Recruiting Campaign in October 1914 served to divide sympathies further.[37]

These problems are reflected in the difficulties faced by the Bradford trade union movement and
the Bradford Trades Council. The First World War
caught the Trades Council in a quandary. On the
one hand, in November 1912, it had passed a resolution calling for a general stoppage in the event
of an outbreak of war.[38] On the other hand, it was
evident from the outset that many members of the
Trades Council were smitten by patriotic sentiments
when the war began. As a result of this imbroglio
the Trades Council permitted itself to drift with
events. Its commitments to international peace and
the International Socialist Bureau were forgotten.
It generally followed the Labour Party policy of
working with the Government and the authorities to
encourage recruitment; although there were occasional decorous statements from its officials and
delegates about the need to secure a peace as
quickly as possible. In general, the Trades Council
spent the early years of the war dealing with the
practical realities of living under war conditions.
In 1914 and 1915 the main activity of the Council
was to check upon famine prices and food stuff
shortages. This activity later gave way to Anti-
Rent Raising campaigns, the raising of money through
the Lord Mayor's Relief Fund, and to its involvement
in the activities of the Joint Food Vigilance Committee, alongside the ILP, BSP and WMF. Perhaps
the Council's most emotive campaign of the practical
type was its attempt to force the Government to
accept responsibility for providing pensions to war
widows and weekly relief and benefits to soldiers
and sailors injured in the fighting. All these
campaigns reflect the day to day functioning of the
Trades Council.[39] But the Trades Council was also
a litmus-paper to the changing mood of the Bradford
working class to the war.

From the start there was a sizeable minority
of delegates on the Trades Council who opposed war.
The leaders of this group were George Licence,
Charlie Glyde and J.W. Ormanroyd. The anti-war

sentiments of Fred Jowett, expressed in the Year
Book for 1914, also tugged the heartstrings of many
delegates, although he was subsequently equivocal
about the war. [40] Yet the silent majority gave their
tacit approval to the war effort, and activists,
such as Alderman J.H. Palin, went to fight in France
alongside Bradford ILPers and trade unionists. [41]
By 1916 and 1917, however, the attitude of the
Council was beginning to change.

The threat of military and industrial conscription, first discussed in 1915, was pivotal in changing the attitude of the Trades Council, although
several other issues conflated to compound the
shift in thinking. In June 1915 the Trades Council
passed a resolution opposing conscription 'in any
form, military and industrial, and urged Parliament
to offer their utmost opposition to any proposal
to impose upon the British people a yoke which is
one of the chief concerns of Prussion militarism'. [42]
This was partly a reaction to the Munitions Act of
1915, which had suspended trade union rights and
prevented vital workers from moving from job to job
without a certificate of approval from their employer but also a response to the threat of military
conscription. The Trades Council delegates began
to drift away from supporting the TUC Parliamentary
Committee's circular calling for trade union help
in army recruitment and, in a series of votes and
a ballot in 1915 and 1916, indicated its withdrawal
from army recruitment campaigns. A vote of delegates towards the end of 1915 produced an equal
number of votes for and against the recruiting campaign. [43] A Trades Council circular to affiliated
trade unions in December 1915, requesting the opinions of societies to the recruiting campaign was
voted upon by just over one-third of the societies
and produced a result of 19 societies for and 11
against, though those unions in favour only represented 6,757 members compared to the 11,157 members
of those unions opposing the recruitment campaign.
Many small societies did not vote on the issue
and three abstained. [44] Yet although the vote was
inconclusive the introduction of conscription
led to the Trades Council's withdrawal from direct
involvement in helping army recruitment.

The anti-war section of the Trades Council
drew strongly from the opposition to conscription,
though this did not necessarily signify opposition
to the war. The Trades Council pressured the
Yorkshire Federation of Trades Councils to hold a
No-Conscription Conference at the Textile Hall,

Bradford in December 1915 and January 1916. It also
sent delegates to an ILP No-Conscription Conference
at Leeds.[45] As the 1916 Annual Report indicates,
there were still 'differences of opinion on the
war', but it is also clear that the anti-war position was burgeoning in the Council's meetings.

William Leach, editor of the Bradford Pioneer,
was permitted to present the views of the Union of
Democratic Control to the Trades Council, and in
September 1915 the Council affiliated to the UDC.[46]
By 1916 it was possible to organise a Peace Conference under Trades Council auspices. That conference decisively condemned Labour MPs for joining
the Government and pushed strongly for peace negotiations.[47] The Trades Council also sent delegates to the Leeds Conference in June 1917, at
which the Workers' and Soldiers' Council was formed,
in the hope of forcing forward the demand for international peace negotiations.[48]

By 1917 the Trades Council was increasingly
being dominated by, what Palin dubbed, 'militant
pacifists'. The 'peace movement' was prevalent
within the Trades Council, though there was still a
substantial commitment to the war effort by some of
the affiliated unions. Many of those Bradford
trade unions who became committed to the Peace campaign of 1917 were not so much pacifists, or even
opponents of the war, so much as opponents of the
Government's military conscription policy. The
imprisonment of Revis Barber, the son of Walter
Barber who was the Secretary of the Trades Council,
as a conscientious objector did much to win trade
union support for the 'peace movement'.[49] Thus by
the end of the war, Bradford had become one of the
centres of the anti-war movement.

The experiences of the Bradford Trades Council
may not have been repeated in every West Yorkshire
trades council, nor in all the major unions, but
the general pattern of events was not unusual. In
some areas, such as Huddersfield, the Trades Council appears to have established a much closer relationship with bodies which opposed conscription
and aimed at protecting civil liberties than was the
case in Bradford. After some early ambivalance over
the war, the Huddersfield Trades and Labour Council
was in the thick of the activities which led to the
formation of the Huddersfield and District No-
Conscription Council in January 1916. This new
anti-war organisation was in fact formed at a meeting
in the Friendly and Trades Societies Club, and
Alfred Shaw, of the Trades Council, was in the

chair.[50] Moreover, the Trades Council had actually
called the meeting. Along with the ILP and the
BSP, the Huddersfield Trades Council campaigned
against military conscription within the No-Conscription Council, sent a representative to the
Workers and Soldiers' Council Conference of June
1917 and helped to form a local branch of the Workers and Soldiers' Council in Huddersfield.[51] It
also appears to have formed the Huddersfield and
District Council for Civil Liberties, in place of
the No-Conscription Council, towards the end of 1918
- the officers of both organisations being practically one and the same.[52]
     Several points emerge about the attitude of
trade unions towards the war. The first is that the
attitude of the trade union movement was less del-
phic than that of the ILP. Trade unions, on the
whole, appear to have supported the war effort in
the first two years before giving way to the peace
initiative during the last two years. This was the
case in Halifax, Bradford and Huddersfield. Secondly, it is clear that whilst the national trade
union leaders generally campaigned for the war
effort their influence was to some extent countered
by the strong local associations between the ILP
and the trade union movement. The impact of the
latter was not always immediate, and the attitude
of ILP leaders towards the war was often ambivalent,
but one must remember that many of the local ILP
leaders, Fred Jowett for instance, were active
trade unionists. Thirdly, the war does not appear
to have unduly injured relations between the ILP
and trade unions in West Yorkshire. There was no
parting of the way as a result of the war. Rather,
we would suggest that other factors led the Labour
Party to replace the ILP as the vehicle of working-
class aspirations in West Yorkshire. Indeed, by
1917 and 1918 the strong emphasis in favour of
peace negotiations was being supported by the ILP
and trade unions alike.

Anti-war sentiments reached their climax in West
Yorkshire in the ill-fated Workers' and Soldiers'
Council Conference which was held at Leeds in June
1917. Amongst the 1,150 delegates who attended the
Conference on 3 June 1917 were many members of the
West Yorkshire Labour movement.[53] Most of the
West Yorkshire trades council, ILP and Labour Party,
organisations were represented. The Leeds Labour
Party decided to attend by 75 votes to 15, the
Leeds Trades Council by the much narrower margin of

37 votes to 30. The Bradford and Halifax trades councils and ILP organisations also attended.[54] Prominent West Yorkshire figures such as Fred Jowett MP and Fred Shaw were present, and Jowett and Joe Fineberg, both of Bradford, were appointed as members of the Central Committee of the Council of Workers' and Soldiers' Delegates.[55]

The conference was the confluence of a number of political tributaries. Its origins are to be found partly in the failure of the British Socialist Party to secure a mass following before the First World War. By 1913 the BSP, under the leadership of H.M. Hyndman, had decided to apply for affiliation to the Labour Party and to establish a United Socialist Council with the ILP and the Fabians.[56] Although the formation of the United Socialist Council had been announced with a fanfare of political demonstrations and meetings organised by the ILP and the BSP, it was quickly shelved as the pro-war stance of the Hyndman-dominated BSP clashed with the more anti-war attitudes of the ILP. It was only the defeat of the Hyndmanite section of the BSP, and the success of the international Socialist section, which permitted the Council to be resurrected as the basis of the Workers' and Soldiers' Council and the Leeds Conference. The immediate context of this resurrection was, of course, the Russian Revolution in March 1917, which symbolised the meeting of revolutionaries and reformists, and raised the prospect of moves towards an international peace settlement. But this event would have been of little significance had there not also been a general desire for peace, which the Spen Valley Trades Council delegate to the Leeds Conference, reflected when he reported that the working class was 'sick and tired of the war and thought it was time it ended'.[57]

The events, speeches and the resolutions of the Leeds Conference are legion. The four resolutions passed by the Conference - hailing the Russian Revolution, advocating moves towards establishing a general peace 'based on the rights of nations to decide their own affairs', demanding the establishment of a charter of liberties by the British Government and the establishment of Councils of Workmen and Soldiers' Delegates in every town, urban and rural district - were traducingly represented as threatening revolution in Britain by the majority of the national and local press. In reality, of course, this was not the view projected by the majority of those present at the conference.

Indeed, the failure of the movement to establish Workers' and Soldiers' Councils throughout the country indicates this not to have been the case.

The Workers' and Soldiers' Council failed to sustain much interest in West Yorkshire. The reasons for this failure are fairly obvious. In the first place, the conference strongly supported the move towards democratic and civil rights which was occurring in Russia, only to find that commitment undermined by the Bolshevik Revolution in November 1917. But even before the Bolshevik Revolution the aims and objectives of the Leeds Conference had been challenged.

By mid-July 1917 the Labour Party had declared that none of its branches should have anything to do with Workers' and Soldiers' councils.[58] But even before this occurred doubts had been expressed at the efficacy of the putative organisation. Many of the delegates who attended as trade union and trades council representatives were immediately doubtful of the value of the conference. Even before the conference was held, the Leeds Labour Party had expressed its support for the first three resolutions but had refused to support the fourth resolution, setting up Workers' and Soldiers' councils throughout the country. These embryonic soviets were rejected by the Labour Party organisations before the Conference and by trade unionists after the Conference.

The main concern of trade unionists appears to have been that the Workers' and Soldiers' Council organisation might challenge their hegemony in organising workers. Returning from the Leeds Conference, the President of the Halifax Trades Council, G. Kaye, reported his disquiet:

> He was not at all satisfied with the Conference. ... personally, he did not support the resolution of a Workmens' and Soldiers' Council, taking the view that the place for these people was in the Labour and Socialist movement and that if multiple organisations were formed there was a great risk of wasting energy on side issues. The conference ought to be followed up by something on the lines of drastic and revolutionary action. His faith lay in the organised industrial workers, backed up by political action if they liked.[59]

When an attempt was made to set up a District Organisation of the Workers' and Soldiers' Council

in West Yorkshire in the autumn of 1917, the Leeds
Trades Council rejected the move for similar reasons to those referred to by Kaye. It was unani-
mously resolved that the propaganda work of the
Soldiers' Council 'can and will be done best by the
existing Labour organisations'.[60]

Most other trade unions and Labour organisations in West Yorkshire seem to have taken a similar
view. Indeed, the Workers' and Soldiers' Council
movement waned so quickly that the editor of the
Yorkshire Factory Times reported at the end of 1917
that 'he had been 'wondering for a considerable
time' what had occurred 'in connection with the
great conference held in Leeds ... Somehow or other
it does not seem to have gripped the public'.[61]
The fact was that the Leeds Conference, and its
resolutions, had been largely rejected by the organised Labour movement.

The failure of the Workers' and Soldiers'
Council movement, both at the national and local
level, had much to do with the internal struggles
and demarcation disputes within the Labour movement. Yet there was some outside pressure upon
events. The national and local press generally
reported upon the Leeds Conference with undisguised
hostility. In addition, there were attempts to
undermine the peace campaign by bodies such as the
British Workers' League, the Socialist National
Defence Committee and the British Empire League.

The British Empire League had sent its representatives to Leeds to prevent the Conference
being held in Albert Hall, and succeeded.[62] The
Socialist National Defence Committee, a patriotic
group of Socialists, threatened to put forward
parliamentary candidates against ILP/Labour Party
candidates who opposed the War. One of the notable
figures in this organisation was Joseph Burgess,
who had had a long association with the ILP since
his newspaper, The Workman's Times, had been responsible for paving the way for the Bradford ILP
Conference of 1893. Burgess had worked in Lancashire and London for many years before coming to
live in Bradford prior to the First World War. He
was editor of the Bradford Pioneer until the
summer of 1915, and was elected as President of the
Bradford ILP branch. Though Burgess had initially
criticised British involvement in the war, pro-
claiming that 'We have no quarrel with Germany', he
had radically altered his position by the summer
of 1915 and had joined the Socialist National
Defence Committee.[63] The Bradford ILP was very

sensitive to the antics of a man who had so recently
been at the centre of its activities. Not surprisingly, the pages of the Bradford Pioneer were filled
with letters and articles in connection with what
became known as the 'Burgess Comedy'.[64]
    Yet it was the British Workers' League which
posed the biggest threat to the peace campaign in
West Yorkshire. Formed to unite patriotic trade
unionists in the war effort, this organisation
quickly found itself in vitriolic exchanges with
the ILP. A. Howarth, of the BWL, said that 'Bradford
had disgraced itself more than any other town in
the country', whilst Victor Fisher, Secretary of
the BWL, announced to a Bradford audience that
'Sinister pacifism is more rampant in your midst
than in any other part of the United Kingdom with
the exception of the Clyde and South Wales'.[65] It
is hardly surprising then that the League should
form a Bradford branch towards the end of July
1917.[66] This event in itself was probably not that
significant and would have almost gone unnoticed
had it not been for the fact that E.R. Hartley, a
noted Bradford Socialist who, as we have already
stressed was connected with the Dewsbury controversy of 1901 and 1902, was appointed as the organising secretary of the BWL in the Bradford area.
Hartley was a powerful orator and a much-respected
figure in the Bradford area but his death in early
1918 must have robbed the BWL of some of its
impetus.[67]
    Despite the efforts of the numerous organisa-
tions which proliferated in the attempt to arrest
the development of the 'peace campaign', it is
clear that the major reasons for the disintegration
of the peace movement was more to do with the internal dissension within the Labour movement than
outside pressure. What is equally evident is that
the war as such does not appear to have distanced
the working classes in West Yorkshire from the political Labour movement. Yet there were political
changes occurring within the West Yorkshire Labour
organisation.

Much attention has been focused upon the fact that
the Liberal Party splintered during the war and
that a section, sometimes known as the '1918 Liberals', joined the ILP and the Labour Party.[68] The
best example of such a defector in West Yorkshire
is C.P. Trevelyan, Liberal MP for Elland between
1899 and 1918, who, through his work with the Union
of Democratic Control moved into the Labour camp,

en route to becoming a Labour Education Minister
during the inter-war years. Yet whilst this drift
from Liberalism to Labour was important it is also
clear that, in West Yorkshire at least, there was
a similar drift by trade unionists from the ILP to
the Labour Party.

Such a switch was, of course not entirely new
or totally unexpected. The Labour Party had effectively replaced the Liberal Party as the real
fulcrum of Labour politics in Leeds before 1914.
Yet in Bradford and Halifax, the main centres of
ILP strength in West Yorkshire, there were no Labour Party organisations as such before the war.
The ILP organisations ruled supreme in Labour politics.

What the war did was to undermine the established links between the ILP and trade unions.
Whilst it is true that both the ILP and trade unions
were divided on the issue of supporting the war
effort, it is equally true that many pre-war ILP
stalwarts, such as J.H. Palin and Michael Conway of
the Bradford ILP, turned their attention to the
Labour Party. In addition the ILP took in a significant number of anti-war Liberals who, by their
very prominence, brought about an increasing div-
orce of the ILP and the working classes. Some of
these ex-Liberals had more in common with the
middle-class pacifist strand of the ILP than with
the average working-class trade union member of the
party.[69] This dichotomy was undoubtedly hardened
with the return of many young male members of the
ILP from the war.

Thus World War One had profound consequences
for the Bradford ILP and served to disturb the long-
established relationship between the ILP and the
trade union movement. The war had had an unsettling
effect upon the alliance. But it was other factors
which led the trade union movement to sever its
traditional links with the ILP in West Yorkshire.

Ross McKibbin has amply demonstrated that the
new Labour Party Constitution of 1918, in enhancing
the control of the trade union movement within the
Executive at the expense of the more middle-class
dominated Socialist societies, created tensions
between the ILP, which was opposed to the new Constitution and the trade unions, who benefited most
from it.[70] In addition it paved the way for the
formation of new local Labour parties throughout
the country to which local trades councils became
affiliated. This transference of allegiance from
the ILP to the local Labour parties did much to

undermine the ILP in Bradford and Halifax.

The ILP had run Labour politics in Bradford since the 1890s. During the 1890s it had dominated the political activities of the Labour movement in association with the Trades Council. From 1902 onwards it had shared the control of Bradford Labour politics with the Trades Council and the Workers' Municipal Federation, a body which had been formed to bring non-Socialist trade unionists more directly into Labour politics.[71] From 1907 the Joint Committee of the ILP and WMF made local political arrangements for the Bradford Labour movement.[72] But in 1918 the basis of that alliance was altered. Bradford was to be re-organised into four parliamentary divisions, instead of three, under the Representation of the People's Act, and a Local Labour Conference was held in November 1917 to discuss the changes.[73] At this Conference representatives of the ILP, trade unions and co-operative societies agreed to contest all four seats at the coming general election and formed a committee of twelve representatives to discuss the selection of candidates. However, also out of this committee, and its deliberations throughout 1918, sprang the decision to hold a Conference on the Formation of a Central Labour Party for Bradford in the September.[74] A further committee of eleven representatives was set up to draft a constitution and the Bradford Labour Party officially came into existence on 5 April 1919, formally uniting the ILP, the Trades Council and the WMF into one Labour organisation for the first time.[75] This move was to prove the undoing of the Bradford ILP whose importance within local politics began to diminish in the 1920s as the Bradford Labour Party increasingly became the focus of Labour politics.

The Bradford ILP never fully recovered from the traumas imposed by the war and the developments within the wider Labour Movement during and after the war. It was already conscious that its prominence even within the national ILP organisations was under threat well before the end of the war. It launched the 'Bradford ILP Forward Movement' in 1918, pointing to the countrywide growth of the ILP and the tremendous steps forward which had been made in Leicester and Scotland.

Halifax, the other ILP stronghold in West Yorkshire, experienced a similar fate. James Parker the ILP/Labour Party MP cut across many ILP members by actively participating in the recruiting campaigns during the war. This created dissension

within the Halifax ILP and the Trades Council,
which whilst it intially supported recruiting,
gradually drifted away from that stance, much as
the Bradford Trades Council had done. The disor-
ientation within Labour ranks appears to have been
such that (in the general elections of 1918, 1922,
1923 and 1924) this once powerful Labour centre was
unable to find a candidate to put forward for the
single Halifax seat left by the 1918 Franchise Act.
An unenterprising Labour Party took over from a
declining ILP in 1918 and it was not until the 1928
parliamentary by-election that a Labour candidate,
A.W. Longbottom, stood again and was swept into Parliament.[76] The war, the formation of the Halifax
Labour Party, plus the fact that the Halifax MP,
J.W. Whitley, became Speaker of the House of Commons
in 1921, help to account for the decline of the
Halifax ILP and the initial political hesitancy of
the new Labour Party.

The War clearly had an impact upon West Yorkshire
Labour politics. In 1914 the ILP, despite some
competition for support from the Labour Party,
still carried substantial political weight, particularly in its old-established centres such as
Bradford and Halifax. But the Labour Party had
made deep encroachments into working-class support
in Leeds and many other parts of the West Yorkshire
area which had only really experienced Labour
stirrings with the formation of the LRCs and early
local Labour parties. By 1918, however, the war
had unhinged what had remained of ILP strength by
creating confusion and some detachment between ILP
organisations and their trade-union supporters.
But the war was only one ingredient in the changing
shape of Labour's political organisation in West
Yorkshire. The emergence of a new Labour Constitution in 1918, and the proliferation of new constituency Labour Parties, gradually undermined the
position of the ILP. It is perhaps no wonder that
many ILPers, including Fred Jowett, began to question the need to continue with the ILP.[77] This
anguish which both the national and West Yorkshire
ILP organisations faced over whether or not to
continue as separate organisations from the Labour
Party is indicative of the fact that the ILPers had
come to recognise the fundamental switch of alleg-
iances that had occurred. The end product of this
change is that, despite the fact that the Labour
Constitution included a commitment to the ownership
of the means of production, the trade unions and

the working classes now attached themselves to an
essentially Labour rather than Socialist organisation. R. McKibbin had it about right when he argued that the 1918 Labour Constitution plus the
1918 Franchise Act, which greatly increased the size
of the electorate, led to the Labour Party truly
becoming the party of the working classes and that
class loyalty inhibited Socialist doctrine within
the Labour Party.78
    If West Yorkshire Labour politics became less
overtly Socialist after 1918 than it was before
1914 that does not mean that it was any less successful. The 'coupon' election of December 1918
was extremely disappointing to Labour, with only
one unopposed Labour candidate being returned for
the 23 West Yorkshire constituencies which had just
been reformed.   Yet, despite its problems, the
Labour Party had weathered the war rather better
than the Liberals, had enhanced its working-class
support, and was clearly to be seen as the liber-
ating force for the working classes in the future.
The ILP, which figured prominently in shaping
Labour politics before 1914, was left to dwell upon
the role of Socialists inside, and outside, the
Labour Party.

NOTES

    1. Trevor Wilson, The Downfall of the Liberal
Party, p. 29.
    2. Yorkshire Observer Budget, 13 Apr. 1914.
    3. Bradford Trades and Labour Council,
Minutes, 7 Nov. 1912.
    4. Photocopies of newscuttings, normally
without date or source, from A. Gardiner's scrapbook. Copies are held by Dr. K. Laybourn.
    5. Roberts joined the ILP in the mid 1890s,
was a member of the Bradford School Board, along
with Margaret McMillan, between 1897 and 1903, but
left the ILP in 1903 due to its unwillingness to
co-operate with the Liberals. He drifted back to
the Labour ranks on the eve of the First World War.
    6. Bradford Pioneer, 9 Jan. 1914.
    7. Georges Haupt, Socialism and the Great
War: The Collapse of the Second International
(Oxford University Press, London, 1972), pp. 195-
215.
    8. Bradford Pioneer, 9 Jan. 1914.
    9. Cross, Philip Snowden, p. 129.
    10. Bradford Labour Echo, 23 Nov. 1895; Brad-
ford Daily Telegraph, 4 Oct. 1912; Bradford Pioneer,

25 Jan. 1918; K. Laybourn, 'The Defence of Bottom Dog: The Independent Labour Party in Local Politics', pp. 234-5.

11. Bradford Pioneer, 22 Oct. 1915.

12. Ibid., 26 Oct. 1917.

13. Ibid., 19 Apr. 1918.

14. Bradford Daily Telegraph, 30 Dec. 1918.

15. Bradford Pioneer, 14 Aug. 1914.

16. Yorkshire Factory Times, 27 Aug. 1914.

17. Bradford Pioneer, 28 Apr. 1916.

18. Dr. Hector Munro took the first Volunteer Motor Ambulance Corps to the front and a Dr. Munro Fund was formed to provide financial help for this unit.   See the Bradford Pioneer, 8, 15 Jan. 1915.

19. Bradford Pioneer, 25 Feb. 1916.

20. Ibid., 1 Mar. 1918.

21. Yorkshire Factory Times, 8 Oct. 1914.

22. ILP Archive, Francis Johnson Collection, 1915/72.

23. Yorkshire Factory Times, 3 Sep. 1914.

24. Ibid., 12 Nov. 1914.

25. Bradford Pioneer, 9 Apr. 1915.

26. Ibid., 2 Jun. 1916.

27. Brockway, Socialism over Sixty Years, p. 152.

28. Bradford Pioneer, 2 Jun. 1916.

29. Ibid., 2 Jun. 1916, 13 Apr. 1917.

30. Republished from the Merthyr Pioneer, in the Bradford Pioneer, 21 Apr. 1914.

31. Bradford Pioneer, 2 Jun. 1916.

32. Ibid., 14 Aug. 1914.

33. Ibid., 16 Oct. 1914.

34. Sowerby Division Labour Representation Association, Calderdale Archives Collection, TU 51/ 1, Minutes, 1 May 1915.

35. Ibid., 29 Jul. 1917.

36. Jowitt and Laybourn, 'The Wool Textile Dispute of 1925', pp. 11-12.

37. Yorkshire Factory Times, 29 Oct. 1914.

38. Bradford Trades and Labour Council, Minutes, 7 Nov. 1912.

39. Ibid., 15 Jan., 13 Feb., 8 Nov., 1915.

40. Bradford Trades and Labour Council, Year Book, 1914 (Bradford Trades Council, Bradford, 1915).

41. Bradford Trades and Labour Council. Minutes, 8 Feb. 1917. Palin took up his duties in France on 12 Feb. 1917.

42. Bradford Trades and Labour Council, Minutes, 17 Jun. 1915.

43. Ibid., 5 Nov. 1915.

44. Ibid., 10 Dec. 1915.

45. Ibid., 8 Nov., 9 Dec., 1915; 3 Jan. 1916.

46. Ibid., 9 Sep. 1915.

47. Ibid., 7, 30 Dec. 1916, 9 Jan. 1917.

48. Ibid., May and Jun. 1917.

49. Ibid., 29 Nov. 1917.

50. Huddersfield and District No-Conscription Council, Inaugural Meeting, 16 Jan. 1916. Deposited in the Polytechnic Library, Huddersfield.

51. Ibid., 2 Jul. 1917.

52. Huddersfield and District Council for Civil Liberties, 6 Aug. 1918. Deposited in the Polytechnic Library, Huddersfield.

53. British Labour and the Russian Revolution: The Leeds Convention: a report from the Daily Herald, with an Introduction by Ken Coates (Spokesman Books, no place or date of publication given), p. 18.

54. Yorkshire Factory Times, 7, 14 Jun. 1917.

55. British Labour and the Russian Revolution, p. 18.

56. Ibid., pp. 6-7.

57. Bradford Pioneer, 8 Jun. 1917.

58. Stephen White, 'Soviets in Britain: The Leeds Convention of 1917', International Review of Social History, vol. XIX (1974), Part 2, pp. 165-93.

59. Yorkshire Factory Times, 14 Jul. 1917.

60. White, 'Soviets in Britain', p. 191.

61. Yorkshire Factory Times, 13 Dec. 1917.

62. Ibid., 7 Jun. 1917.

63. Bradford Pioneer, 7 Aug. 1914, 30 Jul, 29 Dec. 1916; Cross, Philip Snowden, p. 166.

64. Bradford Pioneer, 8 Dec. 1916.

65. Bradford Weekly Telegraph, 9 Nov. 1917; Bradford Pioneer, 13 Jul. 1917.

66. Bradford Pioneer, 27 Jul. 1917.

67. Ibid., 25 Jan. 1918.

68. Bernard Barker, 'The Anatomy of Reform: The Social and Political Ideas of the Labour Leadership in Yorkshire', International Review of Social History, vol. xviii (1973), Part 1, pp. 1-27.

69. Ibid.,

70. McKibbin, The Evolution of the Labour Party 1910-1924, pp. 91-106.

71. Workers' Municipal Federation, Minute Books, 1902-16, in the Bradford Trades and Labour Council Collection, Archives, Bradford Central Library.

72. Ibid., 4 Mar. 1907.

73. Bradford Trades and Labour Council, Minutes, 15 Nov. 1917.

74. Ibid., 14 Sep. 1918.
75. Bradford Pioneer, 11 Apr. 1919.
76. Ibid., 29 Mar. 1918.
77. R.E. Dowse, Left in the Centre (Longman, London, 1966), pp. 35-48.
78. McKibbin, The Evolution of the Labour Party 1910-1924, pp. 236-47.

CONCLUSION

David Howell has noted, in his book <u>British Workers</u>
<u>and the Independent Labour Party 1888-1906</u>, that
the course of early Labour history was indirect
and that each community varied in its response to
the emergence of the ILP.[1] The varied industrial
structures of communities, the role of individual
trade union leaders, the extent to which the paternalism of industrial masters was prevalent, all
helped to ensure different patterns of Labour development. This varied pattern was particularly evident in West Yorkshire where the variety of products
manufactured by the woollen, worsted and engineering
industries supported a variety of local industrial
experiences. The Labour movement in Bradford, dominated by the production of worsted and fancy dress
woollen goods, which gave rise to much female employment, was different in some respects from the
experience of the Halifax Labour movement where the
male-dominated engineering industry of Halifax was
as important as the woollen industry in the local
economy. The experiences of the industrial communities also differed widely from that of more rural
communities such as Colne Valley, giving rise to a
different type of Labour movement. But what gave
this rather amorphous West Yorkshire Labour movement
a recognisable form was the growing involvement of
trade unionism and the increasing direction given
by the national Labour leadership.

  It was trade unionism which underpinned the
burgeoning Labour movement in West Yorkshire. The
ILP's capture of many trades councils in the early
1890s paved the way for the extension of its influence amongst trade unions. Even in areas where
trade unionism was weak, as in Colne Valley, it is
clear that many of the leading local Labour politicians were in fact trade unionists. The only

Conclusion

difference between many Labour strongholds and
areas of patchy Labour support was the strength of
the local trade union movement. In areas where
trade unionism was firmly established and closely
linked with the ILP, as was the case in Bradford
and Halifax, powerful and effective political Labour organisations emerged. In other areas, where
trade unionism was weak and ineffective, or where
the ILP's trade-union links were not widely established, the ILP and Socialist organisations proved
to be less resilient, prone to bouts of frenzied
political activity followed by lengthy periods of
inactivity in the wake of political adversity. This
latter case was particularly evident in Keighley,
and even Colne Valley, despite the return of Victor
Grayson in the 1907 parliamentary by-election,
before the First World War.

The intrusion of Keir Hardie, Ramsay MacDonald,
Philip Snowden, and other members of the Labour
leadership, into the affairs of the local Labour
parties in West Yorkshire, whilst it was much resented, did help to temper the unrealistic political
ambitions of some organisations and to harbour resources for more effective action in the future.
These Labour leaders were able to direct the affairs
of the ILP and the Labour Party by the control they
exercised over the NAC of the ILP and the NEC of
the Labour Party, and by their control over what
was discussed at both ILP and Labour Party conferences. In addition their access to national funds
to support parliamentary contests made their wishes
insuperable to the majority of local Labour organisations. It is evident that in the conflicts
associated with the candidatures for the Leeds
seats, Keighley and Colne Valley, that the Labour
leadership was attempting to exert its will,
couched in terms of the needs of national responsibility, the desire to nurture trade-union support
and, for MacDonald particularly, the need to establish and preserve some type of Progressive Alliance
with Liberalism.

By allying itself with trade unionism, and by
deferring Socialism for a later date, the ILP organisations in West Yorkshire secured increasing political success. From the 1890s to 1906 they made
many local political gains. In 1906 they secured
two parliamentary representatives, to which was
added a third by the Colne Valley by-election of
1907. The euphoria of success was only briefly
tempered by the improvement in some Liberal organisations after 1906 and the local political

204

alliances which Liberal organisations struck up
with the Tories, and from 1910 onwards the ILP and
the Labour Party swiftly eroded the local political
power base of West Yorkshire Liberalism. By the
First World War it was clear that the Liberal Party
was incapable of arresting Labour's growth in West
Yorkshire.

The continued domination of old Liberal ideas
in West Yorkshire, based upon the views of a small
number of industrial magnates, made it difficult
for the Liberals to respond to the Labour challenge.
Whilst an increasing proportion of the working
class were demanding social reforms and collective
action the Liberal· Party remained firmly individual-
istic in its opinions, unwilling to contemplate the
extension of the powers and responsibilities of
the state and local authorities. They preferred,
for instance, to recouch charity by the formation of
guilds of help and proved to be hostile to reforms
such as municipal school feeding. There is little
evidence that their views were tempered by the more
collectivist new-Liberal ideas which were emerging,
though there were some new Liberals in West Yorkshire and though there is some evidence that a
Progressive Alliance operating in Halifax to return
James Parker as MP in 1906. Faced with the obdurate old-Liberal attitudes of most West Yorkshire
Liberal organisations many working-class voters
transferred their political allegiance to the ILP
and the Labour Party.

By 1918 the Labour Party had effectively replaced the Liberal Party as the representative of
the working classes, becoming the vehicle for the
realisation of working-class aspirations. It is
clear that the transferrence of the working-class
vote from the Liberal Party to the Labour Party in
West Yorkshire was only accomplished as a result of
the alliance of trade unions with Labour's political
organisations, and many ILP members would have
concurred with W.H. Drew's image of the ILP and trade unionism as being two aspects of a single homogeneous Labour movement aimed at the emancipation
of the working classes from poverty and exploitation.[2] That alliance ensured that the established
two-party system would have been cracked in West
Yorkshire even if there had been no First World War.

NOTES

1. Howell, British Workers and the Independent
Labour Party 1888-1906, pp. 277-82.

2.   <u>Bradford Labour Echo</u>, 1 Jun. 1895.

EPILOGUE

The inter-war years saw the continued decline of
Liberalism in West Yorkshire. Whilst the Liberal
Party was able to hold on to more than half the parliamentary seats in West Yorkshire at the 1918 General Election it had entered its fissiparous years,
and its parliamentary performance was largely achieved as a result of the support of Conservative
votes for Coalition Liberal candidates. Only one of
the twelve Liberal MPs returned in 1918 was not a
Lloyd George Liberal. Once shorn of the Coalition
Alliance, the Liberal Party in West Yorkshire quickly disintegrated. By the late 1920s and early
1930s the Liberal Party was unable to make much of
a parliamentary splash in the region, and its presence after the 1935 General Election was entirely
confined to three National Liberals, including Sir
John Simon, MP for Spen Valley, whose politics were
almost undistinguishable from those of the Conser-
vative-dominated National Government. The pre-1914
Liberal Party barely survived in West Yorkshire
outside a few local, and isolated, pockets of support in areas such as Hunslet, Huddersfield, Bradford South, and Colne Valley. Even here, the return of Liberal councillors was more of interest as
an historical curiosity than as an augury for the
much vaunted Liberal revival.

The fact is that the old support of the Liberal
Party was now divided between the Conservative and
Labour parties. Much of the old middle-class and
upper-working class vote had been captured by the
Conservatives and the vast majority of the working-
class votes had been secured by the Labour Party.
Not surprisingly, it was these two parties which
shared the major political honours of the inter-war
years. In parliamentary and municipal contests it
was they who dominated the two-party political

207

system and it is clear that, had it not been for the unusual circumstances of the 1931 General Election which returned the MacDonald National Government to power, West Yorkshire would have been regarded as a staunch Labour stronghold during the inter-war years.

Ironically, the ILP which had been responsible for the demise of West Yorkshire Liberalism was itself to become redundant. After the war many members had begun to question the need to continue with the party given that the Labour Party had acquired a Socialist programme. What kept many West Yorkshire members within the ILP was the sense of history and achievement which had surrounded its work. Their commitment was often more a symbolic gesture to the past than a demonstration of their faith that the ILP could continue to shape political events. The thinness of this commitment was demonstrated in the 'Disaffiliation Crisis' of 1932.

The immediate context of this crisis was the decision by the Parliamentary Labour Party to ensure that all Labour MPs pledged themselves to obey the Standing Orders of the party. This followed in the wake of MacDonald's defection to the National Government and could be seen as an attempt to ensure that there was party unity within Parliament. Jimmy Maxton and the ILP leadership saw the move in an entirely different light; regarding it as an attempt to restrict their freedom of expression. Since the political balance of the ILP had moved from Yorkshire and Lancashire to Scotland during the 1920s it is clear that Maxton, and his 'Clydeside' supporters were able to press for disaffiliation within the national movement. Their action was opposed throughout West Yorkshire.

The main critic of the campaign for disaffiliation was Willie Leach, a manufacturer and one-time employer of Fred Jowett, who found the whole idea of disaffiliation unacceptable and undesirable. In a powerful polemic he wrote that

> For some years the I.L.P. has been unhappily losing prestige and membership, due, I think, to two main causes. Firstly a disposition towards the belief that its work as a party was finished when the Labour Party adopted a Socialist programme and secondly because of the irreconcilable and foolish actions of some of its quarrelsome M.P.s. Vanities and disappointed ambitions have played their part. Besides all this the younger end have keenly

desired quicker speed and spectacular action.
Certain spectacular actions have, however,
served to bring discredit. Leadership has a
lot to answer for.
. . .
    I do not know the real will of the I.L.P.
membership. I find it very difficult to believe that a full party plebiscite on the
issue of disaffiliation would endorse the
views of Maxton and Co. I fear that branches
may pass disaffiliation resolutions at tiny
meetings where only the fiery element is in
attendance and decisions will be taken which
never would be taken on a proper plebiscite
vote of the whole membership.
. . .
MacDonald and Co. have gone East, the disaffiliation would go West. All the fruits of ill-
will, antagonism and open war are bound to
follow in both cases. It would be the most
melancholy situation that has ever yet arisen
in British Labour politics.
. . . Suppose the disaffiliationists win.
They will do so, as I think, on a minority
vote of the members. They will march into
the wilderness with less than half of the
membership. It is all very sad and discon-
certing.[1]

    The precise details of Leach's attack were
criticised by Fred Jowett, whose attitude towards
disaffiliation had initially been to oppose the
move but had become one of conditional affiliation.[2]
Since the condition was that the Labour Party should
drop its insistence upon imposing Standing Orders,
this effectively meant that Jowett was in favour of
disaffiliation. The conflict between the two pro-
tagonists was fought out in the press and at the
meetings of the Bradford ILP in July 1932.[3] The
Bradford ILP's Special Meeting favoured disaffiliation by the relatively narrow majority of 112 votes
to 86, and the Bradford Pioneer published an 'Open
Letter' to the delegates attending the ILP Special
Conference at Jowett Hall, Bradford, advising them
not to leave the Labour Party: 'The I.L.P. was born
in Bradford. Have you come to bury it'.[4]
    The decision of the National ILP to disaffil-
iate from the Labour Party was carried by Maxton,
Brockway, Jowett and the 'Suicide Squad', despite
the entreaties of Leach and the Bradford Pioneer.[5]
The events which followed emphasised the prophetic

nature of Leach's polemical article. The Bradford
ILP found difficulties in continuing to meet at
Jowett Hall, lost much financial support, and found
that only one of the 32 members of the Labour group
on Bradford City Council were prepared to leave the
Labour Party.[6] Both the West Yorkshire and the
national ILP organisations collapsed quickly in the
wake of the disaffiliation decision.

It is interesting that Fred Jowett, standing
as an ILP candidate, was unsuccessful in the Bradford East contest in the 1935 General Election,
whilst Willie Leach was returned as Labour MP for
Bradford Central. The fact is that the ILP collapsed as a result of the events of 1932. The Bradford
Pioneer was correct, in commenting on the decision
of the Special Conference, that

> The Independent Labour Party now joins the
> numerous small groups engaged in useless and
> obscure warfare against the organised Labour
> army. Along with the Communist Party, the
> Socialist Party of Great Britain and other
> eccentric groups quite unknown to the general
> public, the total sterility of a once great and
> influential party seems assured.[7]

After more than forty years in the political wilderness the ILP died as a political party in 1975.

NOTES

1. Bradford Pioneer, 8 Jul. 1932.
2. Ibid., 29 Jul. 1932.
3. Ibid., 8, 15, 22, 29 Jul. 1932.
4. Ibid., 29 Jul. 1932.
5. Ibid., 22 Jul. 1932.
6. Ibid., 5, 12 Aug. 1932.
7. Ibid., 5 Aug. 1932.

BIBLIOGRAPHY

Ashraf, M. Bradford Trades Council, 1872-1972 (Brad-
    ford Trades Council, Bradford, 1972)
Barker, B. 'The Anatomy of Reform: The Social and
    Political Ideas of the Labour Leadership in York-
    shire', International Review of Social History,
    vol. xviii (1973), Part 1, pp. 1-27
Bellamy, J. and Saville J. (eds) Dictionary of Lab-
    our Biography, vol. 3 (Macmillan, London, 1976)
    vol. 4 (Macmillan, London, 1977)
    vol. 6 (Macmillan, London, 1982)
Blewitt, N. 'The Franchise in the United Kingdom
    1885-1918', Past and Present, 32 (1965), pp. 27-56
Board of Trade, Report on Trade Unions, 1896
    (c.8644); Report on Trade Unions, 1900 (cd. 773)
Bradford Daily Telegraph
Bradford Labour Echo
Bradford Observer
Bradford Observer Budget
Bradford Pioneer
Bradford Review
Bradford Trades Council, Minutes, Archive Collec-
    tion, Bradford Central Library
———— Year Book for 1914 (Bradford Trades Council,
    Bradford, 1915)
———— Workers' Municipal Federation, Minute Book,
    1902-19, Archive Collection, Bradford Central
    Library
Bradford Typographical Society, Minutes and records,
    J.B. Priestley Library, University of Bradford
British Labour and the Russian Revolution: The Leeds
    Convention: a report from the Daily Herald: with
    an Introduction by Ken Coates (Spokesman Books, no
    place or date of publication given)
Brockway, A.F. Socialism over Sixty Years: The Life
    of Jowett of Bradford (Allen and Unwin, London,
    1946)

Cahill, M. and Jowitt, J. 'The New Philanthropy: The
   Emergence of the Bradford City Guild of Help',
   Journal of Social Policy, vol. 9, Pt. 3 (Jul.
   1980), pp. 359-82
——— 'The Bradford Guild of Help Papers', History
   Workshop Journal, 15 (Spring, 1983), p. 152
Capital and Labour
Clarion
Clark, D. Colne Valley: Radicalism to Socialism
   (Longman, London, 1981)
Clarke, P.F. Lancashire and the New Liberalism (Cam-
   bridge University Press, London, 1971)
——— 'The Electoral Position of the Liberal and
   Labour parties 1910-1914', English Historical Re-
   view, 1975, pp. 828-36
——— 'Liberals, Labour and the franchise', English
   Historical Review, 1977, pp. 582-9
Colne Valley Labour League (Party/Union/Socialist
   League), Minutes, The Polytechnic Library, Hudder-
   sfield, also produced on microfilm by Microfilm
   Ltd, East Ardsley, West Yorkshire
Coneys, M. 'The Labour Movement and the Liberal
   Party in Rochdale 1890-1906', unpublished MA
   dissertation, The Polytechnic, Huddersfield, 1982
Craig, F.W.S. British Parliamentary Election Results
   1885-1918 (Macmillan, London, 1974)
——— British Parliamentary Election Results 1918-
   1949 (Macmillan, London, 1977)
Cross, C. Philip Snowden (Barrie & Rockliffe, Lon-
   don, 1966)
Dowse, R.E. Left in the Centre (Longman, London,
   1966)
Drake, H.J.O. 'John Lister of Shibden Hall, 1847-
   1933', unpublished PhD thesis, University of Brad-
   ford, 1973
Emy, H.V. Liberals, Radicals and Social Politics
   1892-1914 (Cambridge University Press, London,
   1973)
First Annual Conference of the British Socialist
   Party (Communist Party of Great Britain, London,
   1970 reprint)
Forward
Foster, J. Class Struggle and the Industrial Revo-
   lution (Weidenfeld and Nicolson, London, 1974)
Freeden, M. The New Liberalism: An Ideology of Soc-
   ial Reform (Clarendon, Oxford, 1978)
Groves, R. The Strange Case of Victor Grayson (Pluto
   Press, London, 1975)
Halifax Courier
Halifax Guardian
Haupt, G. Socialism and the Great War: The Collapse

of the Second International (Oxford University
Press, London, 1972)

Hill, J. 'Manchester and Salford Politics and the
Early Development of the Independent Labour Party',
International Review of Social History, vol. xxvi
(1981), Part 2, pp. 171-201

Holton, R. British Syndicalism 1900-1914 (Pluto
Press, London, 1976)

Howell, D. The British Working Class and the Independent Labour Party 1888-1906 (Manchester University Press, Manchester, 1983)

Howkins, A. 'Edwardian Liberalism and Industrial
Unrest: a class view of the decline of Liberalism',
History Workshop Journal, 4 (Autumn, 1977), pp.
143-61

Huddersfield Borough Council, Minutes

Huddersfield and District No-Conscription Council,
Minutes

Huddersfield and District Council for Civil Liberties, Minutes

Huddersfield Examiner

Huddersfield Trades Council, Minutes

Hyman, R. The Workers' Union (Clarendon Press,
Oxford, 1971)

Illingworth, A. Fifty Years of Politics: Mr. Alfred
Illingworth: Retrospect (Bradford Newspaper Co.
Ltd, Bradford, 1905)

ILP Manifestoes, Deed Box 13, Case 64, Archive Department, Bradford Central Library

ILP National Archive, F. Johnson Collection, deposited in the British Library and microfilmed by
Harvester Press, Brighton, 1981

ILP News

Independent Review

Inglis, K. Churches and the Working Classes in Victorian England (Routledge and Kegan Paul, London,
1963)

Interview with Mrs Ada Dalby, 1979, in possession of
Dr. K. Laybourn

James, D. 'The Keighley ILP 1892-1900: Realising the
Kingdom of Heaven' in J.A. Jowitt and R.K.S.
Taylor (eds.), Bradford 1890-1914: The Cradle of
the ILP (Bradford Occasional Papers, No. 2, Uni-
versity of Leeds Department of Adult Education &
Extramural Studies, Bradford, 1980), pp. 56-72

——— 'The Emergence of the Keighley Independent
Labour Party', unpublished MA dissertation, The
Polytechnic, Huddersfield, 1980)

Jowitt, J.A. and Laybourn, K. 'The Wool Textile
Dispute of 1925', The Journal of Local Studies,
Vol. 2, No. 1 (Spring, 1982) pp. 10-27

Joyce, P. Work, Society and Politics: The Culture of
    the Factory in Later Victorian England (Harvester
    Press, Brighton, 1980)
Justice
Keighley Labour Journal
Keighley News
Kendall, W. The Revolutionary Movement in Britain
    1900-1921 (Weidenfeld and Nicolson, London, 1969)
King, S.J. 'Bradford Politics and the Boer War'
    unpublished MA dissertation, The Polytechnic,
    Huddersfield, 1983
Labour Leader
Labour Party Archive, Labour Representation Commit-
    tee Correspondence, 1900-7, also microfilmed by
    Harvester Press, Brighton, 1981
Labour Prophet
Labour Union Journal (Bradford, 1891)
Laybourn, K. 'The Attitude of Yorkshire Trade Unions
    to the Economic and Social Problems of the Great
    Depression, 1873-1896', unpublished PhD thesis,
    University of Lancaster, 1973
——— 'The Manningham Mills Strike: Its importance
    in Bradford History', Bradford Antiquary, New
    Series, Part xlvi, 1976
——— 'The Bradford Labour Movement and the Keir
    Hardie By-Election in East Bradford, November
    1896' in J.A. Jowitt and R.K.S. Taylor (eds.),
    Nineteenth Century Bradford Elections (Bradford
    Centre Occasional Papers No. 1, University of
    Leeds Department of Adult & Extramural Studies,
    1979), pp. 74-87
——— 'The Trade Unions and the I.L.P.: The Manning-
    ham Experience', in J.A. Jowitt and R.K.S. Taylor
    (eds.), Bradford 1890-1914: The Crade of the Inde-
    pendent Labour Party (University of Leeds Depart-
    ment of Adult Education & Extramural Studies,
    Bradford, 1980),pp. 24-44
——— '"The Defence of Bottom Dog": The Independent
    Labour Party in Local Politics', in D.G. Wright
    and J.A. Jowitt (eds.), Victorian Bradford (City
    of Bradford, Metropolitan Council, Libraries
    Division, Bradford, 1982), pp. 223-44
——— 'The Issue of School Feeding in Bradford,
    1904-1907', Journal of Educational Administration
    and History, vol. xiv, No. 2. Jul. 1982, pp. 30-8
Leeds Trades Council, Minutes
Leeds Typographical Circular, Leeds Graphical So-
    ciety
Lister, J. 'Early History of the ILP Movement in
    Halifax', MSS copy in Calderdale Archives Coll-
    ection

Lichtheim, G. The Origins of Socialism (Weidenfeld and Nicolson, London, 1968)

Lockwood, E. Colne Valley Folk (Heath Cranton, London, 1936)

Mann, T. Memoirs (The Labour Publishing Co. Ltd., London, 1923)

Mattison, A. Collection, Brotherton Library, University of Leeds

McBriar, A.M. Fabian Socialism and English Politics, 1884-1918 (Cambridge University Press, London, 1966)

McKibbin, R. The Evolution of the Labour Party 1910-1924 (Oxford University Press, London, 1974)

McLellan, D. Karl Marx: His Life and Thought (Macmillan, London, 1978)

Morgan, K. 'The New Liberalism and the Challenge of Labour: The Welsh Experience', in Brown, K.D. (ed.) Essays in Anti-Labour History (Macmillan, London, 1974), pp. 159-82

Morris, A.J.A. C.P. Trevelyan, 1870-1958: Portrait of a Radical (Blackstaff Press, Belfast, 1977)

Parton, C. 'Liberal Individualism and Infant Mortality: The Infant Welfare Movement in Huddersfield 1900-1918', unpublished MA dissertation, Huddersfield Polytechnic, 1982

Pearce, C. The Manningham Mills Strike in Bradford, December 1890 - April 1891 (University of Hull Occasional Papers in Economic and Social History, No. 7, 1975)

Pelling, H. The Origins of the Labour Party 1880-1900 (Macmillan, London, 1974)

Perks, R.W. 'Trade Unionism and the Emergence of the Labour Party in Huddersfield', forthcoming article in J. Halstead and W. Lancaster (eds.) Socialist Studies (Harvester, Brighton, 1984)

───── 'Liberalism and the Challenge of Labour in West Yorkshire 1885-1914, with special reference to Huddersfield', about to be submitted for a PhD, CNAA, The Polytechnic, Huddersfield at the time of preparation

Pugh, M. 'Yorkshire and the New Liberalism', Journal of Modern History, vol. 50, Pt. 3 (1978), D 1139- D1155

Purdue, A.W. 'The Liberal and Labour Parties in North-East Politics, 1900-1914: The Struggle for Supremacy', International Review of Social History, vol. xxvi, Pt. 1 (1981), pp. 1-24

Price, R. An Imperial War and the British Working Class (Routledge and Kegan Paul, London, 1972)

Reid, F. 'Socialist Sunday Schools in Britain, 1892-1939', International Review of Social History, vol. xi (1966), pp. 18-47

Reynolds, J. and Laybourn, K. 'The Emergence of the Independent Labour Party in Bradford', International Review of Social History, xx, Pt. 3 (1975), pp. 313-46

Reynolds, J. The Letter Press Printers of Bradford (Bradford Graphical Society, Bradford, 1972)
—— Saltaire: An Introduction to the Village of Sir Titus Salt (Bradford Art Galleries and Museum, City Trail, No. 2, Bradford, 1976)
—— The Great Paternalist, Titus Salt and the Growth of Nineteenth Century Bradford (Temple Smith, London, 1983), chapter four

Roberts, A.W. 'Leeds Liberalism and Late Victorian Politics', Northern History, vol. v (1970), pp. 131-56
—— 'The Liberal Party in West Yorkshire, 1885-1895', unpublished PhD. thesis, University of Leeds, 1979

Ross, W.D. 'Bradford Politics 1880-1906', unpublished PhD thesis, University of Bradford, 1977

Ruskin, J. The Crown of Wild Olives (George Allen, London, 1886, 1906)

Saltaire and Shipley Times

Saville, J. 'Trade Unions and Free Labour: The Background to the Taff Vale Decision' in A. Briggs and J. Saville, (eds.), Essays in Labour History (Macmillan, London, 1960), pp. 317-50

Sheppard, M.G. and Halstead, J.L. 'Labour's Municipal Election Performance in Provincial England and Wales 1901-1913', Bulletin of the Society for the Study of Labour History, no. 39 (Autumn, 1979) pp. 39-62

Sheppard, M.G. 'The Effect of the Franchise Provisions on the Social and Sex Composition of the Municipal Electorate 1882 1914, Bulletin of the Society for the Study of Labour History, no. 45 (Autumn, 1982), pp. 19-25

Sowerby Division Labour Representation Association, Calderdale Archives Collection, TU 51/1, Minutes

Steele, E.D. 'Imperialism and Leeds Politics, c. 1850-1914', in D. Fraser (ed.), A History of Modern Leeds (Manchester University Press, Manchester, 1980)

Terrill, R. R.H. Tawney and His Times: Socialism and Fellowship (Andre Deutsch, London, 1973)

The Industrial Syndicalist

Thompson, E.P. William Morris: Romantic to Revolutionary (Merlin Press, London, 1955, 1977 edition)
—— 'Homage to Tom Maguire' in A. Briggs and J. Saville (eds.), Essays in Labour History

(Macmillan, London, 1960), pp. 276-316

Thompson, L. The Enthusiasts: A Biography of J & K Bruce Glasier (Victor Gollancz, London, 1971)

Thornton, W.T. On Labour: Its Wrongful Claims and Rightful Dues: Its Actual, Present and Possible Future (London, 1869, 1870 edition)

Todmorden Trades Council, TU 38. 1-11, Minutes and Records, Calderdale Archives Collection

Trade Union Commission, eleventh and final report, Cmnd 4123, xxi, 1868-9

Turner, B. A Short History of the General Union of Textile Workers (Yorkshire Factory Times, Heckmondwyke, 1920)

—————— About Myself (Toulmin, London, 1930)

Wald, K.D. 'Class and the Vote Before the First World War', British Journal of Political Science, vol. 8 (1978) pp. 441-57

Watmough, P.A. 'The Membership of the Social Democratic Federation, 1885-1902', Bulletin of the Society for the Study of Labour History, no. 34, Spring 1977, pp. 35-40

Webb, S and Webb, B. The History of Trade Unionism (Longman, Green, London, 1894)

Williams, J.E. 'The Leeds Corporation Strike in 1913', in A. Briggs and J. Saville, Essays in Labour History, 1886-1923 (Macmillan, London, 1971), pp. 70-94

Wilson, T. The Downfall of the Liberal Party (Col (Collins, London, 1966, 1968)

—————— The Political Diaries of C.P. Scott 1911-1928 (Collins, London, 1970)

White, S. 'Soviets in Britain: The Leeds Convention of 1917', International Review of Social History, vol. xix (1974), Part 2, pp. 165-93

Woodhouse, T. 'Trade Unions and Independent Labour Politics in Leeds, 1885-1914', unpublished paper produced in the mid 1970s

—————— 'The working class' in D. Fraser (ed.), A History of Modern Leeds (Manchester University Press, Manchester, 1980), pp. 353-88

Wright, D.G. 'The Bradford Election of 1874' in J.A. Jowitt and R.K.S. Taylor (eds.), Nineteenth Century Bradford Elections (Bradford Centre Occasional Papers No. 1. University of Leeds Department of Adult Education & Extramural Studies, Bradford, 1980, pp. 50-73

Yeo, S. 'A New Life: The Religion of Socialism in Britain 1883-1896', History Workshop Journal, 4 (Autumn, 1977), p. 5-56

Yorkshire Factory Times

Young Socialist

INDEX

Index